Rabbi Shmuel Herzfeld

Fifty-Four Pick Up

Fifteen-Minute Inspirational Torah Lessons

gefen
publishing house
JERUSALEM ◆ NEW YORK   Est. 1981

Cover Design: Studio Paz
Typesetting: David Yehoshua

ISBN: 978-965-229-558-3

1 3 5 7 9 8 6 4 2

Gefen Publishing House Ltd.
6 Hatzvi Street
Jerusalem 94386, Israel
972-2-538-0247
orders@gefenpublishing.com

Gefen Books
11 Edison Place
Springfield, NJ 07081
516-593-1234
orders@gefenpublishing.com

www.gefenpublishing.com

Printed in Israel

Send for our free catalogue

Library of Congress Cataloging-in-Publication Data

Herzfeld, Shmuel.
    Fifty-four pick up: fifteen-minute inspirational Torah lessons / Shmuel
Herzfeld.
        p. cm.
    ISBN 978-965-229-558-3
    1. Bible. O.T. Pentateuch—Sermons. 2. Jewish sermons, English.
    3. Jewish sermons, American. I. Title.
    BS1225.54.H47 2012
    296.4'7—dc22
                            2011049126

Dedicated in honor of our dear friends

Rabbi Shmuel and Dr. Rhanni Herzfeld,
and their children
Lea, Roey, Elai, Max, Shia, and Kolbi.

Your dedication to your family,
the Washington, DC, Jewish community,
and the Jewish community worldwide knows no bounds.

We miss you every day and are thrilled to be involved
in the publication of this important *sefer*.

Love,
Leelah and Joseph Gitler,
Meital, Elitzur, Ayelet, Yakira and Ziv

The gift of time is one that Rabbi Shmuel Herzfeld has shared, and continues to share, with our family. To learn with Rabbi Herzfeld is an extraordinary experience – he exemplifies a living *Pirkei Avos*. To watch him interact with other people on a daily basis is always a learning experience.

Rabbi Herzfeld is one of those very rare people who spends virtually all of his waking moments trying to improve the world and help the Jewish people. This is a lesson he learned very well from his mentor, Rabbi Avi Weiss. Just recently, when asked about his family, Rabbi Herzfeld remarked, "We are all fine, however the world is not." He went on to describe two immediate challenges to the Jewish community, and his goals to address them that very day.

We feel privileged that Rabbi Herzfeld has reserved a weekly hour of learning with Steve and our son Benjamin for the past three years. Our daughters Rachel and Jessica have learned with Rabbi Herzfeld over the years, and have been able to use their Jewish education from inside and outside of the classroom to act as scholars and leaders in their respective Jewish communities.

We were thrilled to play a small role in helping to bring Rabbi Herzfeld's extraordinary *divrei Torah* to publication. He is one of those rare individuals who follows through on what he preaches, and we can all benefit from his teachings and lessons.

Steven and Sharon Lieberman

CONTENTS

Vayikra

Bamidbar

Devarim

ACKNOWLEDGMENTS

The fifty-four essays contained in this volume correspond to the fifty-four portions into which the Torah is divided. Each and every one of these essays was offered as a *dvar Torah* in synagogue at the Shabbat morning service. They have been only slightly adapted here through the guidance of Ita Olesker at Gefen Publishing House. I am also appreciative of Rachel Lieberman's help in preparing these essays for publication.

A few of the *divrei Torah* were offered at the Hebrew Institute of Riverdale, where I was privileged to serve as an assistant rabbi to Rabbi Avi Weiss from 1999 to 2004. Rabbi Weiss is not only a great visionary and rabbinic role model for all rabbis, he is also my personal mentor and spiritual guide. I mention this here because when I first became a rabbi, Rabbi Weiss spent hours with me helping me understand how to share a Torah thought in an effective and elegant manner. I am forever grateful to him for his ongoing guidance and advice.

The majority of these essays were first offered as *divrei Torah* at Ohev Sholom – the National Synagogue, where I have been so fortunate to serve as rabbi since 2004. Being a rabbi of a congregation is the greatest job on earth. I don't take this for granted at all, and every day I express my thanks to Hashem for this privilege.

Our shul has been good to me and to my family in many ways. One of the ways is the manner in which individuals from the shul helped me sharpen, refine, and sensitize these *divrei Torah*. For this too I am grateful.

Although I would like to list the many people who helped me in the creation of these *divrei Torah* and in my rabbinate, I will refrain from doing so as I do not want to forget or overlook anyone. Please know that I am grateful for all the help I have been given.

I do want to especially thank the two families whose generosity helped make this book a reality.

Steve and Sharon Lieberman not only read virtually all of these *divrei Torah* in advance of my offering them to the congregation, they have also been available to help me twenty-four hours a day throughout my rabbinate. Steve and Sharon's guidance is present on a daily basis in my life and I am deeply grateful for everything they do, not only for me, but for the entire Jewish community. Their dedication to Yeshivat Chovevei Torah is an example of the way in which they are literally changing the world through their active involvement.

I am also thankful to Joseph and Leelah Gitler. Not only for their support of this project but for being such close friends – I can't imagine a closer friendship – to me and Rhanni for over two decades. When Joseph and I roomed together in college he encouraged me to write a book. He promised then that when that happened he would come in from wherever he was in the world and throw a book party. I mention this not to make him honor his word, but to illustrate for you what kind of friend he is and what kind of special people he and Leelah are. It is a source of great pride to me that they started Leket Israel, which through its food rescue program has served over a million meals to hungry people.

Although my name is on the cover of this book, everything I do, I do in partnership with my beloved wife, Rhanni.

We are both enormously aware and grateful to Hashem for His kindness and blessings.

BEREISHIT

FINDING LIGHT

Bereishit

There is a wonderful short story by Joseph Epstein called "Felix Emeritus." In this story there is a conversation between two residents of a retirement home. Both of them are pretty much alone in the world. One is a bitter, divorced man who lost his entire business in a lawsuit. The other is a reflective English professor who keeps secret the fact that he is a survivor of the Holocaust.

The divorced man shares his own very depressing autobiography with the professor. After reading this work, the professor turns to him and says, "They are dark, very dark, your thoughts about life... Does life really seem so unremittingly bleak to you?" To which he responds, "Only when I think about it."

We see darkness all around us. It is very easy to see the darkness.

After all, the world is based upon darkness being everywhere. It was there even before there was light in the world. At the very beginning we are told (1:2), *ve-choshekh al penei tehom*, "and there was darkness over the abyss."

Notice that the Torah never tells us that God created darkness. It says God created heaven and earth. And there was darkness over the abyss. The first words that God utters are "Let there be light" (1:3). But at that point darkness has already been created. Clearly, God must have created darkness – how else could it exist? And yet we are not told that God created darkness. Why not?

The Beit ha-Levi (Rabbi Yosef Dov Ber Soloveitchik, d. 1892), who was for a while a *rosh yeshivah* in Volozhin, explains that God's name is not associated with darkness because God does not want to connect His name with evil, and darkness represents evil. It exists in the world, but God distances Himself from it.

This is the simplest yet most fundamental teaching of the creation story. God is about light, not darkness. The teaching is so simple, but its lesson is often lost. Often God becomes a *kardom lachpor bo*, "an axe to gore with," and God becomes associated with darkness, not light.

Think about when people most often invoke God's name. It can be used in a hurtful manner – to tell people that they are wicked sinners, or that they are infidels, or that they are the ones causing disease to spread. It is often associated with darkness.

This is the exact opposite of the image of God that we know from the creation story. According to the creation story, our responsibility as human beings is to be Godlike.

וַיִּבְרָא אֱלֹקִים אֶת הָאָדָם בְּצַלְמוֹ.

God created man in His image. (Bereishit 1:27)

Our responsibility is to reflect God's image, to bring light into the world like God does, to speak so that there may be light.

So, how do we do that?

An approach to this question is offered by the Beit ha-Levi's colleague in Volozhin, Rabbi Naftali Zvi Yehuda of Berlin (the Netziv, d. 1893), in his introduction to Bereishit.

But first, some background on the Netziv and the Beit ha-Levi.

In 1854, the Netziv took over the famous Yeshivah of Volozhin and the Beit ha-Levi was named assistant *rosh yeshivah*. Their learning styles were very different. The Netziv focused on developing broader concepts from nuances, while the Beit ha-Levi was more casuistic, connecting themes from seemingly unrelated sources. These two different styles led to the creation of two different factions in the yeshivah – Netziv loyalists and Beit ha-Levi loyalists.

It was always the custom that the Netziv gave the Rosh Hashanah sermon in the community to the common families, while the Beit ha-Levi spoke to the students in the academy. In 1857, to the surprise of many, the Netziv spoke to the students in the yeshivah on Rosh Hashanah instead of the Beit ha-Levi. A major controversy ensued. Some people tried to depose the Netziv, and outsiders were needed to quell the internal controversy. Although the two scholars had no ill will toward each other, the great Beit ha-Levi decided to leave the yeshivah.[1]

In the context of internal fighting by the students of the yeshivah of Volozhin, I share with you a teaching from the Netziv. The Netziv notes that the book of Bereishit is referred to in rabbinic literature as *Sefer ha-Yashar*, the Book of the Upright. He wonders why this book is known as the book of the *yashar*, and not the book of the tzaddikim (righteous) or chasidim (pious).

To answer this question, the Netziv delves into Second Temple history. He explains that in the time of the Second Temple, Jews were tzaddikim and chasidim, and they were constantly involved in Torah study, but they were not *yashar*. This defect is what led to the destruction of the Temple: "On account of hatred in their hearts they suspected anyone who did not act like them in matters of faith to be a heretic! Even though they might be acting for the sake of heaven, nevertheless these actions cause *churban ha-beriah*, the destruction of the universe."[2]

The actions of our patriarchs, the Netziv points out, were in fact the exact opposite of such hateful actions. Avraham prayed for the people of Sodom; he was called *av hamon goyim*, father amongst all the nations. Yitzchak was easily appeased by Avimelech, and Yaakov spoke softly with Lavan, who wanted to kill him.

---

1. See *Beis HaLevi: Bereishit*, translated by Yisrael I. Herzceg (Jerusalem: Targum Press, 1990), introduction.

2. *Ha-Emek Davar*, introduction to Bereishit.

The point of Bereishit is not that the patriarchs spread their teachings or that they built a large family. The point is the way they behaved even with the people with whom they disagreed. "They acted with great love towards idolaters. They were concerned for their welfare. In this way they maintained the existence of the world."[3]

The teaching of the Netziv is simple, but it is also profound. The book of Bereishit teaches us how we can maintain our world. We do so by acting like the patriarchs, by loving those with whom we disagree, by looking out for their welfare and benefit.

Ultimately, this is what it means to be Godlike. We spread light in the world by going to places of darkness and bringing out the light that is there.

This sounds easy in theory, but in practice it is very difficult. Our natural tendency is to withdraw from people and ideas that we don't care for. In reality we must do the opposite. When we see someone or an idea that repulses us, we must pursue it. We must seek to uncover the light therein; we must allow ourselves to see the light. This basic message is the essence of what it means to be *yashar*. Before we can be tzaddikim and chasidim, we must be *yesharim*.

Alas, the public face of religion today has become a distasteful one. It has come to be about rebuking people who are sinning. More often than not, it is not finding light amidst darkness. In order to fulfill the mission of God's creation, we must do everything in our power to change that view. We must constantly work to spread the light, to publicize the light, to let the light overpower darkness.

Let us go back to Joseph Epstein's short story. Do you know what the Holocaust survivor said to the depressed businessman? He said, "Maybe each of us brings his own darkness into the world with him. Also his own light. I continue to see life as a gift."

Life is a gift. But it is our job to spread the light. Let there be light.

---

3. Ibid.

FAILURE: IT'S NO BIG DEAL

Noach

One of the great moments in the history of Jewish activism is when the Jewish community rallied on short notice on behalf of Israel in April, 2002.

Here is how that rally happened. After a bomb went off at the Park Hotel in Netanya on the first night of Pesach, Rabbi Avi Weiss and a small group of like-minded rabbis organized a rally for Israel in New York City, which was attended by more than twelve thousand people. At this rally, Rabbi Weiss called for a much larger rally to take place the next week in Washington, DC. He said to the crowd, "The Jewish establishment should do it, and if they do not do it, then we will do it ourselves."

Within twenty-four hours the Conference of Presidents of Major American Jewish Organizations met. I vividly remember driving Rabbi Weiss to that meeting. The leaders of the conference were hesitating about holding a rally in DC; they were concerned that no one would come. What if they called for a rally and no one showed up? They asked, "What if we fail?" Most were against having a rally. One Jewish leader said, "Let's have a rally in Washington for one thousand Jewish leaders." But Rabbi Weiss pressed on. I will always remember Rabbi Weiss telling me that when he played basketball for his high school, he broke the record for shots attempted during a game. He was unafraid to fail. And so he told the leaders who were gathered that if they would not call for a rally, he would organize his own rally. The presidents' conference decided that it would indeed hold a rally in Washington the very next week. The ensuing rally was attended by well over one hundred thousand people and will forever be remembered as one of the bright spots in American Jewish history.

That story relates to a theme of parashat Noach.

The rabbis argue about whether or not Noach was a great man or just a pretty good guy. The Torah calls him tzaddik, a righteous man, but maybe that was only compared to the ruffians of his own generation.

Either way, Noach was certainly not as great a man as Avraham. Rashi reminds us that the Torah says Noach walked with God (*et ha-Elokim hit'halekh Noach*). This is no small feat. However, Avraham walked in front of God (*hit'halakhti lefanai*). And look at their legacy. Noach saw a world destroyed on his watch and then he became a drunk, while Avraham became the father amongst the nations – the great teacher of monotheism.

How come Noach did not succeed like Avraham?

In order to answer this, let us explore another passage from this Torah portion: the story of the tower of Bavel. After the flood came upon the earth, a group of people arose and said, "Let us build a city and a tower for ourselves whose head reaches the heavens, lest we disperse on the face of the earth" (11:4).

According to the rabbis, this generation committed a great sin. Indeed, Rashi says that they were denied a share in the World to Come. What was their sin? Some suggest that their sin was in trying to conquer God, and others offer that it was their arrogance in trying to make a name for themselves. Rashbam suggests, "Their sin was that God had told them to be fruitful and multiply on the earth, but instead they were trying to only stay in place, lest they disperse."

Perhaps we can expand upon Rashbam's idea. The people were afraid to move beyond their city and fulfill God's command to settle the earth out of the concern that they might be dispersed. They thought, *Maybe if we go out we will not be able to settle the earth; maybe we will fail.* So instead of failing, the people stayed inside the city. They said, if we stay here then we will surely succeed.

And that's exactly what God says to them:

וַיֹּאמֶר ה'.... וְעַתָּה לֹא יִבָּצֵר מֵהֶם, כֹּל אֲשֶׁר יָזְמוּ לַעֲשׂוֹת:

> And God said.... "Now there will be nothing lacking
> from them, everything they want to do they will
> accomplish." (Bereishit 11:6)

Well…what is so bad about that? Everything they want to do they will accomplish! What is the sin there?

The sin, of course, was that God wasn't telling them *not to fail*; God was telling them to try to succeed. God had told them to spread out on the earth, but they were afraid to fail. They were worried that it wouldn't work, and so they all stayed together and ignored their mission from God.

This was the same mistake of Noach. Rashi tells us that Noach was *mi-ketanei emunah*, a person of "small faith." Even though God told him to enter the ark, he hesitated and waited until the water physically forced him in. Noach was not a big believer, not in God and not in himself.

After the flood occurred, this personality trait of Noach becomes exacerbated. He no longer tries to build the earth. In fact he doesn't even want to leave the ark. God has to tell him, *"Tzei min ha-teivah – You must leave the ark"* (8:16). And the text implies that Noach and his family were afraid to leave the ark (see 8:17 with Rashi's comments, 8:18, and 9:18). Therefore, God has to tell him: Yes, you have seen a terrible catastrophe, but you must not give up. You must not let your past failure or mistakes define your future. You must go forward.

But Noach doesn't want to go forward. Sure, he plants in the field. But he plants a vineyard in order to get drunk. He wants to go back to his mother's womb and forget about the world. And so he gets drunk and goes into an enclosure – a tent – and lies there naked.

Noach is done with life, and that was his great downfall. Noach's failure was not an action of commission, but omission. He saw the world fail once, and he failed to try again. He gave up on life and on himself. And so he turned to the bottle.

But there is no shame in failing. The greater shame is in not failing – not failing because we never even tried to begin with; because we were too afraid to try.

A friend who owns a successful business once told me that when he interviews people, he asks them to tell him about their biggest failure in life. Sometimes you can tell more about a person from their failures than from their successes. Just because their plans did not entirely succeed does not mean that it was wrong to try; it just means it didn't work out yet.

Let us compare Noach to Avraham. Noach sees the world destroyed, and so he gives up and is afraid to try again. But Avraham never gives up; he is unafraid of failure. God tells him to go and travel to a place where "I will show you" (12:1), and Avraham goes. He doesn't say, "Let me build a tower where I am in case it doesn't work." He isn't worried about failing; instead he is focused on succeeding. And when he gets there his road is not smooth. He encounters famine and war and sins and domestic problems, but he always goes forward.

Noach is the paradigm of fear of failure, while Avraham is the quintessential example of the person who is not afraid to fail. It is Avraham, more than any other figure of the Torah, who teaches us that the only failure is in not trying in the first place.

I recently read a biography about Benjamin Disraeli, a nineteenth-century prime minister of England.[1] If you ask anyone today who Disraeli was, they will tell you he is an amazing success story. He was the only Jew ever to be the leader of England, and even though he was baptized as a boy, he did not hide his Judaism. He was proud of it and advocated for Jews in a more public way than anyone of his generation. He famously responded to anti-Semitic catcalls in the parliament by saying, "Yes, I am a Jew, and when the ancestors of the right honorable gentleman were brutal

---

1. Adam Kirsch, *Benjamin Disraeli* (New York: Nextbook / Schocken, 2008).

savages in an unknown island, mine were priests in the temple of Solomon."

And yet, when I read Disraeli's biography, it is a story of failure after failure.

His first project, a newspaper called *The Representative*, failed and he was saddled with bankruptcy and debt for much of his life as a result. In fact he would have gone to jail for his debts if he did not receive immunity on account of getting elected. His election to Parliament was no small thing either. He ran four times and was soundly defeated each time before becoming elected in 1837. And once elected, he sat on the back bench for thirty years before becoming prime minister.

His life was filled with failures and disappointments, but in the end he was a great success. Each time he failed, he realized that he needed to start again.

This message of viewing failure as just a step in our growing process has been a motivating factor of my rabbinate. Just because something doesn't work doesn't mean it was a mistake to try it in the first place, and it doesn't mean that it shouldn't be tried again.

When I was planning on moving down to Washington to work on rejuvenating our congregation, someone asked my wife, "What if your husband fails?"

The truth is that I never ask myself that question. As long as the attempt is done for the right reasons, then even if it fails spectacularly it is not truly failure. It is just a learning process on the path to serving God more effectively. And only if we are unafraid to fail will we have even a slight chance of success.

So if we fail, it is no big deal. But if we fail to try...now that is inexcusable!

AVRAHAM: AN EVANGELICAL ROLE MODEL

Lekh Lekha

I have a loudspeaker system installed for my car. This allows me to broadcast my message far and wide. When driving through the streets of downtown DC, I sometimes speak into my loudspeaker: "Come and daven with us at Ohev Sholom – the National Synagogue." No matter where I am, the pedestrians always smile when they hear that.

Also just recently, I had to reregister my license plate tags. In doing so I took the opportunity to get vanity plates. The new tags say: "Go 2 Shul."

Yes, I will admit that I am an evangelical rabbi. I believe in evangelizing Jews, unaffiliated Jews, so-called "half-Jews," intermarried Jews, gentiles, and anyone else that might exist.

It is time that the Jewish community as a whole begins to proselytize and evangelize. This is the fundamental message of the life of our patriarch, Avraham *Avinu*.

When Avraham listens to the command of Hashem and travels from Charan on the other side of the Jordan River to the land of Canaan, the Torah tells us:

וַיִּקַּח אַבְרָם אֶת שָׂרַי אִשְׁתּוֹ וְאֶת לוֹט בֶּן אָחִיו וְאֶת כָּל רְכוּשָׁם אֲשֶׁר רָכָשׁוּ וְאֶת הַנֶּפֶשׁ אֲשֶׁר עָשׂוּ בְחָרָן וַיֵּצְאוּ לָלֶכֶת אַרְצָה כְּנַעַן....

> And Avram took Sarai his wife and Lot his nephew, and all the possessions they had acquired, and the souls that they had made in Charan, and they traveled to the land of Canaan.... (Bereishit 12:5)

Who are these souls that they had made in Charan? Rashi tells us that this refers to all the people Avraham and Sarah had converted in their lives up until this point: "He brought them into the Divine Presence.... Avraham would convert the men and Sarah would convert the women."

Indeed, if one reads the commentary of the great Ramban carefully it seems that this is the reason why God selected Avraham to begin with. After all, the text of the Torah itself does not tell us why Avraham was selected to inherit the land of Canaan – it is almost as if God appeared randomly to Avraham and chose him. But Ramban tells us that Avraham was evangelizing all the people around him in Charan and Ur Kasdim, and this is why Avraham was selected to inherit the land of Canaan. He was an evangelical, spreading the idea of Hashem in the world, and for this reason Hashem chose him to go to the holiest land of all, Canaan, and continue his work.

Furthermore, the Talmud in tractate Nedarim (32a) tells us that Avraham committed a great sin in not continuing his missionary work in the land of Canaan.

One of the fundamental questions in parashat Lekh Lekha is how come God doesn't give Avraham the land of Canaan right away? Instead he is told that his descendants will be enslaved for four hundred years in a land that is not theirs, and only then will they inherit the land of Canaan (15:13).

The Talmud understands that the reason why Avraham did not inherit the land right away – and the reason why his children were enslaved for such a long time – is because Avraham committed a sin. The Talmud teaches: "Rabbi Yochanan says: it is because Avraham stopped people from coming into the community of the Divine Presence when the king of Sodom said to him, 'Give me the souls.'"

This teaching of Rabbi Yochanan refers to an incident that happened in parashat Lekh Lekha. There was a battle between five kings who lived in the land of Canaan and four kings who also lived in the land. The four kings conquered the five kings, and in doing so they also took Lot and the king of Sodom captive. After hearing this, Avraham wages war against the four kings, utterly defeats them, and rescues all the captives.

Upon the completion of this incredible military victory, the whole land recognizes Avraham's greatness. All the kings of the land gather to anoint Avraham king (see Rashi's comments on 14:17, "emek shaveh"), and the priest of the land, Malki Tzedek, blesses and praises Avraham. The king of Sodom says to Avraham, "You keep the wealth, just give me the people – ten li ha-nefesh" (14:21). However, in an apparently magnanimous manner, Avraham refuses to take the spoils of the war, and so he personally turns down both the people and the wealth.

In reality, Rabbi Yochanan sees this acquiescence on Avraham's part as a great sin. How could Avraham have turned away the opportunity to connect to those souls? Avraham could have changed those people's lives forever. He could have brought them into the Divine Presence of Hashem. Instead he let them go back to the king of Sodom, where in just a few years they would all end up being killed. He let them return to a life of debauchery; he let them return to a life of darkness and emptiness. Avraham could have saved all their souls, both physically and spiritually. But he turned away from his ultimate mission, and for this reason his own children were exiled for four hundred years!

Avraham abandoned those lost souls to the king of Sodom and as a result his descendants were enslaved in Egypt; the same way he abandoned the souls of Sodom, his descendant's souls were also abandoned in the land of Egypt.

In short, Avraham was selected to enter and inherit the land of Canaan because he understood and lived the evangelical idea of spreading the message of Hashem. But then he and his children were punished because he abandoned his evangelical message.

Practically speaking – what does this message mean? What does it mean for us to accept the evangelical mission of Avraham?

First, it means we need to reorient ourselves as a community.

People often say Jews don't proselytize. And that is true. We generally don't proselytize. But that doesn't mean we shouldn't proselytize.

In the post-Temple and pre-modern era, we didn't proselytize because we were often living precariously on the edge of another pogrom or expulsion. It was extremely dangerous to proselytize when living under the sword of Latin Christendom or Islamic rule. But now that we can freely worship our religion and live without fear as Jews, we can proselytize.

Some of you might still question this, as there is a tradition that when a potential convert comes to the rabbi, the rabbi is supposed to push him or her away from converting. This idea is based upon a text in the Talmud, tractate Yevamot (47b). The Talmud tells us to warn the potential converts about the dangers of joining the Jewish people. When the convert appears before us, says the Talmud, we are supposed to challenge the convert, "Why are you converting?" And then we are supposed to remind the convert: "*Ha-am ha-zeh devuyim* (the Jewish people are afflicted), *dechufim* (oppressed), *sechufim* (downtrodden), *u-meturafin* (and oppressed)."

The reason we are warning the potential convert is not because we don't want him to join; just the opposite. The reason is we want him to join only after careful deliberation and full knowledge of what is at stake; we want him to fully understand what he is getting involved in. We don't want him to commit to something that is beyond him.

If, after all of these warnings, the convert still desires to join, then the Talmud says "*mekablin oto miyad*" – we must accept the convert immediately. And if he is a man we should circumcise him right away. Why the need to circumcise him and convert him right away? Says the Gemara, "We should not delay a mitzvah." In other words, the act of conversion itself is a mitzvah, and so once the convert is ready we should not delay it at all, because we don't want to delay a mitzvah.

Logically speaking, if the act of conversion is a mitzvah, then of course we should be encouraging gentiles of all stripes to engage in this mitzvah.

Let's take this whole discussion one step further. As we know, the Jewish people have been in exile since the destruction of the Temple in the year 70 CE. There is even a theology put forth in the Talmud that argues that the reason we are in the Diaspora at all is for the primary purpose of being able to spread ourselves around the world in order to convert as many gentiles as possible.

We see this cited in the medieval commentary Tosafot to tractate Kiddushin (70b). There is a complicated phrase about converts in the Talmud that states *"kashim geirim le-Yisrael ke-sapachat,"* which roughly translates as "converts are difficult for Israel, just like a skin disease."

Many different beautiful explanations are offered for this difficult phrase, but Tosafot records the following answer: It is the converts' fault that we are in exile to begin with, and the reason is because of a statement in tractate Pesachim (87b): "The only reason that the Jews were sent into exile was in order to increase the number of converts." Thus, according the Talmud, Hashem placed the Jews in exile in order for us to mingle with the gentiles and entice them to convert to Judaism.

That is the ideal. Ideally we should be acting as missionaries to all our gentile neighbors.

But I am a practical person and recognize that we need to live in the real world. Idealism must meet our reality. Realistically speaking it is very hard to overturn centuries of practice of not acting as missionaries. Perhaps we recoil at the idea because, as Jews, missionaries were often thrust upon us, and so we are turned off at the idea of ourselves acting like missionaries. And from the perspective of our own energy level and practical use of community resources, before we focus and evangelize the gentiles, we should first focus on our own community and act as evangelicals to our own brothers and sisters. We should focus on the Jews within the walls of our own synagogue who are feeling disaffected. This includes warmly welcoming newcomers to our synagogue and into our spiritual community and connecting to our friends in the community who themselves feel spiritually disconnected.

Then we should focus on the thousands of unaffiliated Jews in our own city who for all intents and purposes are living like gentiles.

After that, if we still have time, we can turn to the intermarried couples whom we all know, and to their children. It is a special mitzvah to convert a child from a Jewish father and a non-Jewish mother. Such a child, while not halakhically Jewish, is still considered *zera Yisrael*, the seed of Israel.

After that task is accomplished (and only after that), can we turn our focus and evangelical message to the gentiles of the world.

Ramban, in his commentary to this parashah, reminds us of the concept known as *ma'aseh avot siman le-banim* – what happened to our forefathers will happen to their children as well. This fundamental teaching is a reminder to us that we must look at the lives of the patriarchs and matriarchs as inspirational models: what they valued we should value.

Front and center to Avraham's life was a message of evangelism. That too should be a guide to our lives. Our souls must always be seeking to spread the message and teachings of Hashem.

How to Increase
Your Love of Hashem
Vayeira

We recently undertook a novel project in our shul, making us the first Orthodox synagogue in the world to participate in this project.

I am referring to the Kesher Tefillin project with Noah Greenberg. Noah Greenberg is a world-renowned artist who lives in Israel in the city of Tzfat. He is well known for the unique *shtender* he built with another artist named David Moss. This spectacular piece of usable art now sells for $60,000 – and the price is going up.

A couple of years ago, as Noah was preparing to purchase a pair of tefillin for his son's bar mitzvah, he wondered to himself: How did the Jewish people make tefillin when they lived in the desert? When they didn't have fancy machinery and hydraulic presses, what did they do? So Noah, being the creative genius that he is, worked closely with Torah scholars and figured out how one can make absolutely kosher tefillin in a manner consistent with the way the Jewish people made their tefillin in the desert.

After discovering this, Noah realized that our connection to the mitzvah and our understanding of tefillin would be that much greater if we actually constructed the tefillin ourselves. So Noah designed an educational program that over a period of twelve to fifteen hours allows one to both make tefillin and understand the laws and deeper symbolism of tefillin. It is this course that we held in our shul.

Now you might wonder: Why do I need to make my own tefillin? I can just purchase them in a store. Especially since, while these tefillin will be kosher, they will be more fragile and thus are not even recommended for everyday use.

Here is my response to that:

Parashat Vayeira discusses the *akeidah*, the near sacrifice of Yitzchak. In this story, Hashem tests Avraham and asks him to bring his son up to Mount Moriah as an *olah* offering. Avraham willingly brings his son up the mountain and so he passes the test. The commentators ask: Why does Hashem have to test Avraham? After all, Hashem is omniscient, and so He already knows whether or not Avraham will pass the test. Why make Avraham go through with this gut-wrenching trial?

A well-known answer to this question is the explanation of the great Ramban. Says Ramban: Of course, Hashem knew what Avraham was going to do but He still gave him this challenge, *ke-dei lehotzi mei-ha-koach el hapoel*, in order to help Avraham take his innate potential and actualize it. In other words, Hashem knows Avraham has the potential to pass this supreme challenge, but He still challenges Avraham with this difficult task so that Avraham's innate talent can be actualized.

This idea of Ramban is very powerful, but it needs to be properly understood. If Hashem already knows what it is in our hearts, what value is there in actualizing our potential?

Rabbi Yaakov Neuberger, a *rosh yeshivah* at Yeshiva University, explains that the way to understand this Ramban is through a verse that appears in Devarim. The Torah states that sometimes Hashem will allow a false prophet to perform a miracle in order to test us, but the miracle should not distract us from the fact that this prophet is false:

כִּי מְנַסֶּה ה' אֱלֹקֵיכֶם אֶתְכֶם לָדַעַת הֲיִשְׁכֶם אֹהֲבִים אֶת ה' אֱלֹקֵיכֶם
בְּכָל לְבַבְכֶם וּבְכָל נַפְשְׁכֶם:

"God has tested you in order *for you* to know if you love Hashem with all your heart and all your soul." (Devarim 13:4)

The purpose of the test from Hashem is for *us* to see how much we love Hashem; it is not for Hashem to see how much we love Him. It is for us to show it to ourselves. That is the idea behind taking something from the potential to the actual. It is Hashem's way of showing us how much we love Him. For the more we realize how much we love Him, the better we can serve Him and the more reward He can give us.

According to Ramban, God tests us in order to bring out our potential, so that we can in turn feel good about ourselves and love God even more, and thus gain more reward from God.

The rabbinic idea behind this is that "thoughts follow the actions" (*Sefer ha-Chinukh*, mitzvah 16). Thus, the more mitzvot we do, the more our souls broaden (*marchiv nefesh*), the more spiritual we become, and the more we grow closer to Hashem.

On a practical level this is why the rabbis emphasize the need to perform mitzvot as frequently as possible. The rabbis encourage one to perform as many mitzvot as possible rather than doing the entire mitzvah all at once. For example, all things being equal, it is better to study Torah every day for one hour than to study Torah one day a week for seven hours. And, so too, it is better to give ten different poor people a single dollar than to give one poor person ten dollars.

The Chafetz Chayim once told a person it is appropriate to take a job as a bank teller so that he could accustom himself to handing money out to other people. In this way, he would be more likely to give charity to others as well.

The more mitzvot we do, the more we are conditioning ourselves and actualizing our spirituality.

Avraham understands that the *akeidah* is a command from Hashem in order to help him concretize his spirituality. Since it is a command, a mitzvah, he also realizes that the more he personally does himself, the closer he will come to Hashem. Turning the potential into the actual requires Avraham to personally do many of the necessary actions for the *akeidah* himself.

Thus, in this context, the verses highlight all the physical activity that Avraham personally did for the *akeidah*:

וַיַּשְׁכֵּם אַבְרָהָם בַּבֹּקֶר וַיַּחֲבֹשׁ אֶת חֲמֹרוֹ...וַיְבַקַּע עֲצֵי עֹלָה וַיָּקָם וַיֵּלֶךְ אֶל הַמָּקוֹם אֲשֶׁר אָמַר לוֹ הָאֱלֹקִים:

Avraham woke up early in the morning, and he saddled his donkey…and he chopped the wood for the offering and he arose and journeyed to the place that God had told him. (Bereishit 22:3)

Rashi explains: "He did these actions himself, and he did not command it to any of his servants." Avraham understood that the way to achieve a greater love of God is to take our inner spiritually and concretize it. The more we perform physical actions in service of God, the closer we will come to Him. This is why Avraham embraces the seemingly menial tasks surrounding the *akeidah* as ways to serve Hashem.

There are many examples of this in Judaism. Take a funeral. This is the reason why we ourselves carry the coffin to the grave; and this is the reason why we fill up the grave with earth rather than allowing the cemetery workers to perform this task. On a personal note, one of the most spiritual moments of my rabbinate is when our synagogue engages in the baking of matzah on the eve of Pesach. The more we physically partake in actions in service of God, the closer we will come to Him and the more we will love Him.

In that context I urge all of you to engage in this practice of making your own tefillin. The act of participating in the making of tefillin will bring you to a greater love of Hashem; the more you fold the leather and shape it and lovingly put together a kosher pair of tefillin, the more you will love Hashem. The tefillin that I made are very dear to me. I take them out only once a year on a special occasion and place them on my head. My prayers that day are infinitely better and more focused. I believe that everyone who engages in this activity will also have a deeper and more meaningful relationship with Hashem.

Some of you might wonder if the making of tefillin is an actual mitzvah.

My answer to that is that this act of making tefillin isn't necessarily a mitzvah; rather, it is a way of increasing our love of Hashem. The lesson of the *akeidah* is that we need to act in service of Hashem out of great love for Him, even more than out of a *command* to do His will.

God didn't just tell Avraham, "*Kach et binkha* – Take your son." Instead He said, "*Kach* na *et binkha* – Please take your son" (22:2). Why the word *na?* Since when does Hashem have to say "please"?

Rabbi Herschel Schachter (*rosh yeshivah* of Yeshiva University) cites the medieval authority known as the Ran, who explains that Hashem is asking Avraham to do Him a favor. He is telling Avraham: "This isn't a mitzvah. I am not commanding you to do this. But if you want to, you can do this." The test of Avraham is whether or not he will do something even though Hashem does not require it of him. That is the idea of loving Hashem. The classic work *Mesillat Yesharim,* written in 1738 by Rabbi Moshe Chaim Luzzatto, states this clearly: *Ahavat Hashem* means we perform an act for Hashem even without a specific command.

There are different ways to show love in this world.

When a wife asks a husband to pick up flowers for her at the store and he does so, that is one expression of love. But when the husband surprises his wife with flowers for a special occasion… that is an even higher expression of love.

Getting to a higher level of love in all our relationships is always a good thing.

When it comes to Hashem we are encouraged to seek out new ways of increasing our love for Him. An act that helps us have more love for Hashem is a great thing to do even though it is not an explicit mitzvah. According to some, such an act is even greater than a mitzvah, for the highest level of serving Hashem is to do things out of love of Hashem, even though we are not commanded.

When we lovingly create our own pair of tefillin, we will be doing an action that concretizes our love of God. We will be saying: "We know we can just walk into any Jewish bookstore and purchase a pair of tefillin. But, for Hashem, that simply isn't enough. We want to grow closer to Him and serve Him to the greatest extent possible. So we will learn everything we can about this mitzvah. All in the hopes that as a result we will come just a little bit closer to Hashem, the Holy One, Blessed be He."

THE PROHIBITION OF INTERMARRIAGE

Chayei Sarah

In my time as a rabbi, there is a scene that I have witnessed time and time again. A parent whose child has grown apart from Judaism relates his or her disappointment to me, and then the parent says, "I tell my child you can do anything you want, but whatever you do, don't marry a non-Jew – whatever you do, don't intermarry!"

This type of comment has a biblical precedent. The first Jew, Avraham, commands his loyal servant Eliezer to find a wife for his son Yitzchak. But first Avraham makes Eliezer swear that he will not select a wife for Yitzchak from the Canaanites. The verse says:

וְאַשְׁבִּיעֲךָ...אֲשֶׁר לֹא תִקַּח אִשָּׁה לִבְנִי מִבְּנוֹת הַכְּנַעֲנִי.... כִּי אֶל אַרְצִי וְאֶל מוֹלַדְתִּי תֵּלֵךְ וְלָקַחְתָּ אִשָּׁה לִבְנִי לְיִצְחָק:

> "Swear to me...that you will not take a wife for my son from among the daughters of Canaan.... Instead you shall go to my homeland and birthplace and select [from there] a wife for my son, Yitzchak." (Bereishit 24:3–4)

Many commentators are troubled by this exchange between Avraham and Eliezer. Why did Avraham command Eliezer to exclude only the Canaanite tribe from marrying his son? If the reason was because the Canaanites worshiped idols, then Avraham should have said to Eliezer, "Don't take a wife for my son from a tribe that worships idols." In fact, why single out the Canaanites? Indeed, there were many other tribes at the time that also should have been excluded from marrying Yitzchak because they prayed to idols. Finally, what did Avraham hope to accomplish by sending for a bride from his homeland? After all, Avraham himself left his homeland precisely because the people were so idolatrous!

The real difficulty with this passage is that it raises the troubling question of purity of blood, or racism. Does Avraham exclude the Canaanites solely on the basis of race? And does Avraham command Eliezer to return to his homeland solely because he wants to maintain the purity of his lineage?

I raise these textual questions within the context of the consciousness of multicultural American society, which views prohibitions on intermarriage with general disgust. George Bush almost lost his presidential election because he appeared at Bob Jones University, an institution that prohibits intermarriage between religions. And Joe Lieberman was severely handcuffed when he ran for president when he tried to explain to the world why Judaism protests against intermarriage.

All of us should really ask ourselves: Why are our protests against intermarriage not an elitist, almost racist ideology? After all, one could argue that prohibitions against intermarriage made sense in the times of the Torah, when our neighboring tribes were literally sacrificing their children to pagan gods, and when paganism deified a life of ritualistic, sexual orgies. But in today's world, I see some very positive values in Western society – in the values of democracy, equality, and freedom. In today's society does this prohibition against intermarriage really make sense?

It is important to understand how this prohibition evolved. According to some authorities, like Rambam, there is a biblical prohibition against intermarriage (*Hilkhot Issurei Biah* 12:1), but others argue that intermarriage in the colloquial sense of the word is only rabbinically prohibited. The Torah does say *"Lo titchaten bam* – Do not marry them"* (Devarim 7:3), but that is interpreted by some rabbis as a reference only to the seven tribes who inhabited the land of Canaan (see tractate Avodah Zarah 36b and Tur, *Even ha-Ezer* 16).

The prohibition is discussed by Rabbi Moses of Coucy (Semag), who in the year 1236 left his home in France and traveled to preach to the Jews of Spain. When Semag arrived in Spain he saw that many of the Jews there were marrying the local Spanish non-Jewish women. Semag started preaching vociferously against this practice, and he attributes the prohibition to a decree instituted by the Hasmoneans, who were fighting against Hellenistic Jews. He quotes the Talmud, in Avodah Zarah (36b): "The court of the Hasmoneans decreed that one is not permitted to have relations with a non-Jew."

The most important thing to be clear about is that intermarriage is absolutely forbidden. True, according to Semag, it is a rabbinical prohibition, but the Judaism that we practice today is wholly rabbinic Judaism. Nevertheless, the understanding of the evolution of the prohibition is crucial for us to plan a strategy to best counteract intermarriage.

Right now to combat intermarriage there can be two possible approaches. We can either say, "Don't intermarry. The other nations are immoral. It's a terrible sin, and if you intermarry the anti-Semites will have won." But that approach is not working: a study of the American Jewish Committee in 2000 shows that 56 percent of American Jews who responded to a survey do not see intermarriage as a terrible sin. And not only is this approach not working, it comes close to being a racist ideology. It's also not what the Torah is saying.

This is exactly why it is important to note that our constant complaining about intermarriage does not reflect the approach of the Torah or the rabbis. The Torah's complaints against intermarriage are always within the context of immorality. Our complaints in today's world lack that context, and therefore the response of most Jews today is "Why shouldn't I intermarry?" And so the mantra that is repeated time and time again – "Whatever you do, don't intermarry" – falls on deaf ears.

Let me suggest what I believe is the Torah's response to the great danger of intermarriage that is facing the Jewish community. The Torah's approach is to emphasize that the beauty and vitality of Judaism can best be taught through a marriage with shared religious beliefs.

Again, I revisit the context of Bereishit. Eliezer has been sent to find a wife for Yitzchak with specific instructions not to take a wife from the Canaanites. But notice Eliezer's actions. He arrives at Avraham's homeland, Aram Naharayim, and establishes his own system for selecting a bride. Eliezer says: If I ask a girl for a drink of water and she responds, "Here is drink for both you and your camels," then I will know that that girl is the right bride for Yitzchak (24:14).

Many commentators are greatly troubled by Eliezer's actions. For Avraham gave Eliezer one criterion in selecting a wife: not to take a wife from the Canaanites. And here Eliezer is creating his own criteria for selecting Yitzchak's wife!

Perhaps the way to understand Eliezer's actions is to say that he is translating Avraham's instructions from a negative to a positive formulation. Avraham's command not to marry a Canaanite is understood by Eliezer to mean that Avraham wants a bride for Yitzchak who will retain the same values that Yitzchak and Avraham share. So Eliezer translates Avraham's prohibition into a positive commandment: *Find someone who will share my values of hospitality and graciousness.* In the ancient world these were defining elements of the worldview of Avraham's community.

This is also the way we should be responding to the questions of intermarriage that surround us today. How can we decrease the number of Jews who are intermarrying, and how can we justify the prohibition of intermarriage to a world that worships multiculturalism and diversity?

My suggestion is that we can justify our position by stopping to use guilt, anti-Semitism, and the immorality arguments in educating people about intermarriage. The only answer and the only way we can justify prohibiting intermarriage is to take a positive approach: to encourage Jews to marry other Jews for the purpose of maintaining the religious values of Judaism. To tell Jews that marrying Jews is the best way to properly ensure a rich religious environment in the home. To teach that marriage is the sharing of a spiritual destiny.

Our community should teach people to marry Jewish because that is the best way that a proper religious and Jewish environment can be maintained. If Judaism is just a culture, then the prohibition against intermarriage is bigoted. But if Judaism is religious and spiritual, then it becomes perfectly obvious that the best way to lead a Jewish life is with a spouse that shares those values.

So when parents inform me that they tell their children, "Whatever you do, don't marry a non-Jew," I try to explain that this approach is insufficient. The message must be that Judaism is so magnificent, so beautiful, and so meaningful, and it is your responsibility and privilege to carry on this mission. And once we transmit that message, then our children will naturally and proudly marry Jewish.

A Crowning Achievement
Toldot

If you asked me what is one of the most consistently spiritual experiences of my life, I would tell you that, above all else, it is fatherhood. Acting like a father to my children, being involved in their lives, studying Torah with them, teaching them how to daven, being their counselor in camp, being their baseball and football coach, and just sitting down with them every night and discussing their day. All these activities remind me that life is not about the "me," but about the service to Hashem. All these activities are about service to another, educating the next generation, and ultimately about drawing closer to God.

So being an active father has enormous spiritual benefits. What are the spiritual goals of fatherhood? What do we want spiritually from our children? This question is answered in two ways in parashat Toldot.

The opening verse of the portion begs for commentary. The verse says:

וְאֵלֶּה תּוֹלְדֹת יִצְחָק בֶּן אַבְרָהָם אַבְרָהָם הוֹלִיד אֶת יִצְחָק:

This is the lineage of Yitzchak the son of Avraham, Avraham begot Yitzchak. (Bereishit 25:19)

First problem: We have learned in the previous two portions that Yitzchak is the son of Avraham; since we already know this, why the need to repeat this basic fact? And second: The verse itself is redundant. Why the need to tell us Avraham begot Yitzchak, if it already mentioned this in the verse when it stated, "This is the lineage of Yitzchak the son of Avraham"?

The Midrash (Bereishit Rabbah 63:2) answers this question and at the same time introduces us to a powerful idea about raising children.

The Midrash quotes the verse from Mishlei (17:6):

עֲטֶרֶת זְקֵנִים בְּנֵי בָנִים....

Children's children are the crown of elders....

Explains the Midrash: We learn from this that children are the crown of their parents; a person is exalted via his or her progeny. A child or a grandchild or even a great-grandchild can act in a righteous manner and thus crown the life of his or her ancestors.

Thus, the verse in our portion is telling us that Yitzchak's achievements crowned the life of his father, Avraham.

How did Yitzchak crown Avraham's life? In many ways, Yitzchak's life was about continuing the holy work of his parent and thereby making a crown for his life. Yitzchak's main task in life was to continue his father's holy work. This is why the Torah tells us seemingly uninteresting facts about the lives of Avraham and Yitzchak. It is to emphasize the parallel nature of their lives.

About Avraham we are told (21:33), "and he planted an orchard in Beer Sheva." This verse informs us that Avraham was taking ownership of the land of Canaan, literally laying roots down for future generations. Likewise, about Yitzchak we are told (26:12) that he continued this tradition: "and Yitzchak sowed the land."

The verse tells us (14:20) that Avraham gave a tithe to the *kohein* of the land, Malki Tzedek: "and he gave him a tenth of everything." With this act Avraham established in the world the principal of giving charity to religious institutions; he gave a tenth of his wealth to charity. So, too, in reference to Yitzchak, the verse says (26:12) that he found *"meah shearim."* Rashi explains this to mean that he measured out a tithe to charity.

And finally a third example relates to the wells that Yitzchak dug. We are told that the Philistines plugged up all the wells that

Avraham had dug. So Yitzchak went to those same wells and redug them (26:17): "And Yitzchak returned and redug the wells that his father had first dug."

This paradigm of Avraham and Yitzchak is a model for parents and children. In these three examples, Yitzchak understands that his mission in life is to continue the important work – spiritual and physical – begun by his father. Similarly in our own times, many parents want their children to understand that one of their purposes in life is to continue the important, spiritual work of their parents. Especially in the religious community, this idea is emphasized again and again. We can point to this week's portion and tell children that if they continue their parents' holy work, then they will be fulfilling the words of Mishlei: they will become a crown to the life of their parents.

But what about children who don't want to continue the work of their parents? First of all, maybe their parents were flawed and on a bad path, and they don't want to go down that path. Or maybe the children just want to do things on their own, a little bit differently. The father was a rabbi and the child wants to be an artist; or the mother is a doctor and the child wants to work in computers. Then what? Is it any less of a crowning achievement?

Of course not. There are ways for a child to be a crown for the life of his parents even if he does not continue their work and repeat their life story.

This is another lesson of the life of Yitzchak and Avraham.

The verse "Children's children are the crown of elders..." can be an aspiration for all of us; it is something to strive for in our own lives. It can be an injunction to children to better the lives of their parents. They can strive and overtake their parents. Children and grandchildren can live a purer life, a more holy life, and thereby correct the flaws and mistakes of their parents and older generations.

When we look at the life of Yitzchak, we notice that although his life was very similar to Avraham's, in reality he was refining and elevating many of the missteps of his father. Now it goes without saying that Avraham was a holy tzaddik. His righteousness goes beyond anything we can comprehend; his accomplishments are unbelievable. But the greater one is, the more one's sins are magnified, and Avraham committed some mistakes.

One way to think about Avraham is to imagine him as an immigrant to the United States after World War II. We all know people who immigrated with nothing in their pockets. They became entrepreneurs, hard workers, survivors who built incredible businesses and empires. From a spiritual perspective, sometimes these people took short cuts. Sometimes they worked on Shabbat because they just felt they had no choice. Sometimes they felt the need to assimilate into American culture. Sometimes they set up Jewish organizations that were devoid of religion and observance. Deep down they knew better; but they didn't focus on the spiritual because they were more focused on survival.

To a certain degree that was Avraham. He was the ultimate entrepreneur. He started monotheism. He moved to Canaan. He fought the battles with the local kings. He took enormous risks. He willingly sacrificed himself and his son. We all know people like Avraham. They are tough beyond our own imagination.

But in climbing the ladder he took some shortcuts and made some mistakes. Ramban says Avraham committed a great sin in going down to Egypt when famine hit the land of Canaan. He should have never left the land. And when he was in Egypt, Avraham passed off his wife, Sarah, as his sister. He took money for her and in return handed her to Pharaoh. This, too, was a great sin.

Sarah herself rebukes Avraham for another mistake. After Sarah is unable to conceive a child, Avraham prays to God to have a child. Rashi points out that Sarah rebukes Avraham for only praying for himself and not for Sarah. And thus Avraham has a child from Hagar before he has one from Sarah.

One generation later, Yitzchak is able to live a purer life. He is able to look back at the life of his father and correct these three flaws.

Yitzchak is pure, purer than Avraham. He didn't have to fight Avraham's wars; he didn't have to move to the land of Canaan. He was able to move at a slower pace. The rabbis call Yitzchak an *olah temimah*, a pure sacrifice.

When Yitzchak faces a hunger in the land, he doesn't go down to Egypt. Hashem says (26:2), "*al teireid Mitzraymah* – do not go down to Egypt." You, Yitzchak, are pure, you can't leave the land.

When Yitzchak goes to the land of the Philistines, he also says that Rivkah is his sister. But while at first glance this action looks like it is the same as Avraham saying that Sarah was his sister, in reality it is very different. Avraham had willingly volunteered the "Sarah is my sister" line to both the Egyptians and the Philistines. He told them this even before they asked about Sarah. In contrast, Yitzchak waited for them to ask about Rivkah before saying she was his sister. Avraham became rich as a result of passing Sarah off as his sister. In contrast, Yitzchak received no gifts from the Philistines when he said Rivkah was his sister. And in fact, most telling of all, Yitzchak continued to live with Rivkah as his wife. This is why Avimelech looked out of his window and noticed Yitzchak and Rivkah behaving as husband and wife (26:8).

Avraham passed Sarah off to the Egyptians and Philistines as his sister in return for money, while Yitzchak remained with Rivkah and expressed his love for her even in the face of great danger.

And when Rivkah was barren, Yitzchak prayed for her to have a child – *le-nokhach ishto* – on behalf of his wife (25:21). Avraham prayed for himself and he takes another woman as a concubine. Avraham couldn't risk not having a child. For Yitzchak it is different, perhaps because less is at stake or perhaps because he has a better relationship with his wife, but Yitzchak prays for Rivkah to have a child and he does not take a concubine.

In many ways, Yitzchak's life is about correcting and refining the spiritual imperfections of his father. Yitzchak crowns his father's achievements, not by imitating them, but by fixing them. And the same way Yitzchak does this for Avraham, Yaakov will do this for Yitzchak, and Yehudah will do this for Yaakov. The ultimate crown is when a child refines the flaws of his or her parents.

Rabbi Joseph Soloveitchik once taught that the reason we are told the stories of the patriarchs is to learn from their life stories how to experience God.

From the Avraham and Yitzchak story we learn that it is the responsibility of a child either to continue the work of their elders or else to polish the imperfections of their parents, however small or great they may be. Fixing the work of our elders can literally mean repairing their sins, or it can mean seeing an area of the world that was neglected by our parents and working to fill in that area.

Every person's life story is incomplete. Many of us are the next generation; we are the Yitzchaks of the world. Our job is to look at the previous generations – our parents, our teachers – and ask ourselves each and every day: How can we be an *ateret zekeinim*, a crown for our elders? And our job is then to turn to the next generation each and every day and tell them what we hope for from them. We should turn to our children on a regular basis and say: "We love you. We have high hopes for you. We know what you are capable of doing. We know how talented you are and how you can be a crown to all the work of our ancestors. We want you to be our *ateret zekeinim*."

Yaakov's Synagogue:
A Model for All of Us
Vayeitzei

This might surprise you, but there has been some controversy about our synagogue since I came to Washington, DC.

Actually, it started even before I came to DC, when I started referring to our shul as the National Synagogue.

Then as we started doing more and more programs on the streets of DC, to my great chagrin even more controversy was generated. The more programs we did outside the shul, the more controversy we generated.

When we handed out matzah on K Street, people were offended. When we held a Purim parade on Connecticut Avenue, people were offended. When I started driving an old taxi that was repainted with Jewish symbols and had a giant shofar on the top of the car, people got offended. And when we built a sukkah for hundreds of people in Farragut Square, which was covered on the front page of the *Wall Street Journal*, people were REALLY offended.

Some people have even attacked me personally. At first I thought I should just ignore their criticism. After all, it comes only from a distinct minority of the Jewish community, and, in contrast, the feedback from our programs has been overwhelmingly positive.

But after grappling with it, I decided that maybe what I take as self-evident is not as obvious as I thought. Perhaps it is important to discuss the reason why we go out to the streets; perhaps it is important to lay out why we do what we do. In fact, when we go out to the streets it represents a core value of who we are as a shul.

Let me explain through the context of parashat Vayeitzei.

Did you ever wonder why the Jewish people are called *bnei Yisrael*, children of Israel? Israel is a reference to Yaakov, who was also called Yisrael. But why aren't they called children of Avraham? After all, he was the founder of the faith. For that matter, we can also wonder why we are not called children of Yitzchak.

There is an interesting text from the Talmud, tractate Pesachim (88a), that offers us insight into this question. The Talmud comments on a verse from Isaiah that discusses a future era. Isaiah says that there will come a time when all the nations of the world will say, "*Lekhu ve-na'aleh* – Come, let us go up to the mountain of Hashem, to the House of the God of Yaakov" (Yeshayahu 2:3).

Explains the Talmud: It doesn't say, let us go to the House of the God of Avraham or of Yitzchak, but to the House of the God of Yaakov. This is because Yaakov is the only one who actually referred to a House of God. In this week's portion, Yaakov dreams of a ladder with angels going up and down, and when he awakens, he says:

אָכֵן יֵשׁ ה' בַּמָּקוֹם הַזֶּה וְאָנֹכִי לֹא יָדָעְתִּי.... אֵין זֶה כִּי אִם בֵּית
אֱלֹקִים....

"God is in this place and I did not know.... Indeed this is the House of God...." (Bereishit 28:16–17)

Yaakov then builds an altar to Hashem on that very spot.

Yaakov is the first one to refer to a House of God, *Beit Elokim*. Avraham worshiped God on a mountain and Yitzchak worshiped in a field. But the Talmud notes that it is Yaakov who is the first to recognize the power of worshiping God in a house. We can say, then, that Yaakov built the first synagogue. It was Yaakov who recognized that we need a house to worship God.

This leads us to our next question: Why is Yaakov the first patriarch to need a House of God? Why not Avraham or Yitzchak?

Perhaps Yaakov needed a House of God because he spent so much time living away from the spiritual center of the land of Canaan. He spent twenty years with the wicked Lavan, and at the end of his life he lived in Egypt. Of all the patriarchs, only Yaakov spent time with his children outside the land of Canaan. More than the others, Yaakov needed a House of God to reinforce his spirituality. It wasn't enough for him to have a field or a mountain. Yaakov needed something tangible – a *Beit Elokim* to strengthen his spirituality.

Yaakov is the symbol of someone who retains his Judaism in the midst of the world at large. He doesn't seclude himself and meditate on a mountaintop or contemplate in a field. Instead, he is a businessman who deals with the chicaneries of Lavan. Yaakov says, "*Im Lavan garti* – I lived with Lavan" (32:4), and Rashi explains that Yaakov is also saying "*ve-taryag mitzvot shamarti* – even though I lived with Lavan, an evil man, I nevertheless observed the Torah. I kept God's mitzvot. I retained my Judaism."

Obviously, Yaakov's House of God is a far cry from today's modern synagogue. But we can look at it as our forerunner. It is not surprising that the synagogue phenomenon is for the most part a Diaspora phenomenon. While Israel certainly has great synagogues, it is the Diaspora community that feels the need for a synagogue with greater urgency. We Americans are not protected spiritually by the Land of Israel and so we need the synagogue to be our spiritual locus; the synagogue is our lighthouse in the midst of the world. Certainly in America, it is the center of American Jewish life.

And yet, when the synagogue model is pushed too far, it is also the root of the problems of the American Jewish community and can be blamed for such calamities as high assimilation rates. Perhaps the biggest mistake of American Judaism is that the synagogue became "the" place for Judaism. Everything Jewish had to happen in the synagogue, and as a consequence American Jews felt free to confine their Judaism exclusively to the synagogue.

For too long, many American Jews have taken only one part of Yaakov's message: the necessity to build a House of God. But this is obviously a distortion of Yaakov's dream. The point of Yaakov's *Beit Elokim* was that it be a locus of inspiration for him when he went out into the world. It was the center of his Judaism, but it wasn't the ONLY place he would practice his Judaism.

Judaism must gain its strength from the synagogue and then bring that strength to the world at large. For the synagogue model to succeed, it must reach beyond its walls and seek to impact people in their lives outside of the synagogue. For the synagogue to succeed, it must have a presence outside the synagogue.

This is why we are called the children of Yaakov. Yaakov understood the need for a *Beit Elokim*. But he also carried the message of the synagogue into his daily life. He carried it with him when he lived with Lavan for twenty years, and later on when he lived with Pharaoh. We need to carry this message of building a *Beit Elokim* that impacts us when we are outside the synagogue.

Practically speaking, what does this mean for the Jewish community?

One thing it means is that the synagogue must be our center of religious and ritualistic life, but not the beginning and end of our religious and ritualistic life. We must work very hard as a community to take not only the values of the synagogue, but also the rituals and prayers of the synagogue, wherever we go, and especially into our homes. To give an obvious example: we can't just daven when we come to shul; we should daven three times a day, no matter where the day may lead us.

Second, the presence of a synagogue must not be felt *only* in the synagogue. It has to serve the whole city; its presence must be felt everywhere. It must be a model that moves beyond the building and reminds Jews that Judaism should interface with their lives wherever they are.

Above all, a synagogue must be a House of God, whose presence does not end at its walls.

OUTSIDE THE BOX
Vayishlach

On my desk I keep a picture of myself with a very dear friend who is also a highly successful entrepreneur. This friend signed the picture to me: "To Rav Shmuel: Who taught me everything I know about thinking out of the box."

In actual fact, I taught this man nothing about "thinking outside the box." But that is not the point. The point is that he meant to compliment me. To say someone thinks outside the box is to say someone is creative and is able to bring a new perspective to problem solving.

The origins of this phrase are not clear. But many think it goes back to a puzzle – called the nine dots puzzle – that was first introduced in the early 1900s and later became popular in the 1960s. The challenge of the puzzle is to connect dots by drawing four straight, continuous lines that pass through each of the nine dots without ever lifting the pencil from the paper. The solution is simple, but only if you "think outside the box," i.e., if you draw the lines outside the confines of the square area defined by the nine dots themselves. The puzzle only seems difficult because we imagine that we are confined to the box, when really we need to think outside the box.

I would like to propose a new definition of what it means to think outside the box, based upon a *Rashi* in this week's portion.

The verse states that Yaakov crossed over the Yabok River in order to meet his brother, Esav.

וַיָּקָם בַּלַּיְלָה הוּא וַיִּקַּח אֶת שְׁתֵּי נָשָׁיו וְאֶת שְׁתֵּי שִׁפְחֹתָיו וְאֶת אַחַד
עָשָׂר יְלָדָיו וַיַּעֲבֹר אֵת מַעֲבַר יַבֹּק:

> And [Yaakov] awoke that night and he took his two
> wives and his two concubines and his eleven children
> and he crossed over the ford of Yabok. (Bereishit 32:23)

Rashi wonders: By this point Yaakov had not eleven, but twelve children. He had eleven boys and one girl. So Rashi asks, "*Ve-dinah heikhan haitah* – and where was Dinah?" Rashi answers, "*Netanah be-teivah*" – Yaakov had placed Dinah in a box so that Esav would not desire to be with her.

Can you imagine that? Yaakov hid his own daughter in a box!

This action is not looked upon favorably by the rabbis. Rashi continues: "It is for this reason that Yaakov was punished." Because Yaakov held Dinah back, he prevented her from having a good influence upon Esav, and in the end Dinah "fell into the hands of Shechem" (Rashi, 32:23).

Rashi is telling us that Yaakov had no right to place Dinah inside a box. Dinah was put on this earth by Hashem for a reason. Maybe she was put here to change the world, to have a positive influence upon Esav. Whatever the reason, she surely was not created by God in order to be placed inside a box. Yaakov acted in a selfish manner. He didn't want Esav to see her, so he removed her from the world and put her in a box. Dinah was capable of tremendous good, but Yaakov did not let her accomplish it because he kept her inside the box.

I thought about this teaching of Rashi in the context of being personally involved in the creation of a new pair of tefillin. As part of the process of making tefillin we literally made the *batim*, or the boxes of the tefillin. To make these boxes we took sheep skins and pounded them out into a specific shape. We then painted them black and folded them into the shape of a box – a tefillin box.

But then came the hardest part. Each box of tefillin contains within it four paragraphs from the Torah written upon parchment. The four paragraphs are broken down as follows: the first paragraph is from Shemot 13:1–10 and it is called *Kadesh li kol bekhor*; the second paragraph is from Shemot 13:11–16 and it is called *Ve-hayah ki yeviakha*. The third and fourth paragraphs that go into the tefillin are the first two of the Shema, which contain within them the commandment to wear tefillin.

There are four separate compartments and parchments for the head tefillin (one parchment for each paragraph), and only one for the hand tefillin, for all the paragraphs for the hand tefillin are written on one piece of parchment.

We took the combined total of five pieces of parchment, upon which were written four paragraphs from the Torah, and in accordance with the ancient tradition taught to Moshe at Sinai, we wrapped the parchment in another parchment covering called a *matlis*, and then (again in accordance with a law taught to Moshe at Sinai) we tied up the parchment and its covering with the hair of a calf. We then placed that bundle into a compartment inside the box.

So, in short, in the box for the *tefillin shel rosh* (of the head) we placed four pieces of parchment, with each piece of parchment containing a separate paragraph from the Torah, and in the box for the *tefillin shel yad* (hand) we placed one piece, since those same paragraphs are written on one slip of parchment for the *tefillin shel yad*. We then sewed up the box of tefillin using the sinew of an animal.

Before we covered up the parchment with the *matlis* and the calf hair and closed up the box, I remember thinking to myself: this parchment is absolutely beautiful. The calligraphy on it was exquisite and the passages that were written upon the parchment are powerful words from the Torah.

And then I began to feel a little sad: I was about to confine these beautiful passages to the inside of a dark box, never to be seen again. These parchments and their coverings are so beautiful. So why would we go to all this trouble and place them inside a box where no one can ever see them?

The answer lies in the very words written on the parchment.

The first parchment that we placed in the tefillin box contains the passage that opens with the following statement:

קַדֶּשׁ לִי כָל בְּכוֹר פֶּטֶר כָּל רֶחֶם בִּבְנֵי יִשְׂרָאֵל בָּאָדָם וּבַבְּהֵמָה לִי הוּא:

Sanctify for Me every firstborn, the opening of every womb of a human and of an animal; it is Mine. (Shemot 13:2)

Then the paragraph concludes:

וְהִגַּדְתָּ לְבִנְךָ בַּיּוֹם הַהוּא לֵאמֹר בַּעֲבוּר זֶה עָשָׂה ה' לִי בְּצֵאתִי מִמִּצְרָיִם:

And you should say to your children on that day: "It is on account of this that God led me out of Egypt." (Shemot 13:8)

Like Yaakov did to Dinah, we have a natural tendency to take what we love in this world and place it inside a box. We want to protect it and we want to keep it to ourselves. We don't want to share it with the Esavs of the world. But the message of the tefillin box is the exact opposite of this.

We take a box of tefillin and we place inside it the words *Kadesh li kol bekhor*, "sanctify for Me your firstborn." The message that we place inside the box is that we must take our prized possessions – our firstborn children and animals – and take them out of the box; we must take them away from their secret hiding places and share them with the world, sanctifying them not to ourselves but to Hashem.

And the next paragraph that we place in the tefillin repeats this exact same theme:

וְהַעֲבַרְתָּ כָל פֶּטֶר רֶחֶם לַה'.... וְהָיָה כִּי יִשְׁאָלְךָ בִנְךָ מָחָר לֵאמֹר מַה זֹאת וְאָמַרְתָּ אֵלָיו בְּחֹזֶק יָד הוֹצִיאָנוּ ה' מִמִּצְרָיִם.... וְכָל בְּכוֹר בָּנַי אֶפְדֶּה:

> We must dedicate the first of every womb to Hashem....
> And when it will be that your children will ask you,
> "What is this?" you will respond: "For with a strong
> hand Hashem led us out of Egypt.... [Therefore] all
> the firstborn of my children, I must redeem." (Shemot
> 13:12–15)

We sometimes think that our possessions – and we have no more valuable possession than our children – are here to serve us. So we try to keep them to ourselves and keep them inside a box.

So when we make the tefillin box we put the exact opposite message inside the box. The message is that our *bekhorim*, our firstborn children or our prized animals, were put here for a reason. Not to serve us, but to serve Hashem. They were put here not to benefit their parents but to serve God. Our holiest and most precious items are for Hashem and we need to recognize that.

Yaakov placed his daughter inside his box and for this he was punished. He should have allowed his daughter to have an impact upon the world. When we make our boxes of tefillin, we are declaring the opposite message: the possessions that we would naturally want to hide inside the box we are instead dedicating to service of Hashem.

Do you know who carries out this message better than anyone in the Jewish community? Chabad. Chabad parents teach their children from an early age that their responsibility is to serve Hashem. And so Chabad parents willingly allow their children to go off to the four corners of the earth in order to better serve God.

This idea is very hard. What parent doesn't want to have their kids right near them at all times? Who amongst us wants to share our most prized possessions with the world? But that is the message hidden inside the boxes of tefillin: *Kadesh li kol bekhor,* sanctify for Hashem your firstborn.

But you know what else we learn from Rashi? Placing Dinah inside the box didn't work. True, she didn't end up with Esav, but she ended up with a fate that was perhaps even worse.

The classic work *Mesillat Yesharim*, by the great Rabbi Moshe Chaim Luzzatto, states: Because Yaakov placed Dinah in a box to prevent Esav from taking her (even though he certainly meant well), the result was that he withheld his benevolence from his brother, and the Midrash says: "You did not want to marry her off to one who is circumcised so in the end she will be married off to one who is uncircumcised. You did not want to marry her off in a manner that is permissible, so in the end she will be married off in a manner that is prohibited."[1]

Yaakov's excessive caution was not only spiritually sinful but it was also unsuccessful. He thought he was protecting Dinah by placing her in the box. But this overprotection backfired. Placing someone in a box doesn't work. In the end, Dinah eventually left the box, and when she did so she was unprepared for the world.

The next thing we hear about Dinah in the Torah is that she fell into the hands of Shechem the son of Hamor, and that he assaulted her and violated her.

Yaakov's misguided protection of Dinah put her at a greater risk in the world. Dinah was like a child raised in a bubble to ward off infections. Such a child is safe in the bubble, but at a much greater risk outside the bubble. So, too, this was the case with Dinah: the second she left the box she was in great danger. Rashi is teaching us that instead of boxing her in, Yaakov should have taught her how to protect herself in the world.

This is the message of the final two paragraphs of the tefillin (which are also the first two paragraphs of the Shema). We say in these paragraphs that we will take the message of the Torah, *u-ve-lekhtekha va-derekh*, out on the road. As we journey, we will take

---

1. Bereishit Rabbah 71:7. Translation from *The Path of the Just – Mesillas Yesharim*, translated by Yosef Leibler (Jerusalem: Feldheim, 2004), 26.

with us the message of the Torah. The Torah was not meant to be hidden in a box, and as its followers, neither are we. Rather, inside our boxes we write that we have a responsibility to take our Torah and go out on the *derekh*, on the path, on the journey to the world in service of Hashem.

So from now on whenever we hear that seemingly ubiquitous expression – outside the box – let us remember that we Jews have another box, the boxes of tefillin. And it is our job to take the message that is inside that box and share it with the world.

One Shul:
What It Really Means
Vayeishev

On November 19, 2010, the *New York Times* published an article about web-based bar-mitzvah lessons.[1] The article points out that, increasingly, people are turning away from the traditional American route of normal bar- or bat-mitzvah lessons under the rubric of a community synagogue. Instead they are finding their own personal rabbi who might even be hundreds of miles away, but can conduct the lessons and teachings over the web.

I have nothing against technology and there is nothing wrong with conducting a bar-mitzvah lesson over Skype. But the article in the *Times* also spoke about an overall trend in the Jewish community that concerns me and works against the vision that I have for our shul and our community.

The article talks about a group that calls itself oneshul.org and bills itself as "the world's first community-run online synagogue." This group "imagines Web-only bar mitzvahs, with an e-minyan, or group of 10, gathered via Skype." In their words, they are pushing "homeshulin."

The article also quoted Rabbi Joy Levitt of the Jewish Community Center on the Upper West Side of Manhattan, who offered this critique of the new group: "It will accomplish the specific need of a specific parent to get a bar mitzvah.... But from the standpoint of a robust Jewish life that will hold a community and its values into the next generation, we're not going to get there through Skype."

---

1. Amy Virshup, "Bar Mitzvah Studies Take to the Web."

I find myself agreeing strongly with Rabbi Levitt. It is possible for these people to celebrate a bar mitzvah in this manner and completely miss the point of a bar mitzvah.

Let me explain through the context of parashat Vayeishev.

This portion focuses on the fact that Yosef is sold by his brothers into slavery. After he is sold the brothers realize that they need an alibi, so they slaughter a he-goat – or in Hebrew, a *se'ir izim* – and they dip Yosef's coat into its blood. They then trick their father. They take Yosef's bloody coat over to their father and say (37:32): "*Haker na.*" *Lehakir* means "to recognize" or "to know." So they are saying to their father: Do you know whose coat this is? Is this your son Yosef's coat?

But the words *haker na* can also be reversed onto Yosef's brothers, who were themselves incapable of recognizing Yosef's greatness. (See Bereishit 42:8: "For though Joseph recognized his brothers, they did not recognize him.") We can imagine ourselves demanding of Yosef's brothers: *Haker na*, please recognize! Did you know who Yosef was when you sold him into slavery? Did you know what he was capable of becoming? How could you ever do something like this to somebody who you really know?

For this sin of *haker na*, of not recognizing who Yosef was, we the Jewish people are still repenting. We are still repenting for the sin of selling our own brother into slavery and for the sin of not recognizing Yosef's greatness.

Rashi explains that the brothers specifically dipped Yosef's coat into the blood of a goat, because a goat's blood is similar to human blood. Since the sin happened via the blood of a he-goat, the repentance must also happen in this manner. When do we atone for the sin of *haker na* with the blood of a he-goat? On Yom Kippur.

The brothers deceived their father with a goat and so too on Yom Kippur we must repent for this sin. The Torah tells us that on Yom Kippur we are to take two identical he-goats as an atonement offering. One goat is sent off into the wilderness, *azazel*, in order to achieve atonement for our sins; the other goat we slaughter, and we take its blood and sprinkle it in the Temple (Vayikra, chapter 16). This ritual act served as an atonement for the horrible sin of Yosef's brothers.

The actual act was both an animal sacrifice and also symbolic of something even deeper.

Here is the symbolism: The brothers didn't recognize Yosef's greatness, and so we take two goats having no clear difference between them and offer them both as sacrifices, but in very different ways. One goat was offered on the altar and the other goat was sent to the wilderness and thrown off a cliff. The drama of the selection of these goats and the attention surrounding their different fates force the worshipers at the Temple to recognize that the selection of each goat was arbitrary. It is a reminder that we as a people sinned with an arbitrary rejection of Yosef without realizing his greatness. It is as though we are saying that we must really look at people and recognize their greatness and dedication to Hashem, otherwise we are no better than the brothers of Yosef. To a large degree this Temple rite demonstrates how years later the Jews are still being punished for the sin of selling Yosef.

In the time of the Temple, Hashem had mercy upon us and gave us a clear path to repentance. But now we no longer have a Temple, so how are we to repent for this terrible sin?

First, we need to recognize that what we are talking about, of course, goes beyond the actual sin of selling Yosef. That act happened once many years ago. The reason we still need to repent for it is because that act represents another action that we as a community do all the time, on a daily basis. We should understand that this sin of selling Yosef encompasses our community's larger sin of regularly, and in a mundane manner, turning our backs on our fellow Jews and "metaphorically" selling them; i.e., not feeling enough pain when our fellow brothers are in distress.

How often do we not notice the poverty or the pain among us? How often do we not recognize the people in our own community who are in great need and are crying themselves to sleep at night?

This callous indifference to the needs of our own family is akin to selling our brothers into slavery, and it is this sin that we repented for every year with a he-goat in the Temple on Yom Kippur.

But now that we no longer have a Temple and two he-goats, we turn to the text of the Torah, where we see a hint and a path as to how we can repent today.

The Torah itself offers an antidote to the sin of *haker na*.

Right after the incident where Yosef's brothers utter the words *haker na*, the Torah shifts to a different story: the story of what Yehudah does after the sale of Yosef.

The Torah tells us that Yehudah sins by having a physical, intimate encounter with Tamar. Tamar is his widowed daughter-in-law, whom Yehudah was supposed to redeem through Levirate marriage. But he had refused to do so. So she took matters into her own hands and disguised herself as a harlot. When Yehudah meets Tamar at the crossroads, he doesn't recognize her as his daughter-in-law, and he desires to be intimate with her. She tells him that her price is a *gedi izim*, a kid goat. Alas, Yehudah doesn't have his credit card on him, and so instead he gives her his staff, his garment, and his seal as an *eiravon*, a guarantee.

As a result of their encounter, Tamar gets pregnant. Yehudah suspects her of adultery and arranges for her to be executed. So Tamar sends the *eiravon*, the guarantee, to Yehudah and says *haker na*, look closely – do you recognize whose guarantee this is (38:25)?

Tamar is saying to Yehudah: *haker na*, look closely and understand the situation. Don't just kill me; look at me and think about who I am. And when Yehudah looks more closely, he recognizes that it is his *eiravon*, or in other words, it is his responsibility to speak up on behalf of his daughter-in-law. From the union of Yehudah and Tamar the Torah tells us that Peretz is born, from whom ultimately the Messiah will come.

That moment – where Tamar says *haker na*, and where Yehudah listens to her – is the blueprint as to how we can repent for the sin of Yosef's brothers. Yehudah was the mastermind of Yosef's sale. It is Yehudah who sinned by suggesting to his brothers that Yosef be sold – and so he bears responsibility for the sin of *haker na*. The antidote lies in the words *haker na* themselves – we must look closely at the people near us and recognize their greatness.

Too often, we look at a person and see nothing. We are too busy with our own lives to get involved in another person's. So the Torah tells us with this story that the path to redemption for our community comes from being able to look at a person, and say *haker na* – you are our responsibility. We will be your *eiravon*, your guarantee.

How is one moved on a continual basis to feel this idea? It is my belief that the best way to be inspired to feel and live this message on a consistent basis is by gathering for a communal prayer service.

This is one reason why I keep stressing in our own congregation the importance of attendance at daily prayer services, not just Shabbat. When one prays on a daily basis with a mourner and sees his broken heart, then one can truly say *haker na*. When one sees a person crying, praying for the health of a relative, then one can say *haker na*. Coming together and praying for each other's needs is vital for being able to truly recognize the greatness of another.

This is why I am proud that our own synagogue is bucking the trend of other synagogues to have multiple services. In some synagogues, the congregants or the rabbi tell me how proud they are to have multiple minyanim on a Shabbat morning. In our synagogue, I tell them how proud I am that we have one minyan.

In some synagogues, we see a fractioning of Judaism – a "shtiebelization" of Judaism – a further subdivision, each little subgroup forming their own minyan. But I believe such a trend is a cop-out and takes us away from the essence of what a prayer service can and should be. While this might be personally inconvenient for some people, it has a much loftier goal of making the entire community stronger. A prayer service should be about *haker na*, recognizing the people with whom we are praying and holding each other's hands as we walk toward Hashem.

Rambam says that one who doesn't pray with the community and instead prays on his own is a *shakhen ra*, a bad neighbor (*Hilkhot Tefillah* 8:1). Why does he use this harsh terminology?

There is a beautiful *Midrash Rabbah* that explains this *Rambam*:

We read in parashat Toldot that Yitzchak's wife, Rivkah, was barren and unable to have children. So the Torah tells us that Yitzchak prayed to Hashem, *le-nokhach ishto*, on behalf of his wife (25:21). The Midrash tells us what this unusual expression means (Bereishit Rabbah 63:5): Yitzchak and Rivkah prayed in the same location at the same time, for praying in this manner guaranteed that even if only one of their prayers would be worthy of being accepted, the other one would also be accepted. Also, seeing the person for whom one is praying greatly increases the petitioner's concentration and focus, thereby enhancing the quality of his prayer.

This is the essence of *haker na*. We as a community will be stronger when we are able to daven together and not only pray for our own needs but also recognize and pray for the needs of everyone around us.

Often in our shul I see beautiful images that are ordinary images in our shul, but are increasingly becoming rarer and rarer in shuls around the country. I see a recent father who needed help for a moment hand off his son to a much older friend, a Holocaust survivor. And there they sit together, the righteous and holy survivor holding the baby of his neighbor with tears of joy in his eyes, so that his neighbor can finish his prayers. And I also see a young girl come in to shul and hug a grandmother. Not her grandmother, but a grandmother in the community whom she looks up to with great respect and love.

Those scenes are the essence of *haker na*. We need to see beyond our own niche and embrace the larger community.

When we pray as a community, our prayers are more expansive and more beautiful, and they have a better chance of being heard by the Holy One, Blessed be He.

THE MIRACLE OF OVERFLOWING OIL

Mikeitz

In 1990, on the eighth day of Chanukah, a light was extinguished from the world. My Oma, my father's mother, passed away. She was a real character. She had chutzpah and brilliance, warmth and humor.

Thanks to her chutzpah, my father, uncle, and grandfather were able to survive the war, as she helped them run away from the Nazis. There are many legends as to how she and her family managed to survive, but this is my favorite: My grandfather was a diamond dealer in Belgium. One time when the Nazis came to my grandfather's home looking for diamonds, my grandmother had the chutzpah to make sandwiches and hide the diamonds in the sandwiches. The Nazis looked everywhere but could not find the diamonds, which were sitting right there on the kitchen table. She even offered the Nazis some sandwiches to eat, but they refused. The Nazis couldn't see the diamonds right in front of their eyes; all they saw were the sandwiches.

My Oma, whose name was Lea Herzfeld, was a descendant of at least two great tzaddikim. She was a direct descendant of a famous tzaddik, the Chasidic Rebbe, Reb Elimelech of Lizhensk (1717–1786), from his third wife. And she was also a relative of the author of the *Imrei Noam*, Rabbi Meir Horowitz of Dzikow, who was a son-in-law of the Sanzer Rebbe.

Reb Elimelech was himself the third generation of Chasidic Rebbes. He was a student of the Maggid of Mezeritch, who was the primary student of the Ba'al Shem Tov, the founder of Chasidut.

Reb Elimelech is known for being the first to bring Chasidut to Poland and being a driving force in the spread of Polish Chasidut. Some of his students became famous Chasidic teachers in their own merit, like the Chozeh of Lublin and the Koshnitzer Maggid. To this day Reb Elimelech's grave in Lizhensk is visited by thousands of people on his *yahrtzeit*, which is 21 Adar.

Reb Elimelech is revered for his classic work, a commentary on the Torah called the *Noam Elimelech*. The *Noam Elimelech* is a very difficult work to understand because it focuses so much on the concept of a tzaddik, the idea that a righteous person has a special and unique relationship with Hashem.

Reb Elimelech is also known and beloved for the many stories that circulate about him and his brother, Reb Zushya of Anipoli. Just as an example, here is one of the many tales about Reb Elimelech and Reb Zushya.

One time, Reb Elimelech and Reb Zushya were renting a room at an inn. Every night, the anti-Semitic, drunk peasants would come into their room and get their kicks out of beating the one who was sleeping closest to the fire, which was Reb Zushya. So Reb Elimelech decided to switch with his brother so that he would be the one sleeping next to the fire and they would beat him instead of Reb Zushya. That night, as the peasants came in, they said, "Is it fair to always beat the one who sleeps near the fire? This time lets beat the other one." And so, they beat Reb Zushya again! Reb Eliemelech taught that we learn from this that everything is decreed from Hashem, and we cannot change our place in His plan!

Reb Eliemelech has a very special teaching about Chanukah that I would like to share with you, along with a teaching of the Imrei Noam. In order to understand the *Noam Elimelech*'s teaching about Chanukah, we first must review a famous question of the Beit Yosef.

Rabbi Yosef Karo (1448–1575, Tzfat) asks a question in his encyclopedic work that is known as the *Beit Yosef*. This question has become known as "the Beit Yosef's question."

The Talmud in tractate Shabbat (21b) says that we celebrate Chanukah because after the Hasmoneans defeated the Greeks (Yevanim), they "searched the Temple and were able to find only one flask of oil that contained the seal of the *kohein gadol*. There was only enough oil to last for one day. A miracle occurred and they lit it for eight days."

So the Beit Yosef asks: "Why did they establish the holiday for eight days? If there was enough oil to last for one day, then the miracle was only for seven days, so why establish the holiday for eight days instead of seven?"

The Beit Yosef himself gives three answers to this question, which we will not discuss. The *sefer Ner le-Me'ah*[1] records another one hundred answers to this question. One of those answers is a suggestion of the Imrei Noam, a relative of my Oma.

The Imrei Noam writes that there are two different miracles regarding oil in the Jewish tradition. One is the miracle of Chanukah. But there is also a second miracle of oil.

In Melachim Bet, chapter 4, we are told the story of Elisha the prophet and a certain unnamed woman whom he helps. She has no money. Her sole possession is a single jug of oil. So he tells her: "Take all the pots of all your neighbors. Then take your pot of oil and pour it into all your friend's pots." So the woman took *keilim reikim*, empty vessels, and she kept pouring oil into them (verses 2–7). Miraculously, the oil from this pot filled up all the pots that this woman was able to find. The Imrei Noam explains that in this case the original pot was emptied of its oil and then miraculously the oil reappeared.

But he suggests that in the Chanukah story the miracle happened differently. When the oil was poured out of the flask on the first

---

1. Written by Yerachmiel Zelcer (Brooklyn, 1986).

night, the oil in the flask did not decrease, but was miraculously immediately replaced; as the oil poured forth, new oil miraculously replaced it. Thus, even on the first night of Chanukah there was a great miracle in that the flask of oil did not diminish even for a moment, and for this reason we celebrate Chanukah for eight nights.

So there are two miracles relating to oil. In one case, oil appeared in an empty jug. In the other case, oil appeared in a full jug, and made sure that the jug always remained full of oil.

The first case symbolizes a miracle that comes when we are in distress, when our vessel is empty – keilim reikim – and we need the salvation of God. As we say in the special psalm for Chanukah, chiyitani mi-yordi vor, God lifted me out of a pit (Tehillim 30:4). We were in trouble and we needed help. So we turned to Hashem and Hashem lifted us up. This is the miracle that we often think of when we say, "We need a miracle." If we are in distress, and we pray to Hashem, this is the kind of miracle we are hoping for. When people are sick or desperate for financial support, this is the type of miracle they yearn for. When people who were on a plane that survived an emergency landing in the Hudson River came off the plane, they said that they closed their eyes as the plane landed and prayed for a miracle. This is the type of miracle they were praying for. Their jugs were empty and they needed to be rescued by Hashem.

But, explains the Imrei Noam, the miracle of Chanukah was different and even greater. The miracle of Chanukah happened when the jug was full, and so there was no need to ever be in distress in the first place. This is the miracle of having Hashem's salvation come upon us when our cup is overflowing. These are the miracles we often don't notice, because we experience on a regular basis the miracle of the overflowing cup of oil. These are the unnoticed miracles that make up our daily lives.

It is amazing how people misunderstand the miracle of Chanukah. One columnist in the *New York Times* once wrote, "Rabbis later added the lamp miracle to give God at least a bit part in the proceedings."[2] Oy! This shows a lack of a spiritual understanding of the holiday. I am sure the columnist will one day regret those words. Chanukah is not a historical holiday, but a spiritual holiday. The rabbis were the ones who canonized Chanukah as a religious holiday in the first place. So they are obviously the ones who taught us from the beginning what the focus of the holiday should be. It is not about a military victory; it is about the miracle of the oil.

Some people say, "Oh, the miracle of oil is such a minor miracle. Big deal, they found a little bit of oil. Compared to the splitting of the sea, that is not even a footnote."

But that is exactly the point of the Imrei Noam. The miracle of Chanukah's oil is to remind us of the miraculous moments of our daily lives and to appreciate Hashem when our cup overflows. We must not wait for our cup to be empty in order to turn to Hashem and be cognizant of His miracles.

This is essentially the teaching of the *Noam Elimelech* as well. Many people wonder how Chanukah gets the name Chanukah. Some say it comes from the word *lechanekh*, to dedicate, alluding to the fact that the Jewish people rededicated the altar or the Temple on this holiday, and made a *chanukat ha-bayit* (literally, a dedication of the altar). Others say it means, *chanu k"h*, meaning that they rested or camped on the twenty-fifth day of Kislev.

But the *Noam Eliemelech* explains the matter differently. In his opinion, Chanukah comes from the word *chein*, meaning grace: on this holiday Hashem gave us His grace and His kindness. And that is the essence of Chanukah: to recognize the daily gift of *chein* that Hashem gives us; to pause and be appreciative; and then to

---

2. David Brooks, "The Hanukkah Story," December 10, 2009.

thank Hashem for the miracle of the overflowing cups of joy that He gives us in our daily lives.

And if we do that then we will feel the presence of God everywhere and anywhere – as we learn from the following story of Reb Eliemelech and Reb Zushya.

Once they were wandering around with a group of beggars in order to humble themselves and to inspire themselves to repent. And it happened that in their wanderings they were falsely accused and thrown into jail by the anti-Semitic police.

Sitting in the jail, Reb Elimelech arose to daven *minchah*. Reb Zushya looked at him and said, "You can't daven *minchah* here."

"Why not?" asked Reb Elimelech.

Reb Zushya reminded him that in the jail cell there was a pail serving as a waste bucket, and since prisoners had gone to the bathroom in the pail, it was now prohibited to pray in the same room.

Reb Elimelech sat down and began to cry over the fact that he was now unable to pray.

Reb Zushya said to him, "Don't cry over the fact that you can't pray to Hashem. The same God that told you to pray when the room is clean, also told you not to pray when the room is unclean. So by not praying you are fulfilling a commandment of Hashem. So if you truly want to connect to Hashem at this time, you should rejoice over the fact that He has now told you NOT to pray to Him."

When Reb Elimelech heard this he began to smile and laugh. He said, "Reb Zushya, you are absolutely correct. We must rejoice over the fact that this is how Hashem tells us to serve Him."

And so the two brothers arose and began to sing and dance over the fact that they were now performing the mitzvah of not praying where there is a waste pail.

When the prison guards heard the noise and saw them singing and dancing, they asked another cellmate, "Why are these two dancing and laughing?" The other prisoner said, "They are dancing about the fact that there is a waste pail in their room."

When the guard heard this he said, "We'll see about that!" And he immediately removed the waste pail from their cell.

And so, immediately, Reb Elimelech and Reb Zushya began to daven *minchah* in a proper manner.

As I mentioned, my Oma hid her diamonds in the sandwiches.

Valuable diamonds are hidden in the everyday realities of our lives too. Chanukah is a holiday that reminds us that sometimes the real diamonds are hidden in our sandwiches, and in the mundane existence of our lives.

And so perhaps we can say that the smaller the miracle, the more we have to be thankful for.

A SHEPHERDED COMMUNITY

Vayigash

Our synagogue is located in a wonderful DC neighborhood called Shepherd Park. The name Shepherd Park derives from Alexander Shepherd, who was the governor of the territory of DC from 1873–1874. Governor Shepherd and his wife built a great mansion, which they called Bleak House, on the corner of 13th and Geranium. This home was distinctive in the neighborhood and Governor Shepherd was very accomplished, so the surrounding community was given the name Shepherd Park. Alas, eventually the house itself was demolished in 1916.

We know that there are no coincidences in life. It can't be a coincidence that our synagogue and many people from our congregation dwell in Shepherd Park, for the word *shepherd* is a name suffused with biblical meaning.

The importance of a shepherd appears in the haftarah for Vayigash, which comes from the book of Yechezkel, chapter 37. We are told of a prophecy of Yechezkel: that there will come a time in the future when a descendant of David will rule over all of the Jewish people, "and there will be one shepherd for My entire people" (verse 24). This is a reference to the future Messiah, the redeemer of our people. He is called a shepherd, or in Hebrew, a *ro'eh*.

I want to encourage everyone to see the name "Shepherd Park" as a fortuitous name, a call meant to inspire each of us to achieve greatness.

Let us take a closer look at this prophecy of Yechezkel and try to understand what it might mean for all of us on a practical basis as we try to live our lives in the service of Hashem.

59

Before we get into Yechezkel's prophecy, we will first offer a little background. Yechezkel was a prophet who lived in the sixth century BCE. After Shlomo ha-Melekh ruled over the Jewish people, the kingdom of Israel split into two. There was the northern kingdom, which was home to ten tribes and was dominated by the tribe of Efraim (one of Yosef's sons), and there was the southern kingdom where the tribes of Yehudah and Binyamin and Levi lived. Yechezkel shared his prophecies with the exiled people of the southern kingdom more than 140 years after the exile of the northern kingdom of Israel in 722 BCE.

The northern kingdom of Efraim was exiled by Sancheirev, king of Ashur. Now, 140 years later, the southern kingdom of Yehudah was also beginning to be exiled in various stages. When Yechezkel gives the prophecy that is recorded in this week's haftarah, he was already exiled in Bavel but the Temple had not yet been destroyed. That would happen in 587 BCE, and after that catastrophic event many more exiles would follow him to Bavel.

Those were dire times for the Jewish people. The northern kingdom had been destroyed and dispersed more than a century ago, and now Yechezkel was forecasting a terrible fate for the kingdom of Yehudah.

But in the midst of this gloomy scenario, the haftarah tells us of a hopeful prophecy of Yechezkel. As he watched the people of Yehudah being exiled, Hashem tells him to walk in front of his nation with two sticks of wood. On one stick of wood he should write: "To Yehudah and his friends from Israel"; and on a second stick he should write: "To Yosef a tree of Efraim and to all of Israel his friends" (Yechezkel 37:16).The book of Yechezkel tells us that these two sticks of wood will represent the two kingdoms of Israel that have now both been exiled.

Then Hashem tells Yechezkel to hold the sticks close to each other and miraculously Hashem will unite the sticks together. Yechezkel is then instructed to tell his fellow Jews that Hashem will one day unite the Kingdom of Yosef (the northern kingdom) and the Kingdom of Yehudah (the southern kingdom) into one kingdom. And from that point on they will never be separated and they will never fight again. God will save our nation, redeem us, and purify us. And there will be one *ro'eh*, one shepherd, a descendant of David, who will rule over us. God will restore us to our land, rebuild our Temple, and give us a covenant of peace.

Yechezkel's prophecy is a messianic prophecy of a true and complete redemption for which we are still waiting. We are still waiting for the shepherd who will reign over a united Israel. According to some biblical commentators, this prophecy is only referring to one redeemer, a *Mashiach* who will come from the tribe of Yehudah. This person whom we are waiting for is known as *Mashiach ben David*.

But the nineteenth-century Russian commentator known as Malbim teaches us that according to rabbinic tradition, this prophecy of Yechezkel is actually referring to two Messiahs, not one. He explains that before the *Mashiach ben David* will reign over Israel, there will first be *Mashiach ben Yosef*, a *Mashiach* from the house of Yosef. This *Mashiach* will gather up the ten lost tribes that were scattered throughout the world and reunite them with the Kingdom of Yehudah. However, he will be unable to bring about a full redemption, and he himself will be defeated in battle. Then the *Mashiach ben David* will arrive and bring about the full messianic redemption.

Either way, according to Yechezkel the ultimate Messiah, i.e., the complete redemption, will come from the house of Yehudah and not from the house of Yosef.

Today we take this concept as a given, but it wasn't always clear that this was the case. There was a point in our history when Yehudah and Yosef were fighting over who would be the *Mashiach*.

Parashat Vayigash begins with the scene of Yehudah confronting Yosef in Yehudah's attempt to redeem Binyamin. Yehudah says (44:18), "Do not be angry with your servant." Rashi explains that Yehudah was speaking very harshly to Yosef, *dibber alav kashot*. And in fact the Midrash says that Yehudah was speaking so harshly to Yosef that metal was flying out of his mouth. The Midrash explains that they were fighting over the right to be the ultimate king of Israel, the *Mashiach* of the Jewish people (Bereishit Rabbah 93 [middle]).

We select this prophecy from Yechezkel to read along with parashat Vayigash in order to tell us that it will be Yehudah, and not Yosef, who is selected as the ultimate *Mashiach*.

Traditionally, two answers are given as to why Yehudah is chosen over Yosef. One reason offered is because Yehudah has sinned, while Yosef avoided sin; Yosef was perfect. When Mrs. Potiphar tried to seduce him, he held his ground and did not commit a sin. So too, his descendant, Yehoshua, from the tribe of Efraim, was perfect and never committed a sin.

In contrast, Yehudah sinned with his encounter with Tamar. As the Torah tells us, he went off the path and visited a harlot. So too his descendant David committed a sin via his liaison with Batsheva. Yehudah and David sinned and repented. They are the paradigmatic examples of *ba'alei teshuvah*, people who sin and repent. So explains Rabbi Joseph Soloveitchik: The king needs to understand his people. If he will be someone who has never sinned then he won't be able to relate to the people. Yehudah has sinned and repented, and so it is he who is selected as the future king of Israel, because he can better relate to the people.

A second answer given is that Yehudah is the one who says about Binyamin, "*Anokhi e'ervenu* – I will take responsibility for him" (43:9). Yaakov had been afraid to send Binyamin to Egypt until Yehudah stepped in and said that he was responsible for his brother. The words *anokhi e'ervenu* literally mean "I will be the guarantee."

It is for this reason that Yehudah is chosen to be the king and future *Mashiach*. Remember that Yechezkel calls the *Mashiach* a *ro'eh*, a shepherd.

The rabbis explain that a shepherd is chosen as the *Mashiach* because a shepherd feels personal responsibility for each and every member of his flock. So too, it is the Messiah's responsibility as well to feel personal responsibility for each and every member of his flock.

What do these two answers mean for our own lives?

While waiting for the perfect *Mashiach* to arrive and redeem all of us, we too can act like we are each the *Mashiach*. We can act in the spirit of the Messiah and therefore encourage his early arrival. By this, I mean we can turn our community into a true Shepherds' Park.

There are multiple ways that we can act in the spirit of the Messiah. But here are two suggestions that follow in the path of Yehudah.

First, we can each act as though we are personally responsible for our brothers and sisters. We must act as the guarantee for the rest of our family, the Jewish people.

Here is an example of how we can do that. In December 2010, we heard news about a devastating catastrophe in Israel. As a result of a forest fire, forty-two families lost a soul and more than thirty families had an injured family member. More than seventeen thousand people were evacuated from their homes. Seventy-four structures were completely destroyed, 173 partially destroyed, and five million trees are no longer in existence.

This was the worst fire in Israel's history.

The way of the Messiah, the way of the shepherd, is to feel a personal connection to such a tragedy. We should take action. Get involved. Donate to charity to help those of our brothers and sisters who were hurt by this tragedy. That is just one example.

If you want to act like a shepherd it means you must get involved personally when you hear of a tragedy that affects a member of our flock.

And here is a second suggestion of how we can act like the *Mashiach ben David*. In order to act like the Messiah, we can reach out to the Ten Lost Tribes and help them return to Israel.

There is a wonderful organization in Israel called Shavei Israel that reaches out to "lost Jews." They connect with people from India, China, Uganda, and other exotic places, who are descendants of the Ten Lost Tribes of Israel. They help these "lost Jews" reunite with their Jewish brethren. This work is very praiseworthy and deserving of our support. But as shepherds we can also focus on less exotic, but equally important, work. In order to be like the *Mashiach ben David* we need to focus on helping those who are the ten lost tribes amongst us to return to the Jewish people.

Too often, people have fallen and they think that they cannot return to God. They think it is too late. But the message of *Mashiach ben David* is that the *Mashiach* himself will be a *ba'al teshuvah*, just so that he himself can relate to someone who has fallen.

We as a Jewish community tend to forget about the people who are on the fringes – the so-called "have-nots" of the world. It is often the case that the "have-nots" got themselves into trouble. But so did *Mashiach ben David*. And he was selected precisely for that reason. Thus, the true path to redemption is to seek out those people, so that we can pave the way for the *Mashiach* to arrive. Because the *Mashiach ben David* will arrive only once all people – the "haves" and the "have-nots" – are included in our community. And that will only happen when we feel directly responsible for each and every person in our community.

And when that happens, we will be fulfilling our own prophecy of why our community is called Shepherd Park.

RECOGNIZING YOUR CHILDREN

Vayechi

Recently our congregation was given a tremendous gift. The family of Rabbi Gedaliah Silverstone gave us a Torah scroll that they had acquired many years ago in memory of Rabbi Gedaliah. The family had read from the Torah on the High Holidays and memorable family occasions, and they decided that they wanted our congregation to be able to use the Torah, protect it, and watch over it.

This gift has special meaning for us, as Rabbi Gedaliah Silverstone was rabbi of our congregation back in 1906. When we read from this Torah, I feel as thought the *neshamah* (soul) of Rabbi Gedaliah Silverstone is here with us as well.

Rabbi Gedaliah Silverstone came with his wife Rebecca to Washington, DC, in 1901 after first serving as a rabbi in Belfast, Ireland. Together, he and Rebecca had ten children and many more grandchildren.

The rabbi was a great scholar in the strictly Orthodox Lithuanian rabbinic tradition. He is known to have written at least thirty-eight books, and he probably wrote even more than that. He was well known for his brilliance and his devotion to Orthodoxy.

I wonder what it must have been like for him when he got off the train in Washington for the first time. Here was this Lithuanian rabbinic scholar in a place that was, from the perspective of *Yiddishkeit,* a desert. There were no yeshivahs back then in Washington. There weren't any kosher restaurants. And he was *the* Orthodox rabbi. I have seen with my own eyes how Rabbi Silverstone signed his documents: Rabbi Gedaliah Silverstone, chief rabbi of Washington, DC.

He might have been chief rabbi, but he was also in many ways a lone wolf keeping the ancient traditions in a modern land. His granddaughter, Judith White, tells the following story in her book, *Silverstone Stories and Other Mishagos*.[1]

> One time he was invited to President Taft's wedding anniversary celebration, where he was seated with the Archbishop of Washington, DC. Mrs. Taft came over to the table and noticed that Rabbi Gedaliah was not eating the pork. So she told him: "You can eat, it is all kosher." Then the Archbishop asked the Rabbi why he was so stubborn and old-fashioned about not eating pork. The rabbi displayed his keen Talmudic mind and wit and quickly responded, "I promise you that at your wedding I will eat pork."
>
> He was a great scholar of the Talmud living in a strange country with new customs and traditions. In fact he was the 12th straight generation of Silverstone rabbis – his son, Rabbi Dr. Harry Silverstone was the 13th generation. With his black hat, and full grey beard and love of Torah study, he must have felt that this country America, which was so open and welcoming to his family and friends, wasn't really the place for him. This is probably why, in 1937 he moved to Palestine, where he died in 1944. Although he kept in close contact with his ten children while he lived in Palestine, he never saw them again.

Ever since the Silverstone family gave us their Torah scroll, I have thought about Rabbi Gedaliah a lot. What must have been going through his mind as he watched his children and grandchildren growing up in America?

---

1. Eshel Books, 2007, p. 5.

If you look at the Silverstone family today, you will see a wonderful and beautiful extended family. Nice people. Good people; generous people. But in many ways they are the typical story of the American Jewish family – including my own. The original patriarch was a pious grandfather who immigrated. Now a few generations later, for the most part there is no more Orthodoxy. Some of the family members remain connected Jewishly to various degrees, others less so. And of course, as in every American Jewish family, some of the descendants of this very great rabbi are now no longer even Jewish.

If we took Rabbi Gedaliah and via a time machine placed him right in front of his descendants – what do you think he might say?

Lucky for us, we *do* have such a time machine. It is called the Torah, and it is relevant to us in every generation.

Parashat Vayechi records the following interaction between Yosef and his father, Yaakov. Yosef gets word that his father is about to die, so he rushes to see his father, and he brings with him his two sons, Efraim and Menashe. Yaakov says, "Your two sons, who were born to you before I got here, shall be like my sons to me. Efraim and Menashe will be to me like Reuven and Shimon" (48:5).

But then the text says something very strange and difficult to understand:

וַיַּרְא יִשְׂרָאֵל אֶת בְּנֵי יוֹסֵף וַיֹּאמֶר מִי אֵלֶּה:

And Israel saw the children of Yosef and he asked, "Who are these?" (Bereishit 48:8)

Mi eleh? Who are these? What kind of question is that? Yaakov just told us that Efraim and Menashe are like his own children, and now he looks at them and asks "Who are these"?

And Yosef's response is also very strange. Yosef says:

בָּנַי הֵם אֲשֶׁר נָתַן לִי אֱלֹקִים בָּזֶה....

These are my children that God gave me here.... (48:9)

As if his father didn't know that Efraim and Menashe are his children! As Ramban points out, "Yosef doesn't need to tell his father that these are his children that God gave him in Egypt!" What is going on in this strange passage?

The answer is that when Yaakov looked at Efraim and Menashe, he said "*Mi eleh?*" in a different sense of the words. He was asking: Who are these children standing before me? What are their values? Are they really worthy of being my children? Probably he looked at them and they looked like Egyptian children. And he was scared and concerned that they would not follow in his spiritual path. He said "*Mi eleh?*" because he did not know what to make of them.

In many ways the older generation of American Jewish immigrants looked at their younger offspring in America and said "*Mi eleh?*"

And it cuts both ways. Many people bring a picture into my office of an ancestor of theirs from Europe: a pious, bearded Jew with traditional garb. And now, here they are, themselves clean-shaven and dressed in modern clothing. And the descendants ask about their ancestors of just two or three generations ago: "*Mi eleh?*"

This is the checkered story of American Jewry. People look at the pictures of their grandparents or their grandchildren; the facial features are the same, but that is it.

According to Rashi, Yaakov was very uncomfortable with his own grandchildren. The Torah says that his children carried his coffin to the land of Canaan. And Rashi comments that Yaakov only lets his children and not his grandchildren carry him, "and not an Egyptian man or any of your children since they are from the daughters of Canaan" (Rashi, Bereishit 50:13).

Yaakov's grandchildren are partially Egyptians and Canaanites and so he has great concerns about them. He asks himself: *Mi eleh?* Are these my children?

This is why Yosef responds to his father's question by saying, "*Banai hem asher natan li Elokim* – These are my children that

Hashem gave me." These children are from God. This is our fate in this world and we must recognize that. My father, understand that these too are your children.

And when Yaakov hears this he recites a blessing that many of us sing to our children before we tuck them in at night. Yaakov says:

הַמַּלְאָךְ הַגֹּאֵל אֹתִי מִכָּל רָע יְבָרֵךְ אֶת הַנְּעָרִים וְיִקָּרֵא בָהֶם שְׁמִי וְשֵׁם אֲבֹתַי אַבְרָהָם וְיִצְחָק וְיִדְגּוּ לָרֹב בְּקֶרֶב הָאָרֶץ:

May the same God who sent an angel to redeem me, may He bless the lads and let them carry my name and the name of my fathers, Avraham and Yitzchak, and let them increase in the land like fish. (Bereishit 48:16)

Ramban explains that this verse means: "May their seed and name endure forever, and may the name of Avraham, Yitzchak and Yaakov be remembered through them forever!"

This prayer is declaring that even though we know our children will not necessarily follow our spiritual blueprint, we are asking for the angel of Hashem to guide them so that the names of Avraham and Yitzchak and Yaakov are always remembered through them. And when we recite this prayer with our children every night this is what we are requesting from Hashem: that the angel watches them and guides them on their spiritual path.

But of course, this is not only true in the area of spirituality.

Sometimes parents look at their children and they say *"Mi eleh?"* – who are these kids? This is not the path I wanted. This is not the direction I wanted my child to go in. My child is turning out differently than what I had in mind.

And so we turn to Hashem and we pray that the angel guides them and directs them along their paths.

In parashat Vayechi we are taught that we should always bless our male children to be like Efraim and Menashe. Why Efraim and Menashe, and not Moshe and Aharon, or Avraham and Yitzchak?

Aren't Efraim and Menashe minor figures in the greater biblical narrative?

You know why we always bless our children to be like Efraim and Menashe? Because Efraim and Menashe did not turn out exactly like Yaakov wanted them to, but nevertheless he blessed them and he loved them unconditionally. Probably, he felt that by loving them unconditionally he would have a chance to influence them and guide them.

I want to close with another teaching of Rabbi Gedaliah Silverstone. This is a teaching that I have taken to heart and started practicing in my own rabbinate. Whenever Rabbi Gedaliah would visit a home that might not be kosher, he would always partake of a fruit: an orange or a banana. He felt that it would be impolite to completely refuse the host's gesture of hospitality.

In short, he found a way to practice his Orthodoxy and connect to the Jews of the city.

We had a ceremony in our shul to rededicate the Silverstone Torah and we held it on a Saturday night in the winter. That Saturday night it snowed, and so we thought that very few people from the Silverstone family would come. After all, it was snowing.

Boy, were we wrong.

The Silverstone family arrived in droves. Some drove from Philadelphia, while others flew in from Texas. All wanted to be there for the rededication of Rabbi Gedaliah's Torah. What a merit to his *neshamah* that all of these family members so many years later came to partake of the mitzvah of honoring and writing a Torah scroll.

Perhaps soon, in Rabbi Gedaliah's merit, we will have yet another generation of Silverstone rabbis. In the meantime, every time we read from that Torah in our shul, we are fulfilling the blessing of Yaakov (48:20), "*Yesimkha Elokim ke-Efraim ve-khi-Menashe* – May God make you like Efraim and Menashe."

SHEMOT

No Excuses for a
Recalcitrant Husband
Shemot

I met Tamar on Sunday, December 19, 2010. She is a twenty-seven-year-old graduate of Yeshiva University's Stern College and the mother of a three-year-old child. Although she was surrounded by family, friends, and literally hundreds of supporters, she had tears in her eyes.

She said to me, "I never thought it could happen to me. If it could happen to me, then it could happen to anyone."

Tamar is very brave. She is speaking out publicly and defiantly in the face of the terrible ordeal she is going through. She is currently an *agunah* or a "chained woman." By this we do not mean physically chained, but psychologically, emotionally, and legally chained. Despite the fact that she and Aharon have been separated for three and a half years and were civilly divorced more than a year ago, and despite the fact that financial and child custody matters have been settled, he refuses to give her a *get* (a Jewish divorce) and therefore she is not permitted to remarry.

I have been a rabbi long enough to know that when a contested divorce is taking place there are at minimum two different sides to the story. But when either party withholds a *get* and uses that as leverage, then until that matter is settled there is only one side. Period. Otherwise we are effectively giving the spouse veto power over any court's decision. Just as we would not tolerate physical coercion, we cannot tolerate emotional coercion.

I feel strongly that once there is a civil divorce there is absolutely no excuse to withhold a *get*. (I would actually go further and say

73

that once there is no chance for reconciliation a *get* should be given immediately.) The *get* cannot be used as leverage to gain more money or better terms of a divorce settlement. To do such a thing is a desecration of God's name, as it is chaining the woman in an emotional fashion.

Make no mistake about it, being emotionally and psychologically chained can be just as enslaving as being physically chained.

We see this very notion in parashat Shemot. The verse (Shemot 1:13) says that the Egyptians enslaved the Jews *be-farekh*. The word *farekh* is usually translated as "hard labor," as in work *ha-mefarekhet et ha-guf*, that destroys the body. But Rambam translates the word differently as "*peh rakh*, a "soft tongue." In other words, Pharaoh enslaved the Israelites with deception and manipulation and not hard labor. The slavery of Egypt was an emotional and psychological slavery as much as it was a physical one.

And that is what Tamar is going through. She is being emotionally and psychologically enslaved by her former husband and is unable to free herself and move on with her life. By Jewish law the only way Tamar can remarry, short of the death of her husband, is if Aharon gives her a get of his own free will. Yet, Rambam rules that we should physically encourage Aharon to give the get until he says he is doing so of his own volition.

Today, of course, we cannot and should not use physical attacks as a method of coercion. It is illegal and inappropriate, but nonetheless we must not remain passive. When we see such an enslaved woman in our own community, what should our reaction be?

I want to present two appropriate reactions on the basis of parashat Shemot.

First and foremost, when we hear of an *agunah* situation in our own community, we as a community and as individuals must get involved. At the time of the December 19 rally, three rabbis representing the local Va'ad Harabanim of Greater Washington issued a statement to the effect that they are not taking a stand on this matter. But they did take a stand. By issuing such a statement on the eve of the rally, they participated in a smokescreen in support of the husband. None of those rabbis attended the rally for Tamar. Their passivity was in fact a stand in favor of the status quo.

It was only ten months later, on October 5, 2010, that the local rabbinate publically criticized Aharon. This was a tragic and unnecessary delay.

We must take the opposite approach. We must get involved. Don't say "we cannot take a stand on this matter." Such an approach is unacceptable and plays jurisdictional politics with the life of a young woman. It is only by getting involved in these cases that we will bring about the redemption. And what is at stake here is not just Tamar's well-being but the redemption of our people.

It is the awesome, spiritual power of marriage that led to the redemption of the Jewish people from Egypt. The verse says:

וַיֵּלֶךְ אִישׁ מִבֵּית לֵוִי וַיִּקַּח אֶת בַּת לֵוִי:

> And a man went from the house of Levi and married a
> daughter of Levi. (Shemot 2:1)

It is from this union, between Amram and Yocheved, that the great Moshe Rabbeinu, the redeemer of our people, was born.

But the verse itself is difficult. The commentators notice that the word *va-yelekh*, "and he went," is unusual in this context. Explains Ramban: The word *va-yelekh* speaks to the greatness of their act. Pharaoh had just issued a decree that every Jewish boy who was born was to be killed. In this context, Moshe's parents decided to get married and have children even though their actions entailed a great risk.

Ramban (Shemot 2:1) says that the very act of *va-yelekh* was an act of greatness because it was "an act of defiance of Pharaoh's decree." And he writes, "Through this courageous act of defiance the Israelites were ultimately redeemed from Egypt." It is through a courageous commitment to marriage and creating children that the Jewish people achieved redemption in Egypt.

But this positive idea comes with a negative contrast as well. The flip side of this is when people take actions that destroy the core of marriage. By chaining a woman and preventing her from remarrying, a recalcitrant husband is destroying our ability for redemption as a community. It is not just the woman who is denied freedom and redemption; whenever any woman in a community is chained and thereby unredeemed, we are all being chained by virtue of the fact that we are all denied redemption.

In response we must get involved.

More specifically, I spoke directly about Tamar's situation with Rav Herschel Schachter. Rav Schachter is viewed as a *posek* (legal authority) for the Rabbinical Council of America and the Orthodox Union. He encouraged us to publicly raise a voice against Aharon. He also encouraged me to let Aharon's employers know about his unethical behavior. Aharon is a lawyer for a very powerful Republican congressman (David Camp from Michigan). Rav Schachter urged me to pursue this matter with Aharon's colleagues on Capitol Hill.

This is the first point I wanted to make: we must get involved in trying to free Tamar.

But I have a second point as well. In this case simply getting involved is not even enough. It is necessary but insufficient action.

This can also be seen from the verses in this Torah portion.

It states:

וַיְהִי בַּיָּמִים הָהֵם וַיִּגְדַּל מֹשֶׁה וַיֵּצֵא אֶל אֶחָיו וַיַּרְא בְּסִבְלֹתָם....

> And it was in those days that Moshe grew up and
> went out to his brothers and he saw their afflictions....
> (Shemot 2:11)

This verse refers to the fact that Moshe was raised in the palace of Pharaoh, but he then went out and noticed that his own brethren were being enslaved. Famously, Moshe intervenes twice on behalf of his brothers. First he notices that an Egyptian is beating an Israelite. When Moshe sees this, "he strikes the Egyptian" (2:12) and kills him. Moshe then sees two Israelites fighting with each other. Here too, he intervenes. But this time his actions are exposed to Pharaoh and he needs to flee into exile.

So Moshe has acted courageously twice. But he is still not yet picked by Hashem to be the redeemer of His people. Moshe is still not worthy to receive a revelation from God. His actions were noble, but they weren't enough to cause redemption.

Moshe runs into the wilderness of Midian, and according to Ramban (2:24) he was in the wilderness for at least sixty years! For sixty years he wasn't worthy to redeem the people, despite the fact that he had gotten involved. Something more was required. The Torah doesn't mention the intervening sixty years of his life, because he didn't do anything sufficiently of consequence in between.

It is only after the following incident that Moshe becomes worthy of standing in God's presence, receiving revelation, and effectuating redemption; it was only after the following incident that he saw the burning bush and merited to be Moshe Rabbeinu: The first thing the Torah mentions after sixty years of Moshe's life is that he helped seven Midianite women get their water from a well. Says the Torah (2:16–17): "As these [seven daughters] were beginning to fill their troughs and water their father's sheep, other shepherds came and tried to chase them away. Moshe got up and came to their aid and then watered their sheep."

So what was so special about this incident?

Again, Ramban (2:16) teaches us how to interpret this passage. He explains that every day the shepherds were bullying and abusing these seven daughters and stealing their water. Moshe's greatness was that not only did he return the water to its rightful owners, but he also helped them draw new water. In the words of Ramban, "ve-gam daloh dalah lahem – he also drew new water for them." Not only did he fix the injustice of the situation but he did an act of outright kindness to sustain them going forward.

Moshe's greatness was that he didn't settle for fixing a specific injustice; he moved the community so that there would be no more injustices.

We see a similar idea as it relates to the midwives, Shifrah and Puah, who are spoken about in parashat Shemot. Pharaoh had commanded these women to kill the male Jewish babies, but the Torah states that these Jewish women saved the babies, "*va-techayenah et ha-yeladim* – and they allowed the children to live" (1:17).

But Rashi, commenting on the words "*va-techayenah et ha-yeladim*" says "they gave them food." In other words, not only did these midwives (who our tradition understands to be the mother and sister of Moshe) save the lives of these babies, but they also went an extra step of providing them with food and water.

Rav Schachter explained the midwives' actions on the basis of an idea of Rambam in his *Shemonah Perakim*. Rambam states that when there is a character trait of society that is bad in the extreme, we need to change our society by moving to the other extreme. When there is an environment of injustice in the community, it is not enough just to correct the injustice. We must totally change the culture that allows such an incident to happen.

It wasn't enough for Moshe to simply return the water to the seven Midianite daughters; he also needed to draw new water for them. It wasn't enough for Shifrah and Puah to save the lives of the newborn babies; they also had to provide food and sustenance for all the babies they saved. And for us, too, it is not enough just to correct the injustice for Tamar; we must change the environment of our entire community.

This case has shown me that the Rabbinical Council of America's recommended prenuptial agreement is sadly inadequate to protect women from becoming *agunot*. The Beth Din of America recommends this prenuptial agreement which "contains a support obligation that formalizes the husband's obligation under Jewish law to financially support his wife, thus providing an incentive for the timely delivery of a *get* in the event the marriage fails" (http://www.bethdin.org/agreement.asp).

I know of a case where a woman who signed this prenuptial agreement is unable to get a *get* because the husband is claiming the signature was forged. Second, the prenuptial agreement only threatens the husband with a financial penalty. But this is insufficient protection because a vindictive husband can elude such a threat. We need to do better. The status quo is unacceptable.

When there is a tragic event like an *agunah* in our community, it is not just the woman who is chained and enslaved. We are all chained and enslaved and held back from redemption. And such a tragedy cannot just be put right with a mere correction for this specific woman; we need to reach out beyond her case and seek to aid the plight of all *agunot* around the country. We must use this as a springboard to help all struggling women in similar situations – not to just free them from their plight but to draw water for them going forward and to provide them with *mazon* and *mayim*, bread and water.

And only when we do that will we also be worthy of seeing the burning bush and standing in the presence of Hashem.

BUILDING A NOBLE
COMMUNITY
Va'eira

There is a woman in our shul named Anna Yuter, who is ninety-nine years old. Recently, she retired after working in the same job for over seventy-three years. Since 1934, Anna has worked at Hotel Washington. She started working at the hotel back when Franklin Delano Roosevelt's (FDR) vice-president, John Garner, used to live there. Over the years she held many different jobs at the hotel. It is only when it closed for two years of renovations that Anna gracefully accepted retirement.

In honor of Anna, let us pose this basic question about parashat Va'eira: How did Moshe have the courage to approach Pharaoh on behalf of the Jewish people?

In parashat Shemot, we read that after the first time Moshe approached Pharaoh, he was not only rejected by Pharaoh but he was also rejected by his own people. Pharaoh then responded by doubling the workload of the Israelites. He said, previously I supplied you with straw, but now you have to find your own straw and produce the same number of bricks.

The people were infuriated with Moshe. By raising a voice he had made things worse for them. Says the Torah:

וַיִּפְגְּעוּ אֶת מֹשֶׁה וְאֶת אַהֲרֹן.... הִבְאַשְׁתֶּם אֶת רֵיחֵנוּ בְּעֵינֵי פַרְעֹה
וּבְעֵינֵי עֲבָדָיו....

The people of Israel attacked Moshe and Aharon.... "You have ruined our reputation in the eyes of Pharaoh and in the eyes of his servants...." (Shemot 5:20–21)

They were screaming at Moshe: "Shhh. Be quiet. Do not ruin our reputation in the eyes of Pharaoh. Do not raise a voice!" They were being persecuted by Pharaoh and yet they screamed at Moshe to remain quiet. Can you imagine such a thing?

Of course, we can, because this has been a frequent response of leaders of the Jewish community whenever Jews wanted to speak out against anti-Semitism. There are so many examples in history of the mentality that it is better to remain quiet that it seems almost a cliché to repeat it. But it happens over and over again.

Felix Frankfurter reminisces in his memoirs that when word got out that FDR was thinking of appointing him as a supreme court justice, it was the leaders of the American Jewish community who led a delegation to FDR. The delegation did not applaud FDR but (led by the *New York Times'* Sulzberger) instead pleaded with FDR not to appoint Frankfurter *because it would anger Hitler* and make Jews too visible in this country.

Rabbi Avi Weiss told me that when the Student Struggle of the Soviet Jewry movement got started, the leaders of the American Jewish community were at odds with the students who began the movement. The leaders of the community wanted no one to raise a voice about the Jews of the Soviet Union, so they pressured Congress not to act. On the eve of the Jackson-Vanik amendment, the head of the Conference of Presidents of Major Jewish Organizations walked into Scoop Jackson's office and begged him not to sponsor this legislation (which turned out to be the decisive turning point in the struggle for Soviet Jewry) *as it would anger the Soviet leaders.*

And recently, in my own small way, I felt this myself. After I saw press reports that the Jews of Venezuela are being threatened, I called Jewish leaders and leaders of Congress and asked them to raise a voice on behalf of the Jews of Venezuela. The response was, "Let's be quiet *so as not to anger Chavez* and endanger the Venezuelan Jewish community."

In the face of people telling him to be quiet, how did Moshe have the strength to continue to go to Pharaoh? We can broaden this question and ask: "In the face of so many obstacles that face our community, how can all of us have the courage to continue to work on behalf of the Jewish people?"

The truth is that Moshe needed Hashem's help. Hashem tells him, "Go to Pharaoh." And Moshe responds:

הֵן בְּנֵי יִשְׂרָאֵל לֹא שָׁמְעוּ אֵלַי וְאֵיךְ יִשְׁמָעֵנִי פַרְעֹה וַאֲנִי עֲרַל שְׂפָתָיִם:

"Indeed the children of Israel will not listen to me; how will Pharaoh listen to me, as I have clumsy lips?" (Shemot 6:12)

Aral sefatayim literally translates as "clumsy lips," and often people interpret the phrase as Moshe saying, "I have a speech defect." But I really prefer Rabbi Aryeh Kaplan's translation for *aral sefatayim* – "I have no self-confidence."[1]

Moshe has turned to Hashem and exclaimed: "Why should I bother going? They aren't going to listen to me. How can I go? I have no confidence that I will succeed. The people themselves are telling me not to go."

The interesting thing is that the Torah does not directly answer Moshe's challenge to Hashem. Instead, the next verses of the Torah go into the lineage of Moshe and list the genealogy of the tribes of Reuven, Shimon, and Levi. The commentators all struggle with this very strange interruption. How come the lineage appears now? It seems to be out of order and out of context.

Many beautiful answers have been suggested to this question. Just as an example of one approach: Rav Samson Raphael Hirsch,

---

1. See Rabbi Aryeh Kaplan, *The Living Torah* (Brooklyn, NY: Moznaim, 1981), 287.

the great German rabbi (1808–1888), suggests that the Torah presents Moshe's genealogy at this point in order to stress the humanity of Moshe. Moshe is about to become the leader of the Jewish people and cause plagues to rain down on Egypt, but in the end we must never forget that he is human.

Ramban provides another answer. He writes that the lineage of Moshe is given here, "*Likhvod Moshe* – for the honor of Moshe."

Moshe has said, "How can I go?" Hashem responds by telling him who he is and who he came from. Hashem is telling him: "You are not just Moshe who was born as a slave in Goshen, and lived as a shepherd in Midian. No! You are Moshe who is a descendant of Avraham, Yitzchak, and Yaakov. You are the great-grandson of Levi, the grandson of Kehat, and the son of Amram. Your father's name, Amram, means 'great nation.' Your mother is Yocheved the daughter of Levi. You have a distinguished lineage."

When Moshe goes to Pharaoh he is being reminded that he not only represents himself, but he represents his ancestors and his future descendants. He must carry the nobility of his family. If he lacks courage, then he is disrespecting the honor of his ancestors.

That is why Hashem tells Moshe (6:4), "*Ve-gam hakimoti et briti itam* – I will keep my covenant with them," with your forefathers. Hashem reminds Moshe that the covenant He has with Moshe and with the children of Israel is not just a covenant with their generation, but with all of the Jewish people – past, present, and future.

This is the answer that Hashem gives to Moshe. Say to the children of Israel: "I do not only represent you. I am speaking on behalf of the Jewish people, past and future. You are telling me that you prefer to live in danger under Pharaoh. But I tell you that the decision is not yours. The decision was made by your ancestors to have a covenant with Hashem. That covenant requires us to speak up to Pharaoh and to leave his land."

This is the secret to the survival of the Jewish people throughout the millennia. It is the recognition that our primary commitment is to the covenant with Hashem, which is obviously much bigger than any one person or any one community.

The Jewish community is a seamless community, where past and future meet together as one. Even if a local community chooses to remain silent in the face of persecution, the larger Jewish community has a responsibility to not remain silent. As the Talmud says, "Silence is like acceptance" (Yevamot 87a).

The idea that we live as Jews with a transgenerational responsibility is true in both a negative context, when we face persecution, as well as a positive context, as it relates to our responsibility to build and strengthen the Jewish community.

We commit to our community, not only for ourselves, but also as a result of our responsibility to our past and to our future. We make sure that the place where we live is committed to Hashem and doing His will, strong in Torah study, serious about *tefillah*, committed to *tzedakah* and *chesed*. Our community must be a noble one; otherwise we are disrespecting ourselves, our ancestors, and our descendants.

This is the nobility that we recognize in people like Anna Yuter.

When Anna's parents (Itzhik Yankel and Meryl) came to DC from Lithuania in 1900, they chose to settle in Southwest, DC. They left a thriving tradition in Lithuania; it was home to tremendous Torah scholarship and very pious Jews. It was a noble community. They were poor and persecuted, but they were noble.

They came to DC, where there was practically nothing. There were no Jewish schools and just a handful of synagogues. They knew their responsibility; they built a noble community. They became involved in the building of Congregation Ohev Sholom. And when their daughter, Anna, was born in 1913 they practically raised her in the shul.

When they built the shul and their community, they knew that they weren't only building it for Anna, but they were building it for generations and generations to come. And when we build the very same shul and our larger Jewish community today, we feel the same way.

As a community we must always remember that our responsibility transcends our family, our location, and our generation.

We have a covenant with Hashem, and we have a commitment to our ancestors and descendants. That covenant is what gives us the courage and the responsibility to speak to Pharaoh: past, present, and future. This covenant is what inspires us to build our community: past, present, and future.

Do Not Leave Your Doorway until the Morning

Bo

One of the highlights of a recent trip to Israel occurred on Shabbat morning. After davening at the Kotel we went to look for my cousin who studies in a yeshivah in the Old City of Jerusalem. It turns out he was davening in the newly renovated Churvah Synagogue, which is located in the Jewish Quarter of the Old City. We walked over to that synagogue, and as my cousin was walking out of the *petach*, the doorway of the synagogue, we banged into each other. We then entered the synagogue together, and I was blown away by its absolute beauty and its powerful history.

I had not yet seen the synagogue in its rebuilt form, and I was not expecting to see what I saw: a magnificent, towering, and awe-inspiring sanctuary.

The synagogue carries a strange name: *Churvah*, which means "a ruin." How did a synagogue come to have the name "*Churvah*"?

The synagogue was first built in the early eighteenth century by a rabbi named Yehudah he-Chasid (who is not to be confused with the medieval scholar also known as Rabbi Yehudah he-Chasid). It was built with money borrowed from Arab lenders. The worshipers in the synagogue were unable to pay back the money they had borrowed in order to fund their synagogue, so in 1721 the leaders of the community were imprisoned and the synagogue was burned to the ground by the lenders. The synagogue was left in a pile of rubble, and so it became known as the *churvah,* the "ruin."[1]

In 1864, the synagogue was rebuilt, and even though it carried a different name, it was still known as the *Churvah.* In the ensuing years it became known as the main synagogue of the Old City, the center of Jewish life in the entire Land of Israel, and the spot in which the chief rabbis of the land in that period were installed into their positions. But it was again destroyed during the War of Independence in 1948.

Finally in March 2010, the synagogue was again rebuilt and fully renovated. And so when we visited the "*Churvah*" Synagogue, we did not see a synagogue in ruins, but instead one of the most beautiful shuls I have ever seen.

Although the *Churvah* is a modern synagogue, there is an earlier reference to an ancient place of prayer in Jerusalem that is also called a *churvah.*

The Talmud in tractate Berakhot (3a) tells the following story: "Rabbi Yose recounted: One time I was walking along on my journey and I entered into a *churvah* – a ruin – in Jerusalem in order to pray. Along came Eliyahu the prophet and he stood guard by the *petach,* by the doorway, and he protected me until I finished my prayer."

Why was it necessary for Eliyahu to guard the doorway while Rabbi Yose prayed? On a simple level this is because Rabbi Yose was praying in a dangerous place, an abandoned building, and so Eliyahu was guarding him while he prayed to Hashem.

But on a symbolic level it means much more. On a symbolic level the doorway represents the path between two boundaries. One can go on the right path in life or on the wrong path. Rabbi Yose was living in the days following the destruction of Jerusalem and the destruction of the holy Temple. He and the Jewish people could easily have gone off the path. They could have lost their

---

1. See http://www.rova-yehudi.org.il/en/atar-hurva.asp.

connection to Torah and to Hashem. So Eliyahu the prophet stood at the doorway – he stood at the border – and made sure that Rabbi Yose did not go off the correct path.

Eliyahu ha-Navi was not the first person in history to stand by a *petach* – a doorway – and protect his charges.

Let us remember that Avraham himself used to sit at the *petach*. The verse says:

וַיֵּרָא אֵלָיו ה' בְּאֵלֹנֵי מַמְרֵא וְהוּא יֹשֵׁב פֶּתַח הָאֹהֶל כְּחֹם הַיּוֹם:

And God appeared to him [Avraham] in Elonei Mamrei
and he was sitting at the entrance to the tent in the heat
of the day. (Bereishit 18:1)

According to Rashi, Avraham was watching at the entrance to the tent in order to seek out travelers who might need his help. Like Eliyahu he was standing at the doorway in order to protect his charges.

So the *petach* is a doorway that symbolizes the edge of danger. And often our great protectors – like Avraham and Eliyahu – stood there in order to offer help to the vulnerable people of the world.

But there is another reference to a *petach*, and it is found in parashat Bo.

We are told that Moshe commanded the Jewish people to take a paschal lamb and slaughter it on the fourteenth day of the month. Then they were supposed to take the blood of this lamb and spread it on their doorposts and lintel and wait the entire night as Hashem smote the firstborn of the Egyptians. When Hashem would see the blood on the doorposts of the Israelites, He would pass over their homes and spare their firstborn (12:21–22).

The Israelites are then commanded by Moshe:

וְאַתֶּם לֹא תֵצְאוּ אִישׁ מִפֶּתַח בֵּיתוֹ עַד בֹּקֶר:

And you shall not go out from the door of your home
until the morning arrives. (Shemot 12:22)

On a literal level the Israelites are simply being told that they cannot leave the entrance of their homes until morning arrives, for to do so would expose them to the Angel of Death that was traveling around Egypt that night.

But here too, we should look at this verse on a deeper level. The Israelites are not being told that they can never leave their *petach*; they are being told that they have to wait until morning (*boker*) in order to leave their *petach*.

Why is Avraham allowed to leave the *petach* of his home whereas the Israelites were not allowed to? The crucial difference is that Avraham is in the land of Canaan and he is thus in a secure position and able to help others who are in danger. In contrast, the Israelites are in Egypt and so are themselves in great danger. Therefore if they would be leave their homes to protect others they would be exposing themselves to harm. So before they can help others they must help themselves. They must not leave their *petach*. They must first wait until morning when redemption will arrive.

This contrast between the *petach* of Avraham and the *petach* of the Israelites of Egypt points to a fundamental, historical difference between the spiritual life of the Jews of Eretz Yisrael and the Jews of Diaspora.

The Jews of Eretz Yisrael are generally more secure and better protected in their spiritual connection and are thus better able to stand at an open *petach* and look out from the *petach* to help others. In contrast, the Jews of the Diaspora must guard their homes carefully; they must shut their *petach* lest they go out and are destroyed spiritually by the Angel of Death.

This is true as a historical phenomenon and it is true in today's world as well.

On my trip to Israel, as I walked through the streets of Jerusalem I saw scenes that I would never see in the Diaspora. On multiple occasions I witnessed schoolchildren walking through the streets at all hours of the day singing Jewish songs and outwardly displaying their Judaism. Here in America if one displays one's Judaism too openly and publicly it is an abnormality; in Israel it is the norm. I felt that in Jerusalem the people were like Avraham sitting at the *petach*, while in America we are like the Israelites unable to walk outside of our doorposts until the morning.

If we in the Diaspora are symbolically being commanded not to leave our doorways until the morning, what should we do? How can we strengthen ourselves in the Diaspora? How can we live here as Jews even while recognizing that our spiritual life will be qualitatively different than the more secure spirituality of the Jews of Eretz Yisrael?

Here are suggestions about two mitzvot that we in the Diaspora can do in order to better secure our spiritual lives:

First, we should follow what the Torah itself says to do. The Torah tells us to place a mezuzah on our doorposts. A mezuzah is a piece of parchment containing the first two paragraphs of the Shema. The Torah requires us to place this on our doorposts in order to provide protection – spiritual protection – for us. When we walk through the doorposts of our home we are supposed to look at the mezuzah, and kiss the mezuzah, and recite:

ה' שֹׁמְרֶךָ ה' צִלְּךָ עַל-יַד יְמִינֶךָ: ה' יִשְׁמָר צֵאתְךָ וּבוֹאֶךָ מֵעַתָּה וְעַד-עוֹלָם:

> God is your guardian, God is your shade upon your right hand. God should guard your going out and your coming in now and forever. (Tehillim 121:5, 8)

This is a way of praying for Hashem's protection.

If we are punctilious about this mitzvah we will see our entire world through the prism of the paragraphs contained in the mezuzah. We will recognize the unity of Hashem and the centrality that He needs to play in our lives, and we will remember to always be grateful to Him. Proper performance of this mitzvah will help us be more secure within our own doorposts.

What does it mean to be punctilious about this mitzvah? First, we should notice the mezuzah each and every time we walk into a room. Second, we should be careful that we are obeying the mitzvah properly. We should make sure that every room and doorway in our house (excluding a bathroom and closets that are too small) has a mezuzah. We should make sure that our living areas, and if possible our offices, also have mezuzah scrolls. We should learn the laws of the mezuzah and carefully apply them in order to provide spiritual protection for our homes.

Adherence to the mitzvah of mezuzah will better secure our own *petachim*, doorposts.

There is another mitzvah that I want to suggest we all take upon ourselves in order to secure our own doorposts. We should all perform the mitzvah of visiting Eretz Yisrael.

According to some commentators it is a mitzvah to visit Eretz Yisrael because all of our mitzvot are performed in an enhanced manner when visiting the land. In this vein, Rashi writes (Devarim 11:18) that we should perform the mitzvah of mezuzah even outside Eretz Yisrael so that we can properly perform the mitzvah when we eventually return to the land – *"asu mezuzot kedei shelo yehiyu lakhem chadashim ke-she-tich'zeru."*

In other words, all our mitzvot when performed in Eretz Yisrael have an extra spiritual quality to them; they are naturally enhanced by a closer connection to Hashem.

My recommendation is that every Jew should seriously consider visiting Eretz Yisrael as it is a mitzvah and it will boost your own spirituality. By performing this mitzvah you will better be able to come back and guard your own doorpost and infuse it with spirituality.

We are told in the Torah that when we placed the blood of the lamb on our doorposts, Hashem watched for the blood and then passed over those homes. Rashi (12:3) uses the word *dalag*: He "skipped over" the homes. But some commentaries say that when

He saw us performing the mitzvot, He did not skip but jumped for joy over the houses.

In Jerusalem, on Friday night, I went with my son Roey to daven *Kabbalat Shabbat* services at the Kotel. Alas, right when we arrived it started to drizzle. We decided to go to the indoor part of the Kotel in order to be dry, but too many other people also had that same idea. So we decided to stay outside, as it was only a light mist. We started to daven. There were just a few of us in the group, maybe fifteen people. But then it started to rain harder...and harder... and harder. And the harder it rained the more people joined us in singing praises to Hashem. And then it started to really pour. By this time our group had grown tenfold. I thought for sure that the rain would drive people away. But the harder it rained, the louder we sang, and the faster we danced, and the higher we jumped in service of Hashem.

And now that we have returned to DC, every time we go to kiss our mezuzah, we are still jumping in service of Hashem.

DEFEATING EVIL: THOUGHTS ON THE ARIZONA MASSACRE

Beshalach

On January 8, 2011, we saw a senseless act of pure evil in the world. US Representative Gabrielle Giffords was holding an open meeting in a parking lot with her constituents in Tuscon, Arizona, when a mentally unstable person named Jared Lee Loughner opened fire. Nineteen people were shot, six fatally. Representative Giffords was herself shot in the head at point-blank range, and it is a miracle that she survived.

When we hear of such an act it is often emotionally devastating and depressing. We are all affected by it. I want to share with you some thoughts about how we can respond to that terrible act in a spiritual manner.

Since Jared Lee Loughner is in all likelihood mentally ill, we cannot categorize him as purely evil; but the act of intentionally killing innocent people in such a barbaric manner is itself evil. How can a person take a gun and kill in such a manner? It is beyond comprehension. It is pure evil.

Parashat Beshalach makes one thing clear: the idea of pure evil existing in the world is something that has been with us since the time of the Exodus. The Torah portion tells us about Amalek; Amalek attacked the Jewish people after they crossed the sea and were enjoying their first steps of freedom. Amalek is defined by the Torah as pure evil. They are a nation that needs to be destroyed and wiped off the earth (Devarim 25:17–19).

93

The rabbinic commentators debate whether this commandment is still in force today and whether the actual nation of Amalek still exists in the world.

In the years after the Holocaust, Rabbi Joseph Soloveitchik taught that Amalek is still in existence. The reason for this is because the verse states:

כִּי יָד עַל כֵּס יָ-הּ מִלְחָמָה לַה' בַּעֲמָלֵק מִדֹּר דֹּר:

The Hand is on God's throne. God shall be at war with
Amalek for all generations. (Shemot 17:16)

Rashi explains that "The Hand is on God's throne" means that God is making an oath that there will be a war with Amalek for all generations until such time as evil is eradicated from the world. The term "God's throne" is written in an incomplete manner, *kes* instead of *kiseh*, and the verse contains the word *yah* instead of the full four-letter name of God. This means that God's throne will be incomplete and His name will be incomplete until Amalek is totally wiped off the earth. "For all generations," means that God is still waging war with Amalek.

Furthermore, Rabbi Soloveitchik notes that Rambam writes in his *Mishneh Torah* that the seven Canaanite nations no longer exist, as they were mixed up among the other nations of the world. However, Rambam never wrote that this same principle applies with respect to Amalek, and the implication therefore is that even though we are many years distant from the time of the Bible, Amalek is still in the world.

By virtue of the fact that evil still exists in the world, Rabbi Soloveitchik concludes that Amalek must also still exist. And so the war against Amalek is literally still continuing to this day.

How do we know who Amalek is? Rabbi Soloveitchik and many other rabbis expand the category of Amalek and argue that it applies to any nation that is dedicated to destroying the Jewish people and does not fear God. (As the Torah states elsewhere about Amalek [Devarim 25:18], they are *lo yareh Elokim*.)

Famously, Rabbi Soloveitchik applied this teaching to Nazi Germany and even went so far as to apply *some* of the biblical rules of Amalek to Nazi Germany. The rule is that one may not derive material benefit from the products of Amalek. In light of this, Rabbi Soloveitchik told David Ben-Gurion, Israel's first prime minister, that he was not permitted to accept reparation funds from Germany after World War II. Ben-Gurion did not listen to Rabbi Soloveitchik. And some of Rabbi Soloveitchik's later students say that many years after Rabbi Soloveitchik recanted from this position once he saw how much of a salutary effect the reparations had on the infrastructure of Israel. (I heard this description of Rabbi Soloveitchik's views on Amalek and his conversation with David Ben-Gurion in a lecture of Rav Hershel Schachter.)

Regardless, the important factor is that many rabbis expand the concept of Amalek. We all need to be very careful before expanding the category of Amalek and applying it to a specific nation. It is extremely dangerous and when misapplied can lead to evil in its own right.

Amalek represents pure evil. One suggestion about how we should understand the idea of Amalek is to recognize that it represents the Torah's teaching that evil will exist in the world until such time as the Messiah comes to complete God's throne.

So when we come to grips with such horrible tragedies like the murders in Tuscon, Arizona, we remember that the Torah already told us that we can expect that there will be pure evil. And the Torah not only tells us that evil will exist but we can gain insight from the Amalek story as to how we can react to the existence of evil in the world.

The Torah portion offers three reactions that we should have when we see Amalek. In doing so, the Torah is offering us a blueprint for how we can deal with the evil we experience in this world.

First, the Torah tells us we must wage battle with Amalek. Moshe says to Yehoshua:

בְּחַר לָנוּ אֲנָשִׁים וְצֵא הִלָּחֵם בַּעֲמָלֵק....

> Select some men for us and go out and wage war with
> Amalek.... (Shemot 17:9)

From this we learn that we are commanded to wage war with evil. We must not ignore it or pretend it doesn't exist. We must not retreat in the face of evil. Rather, we must "go out" and battle it. The first step in defeating evil is recognizing it and being willing to acknowledge that it is evil.

It is easy to forget this responsibility. This is why the Torah goes out of its way to constantly remind us not to forget our responsibility (17:14): "Write this as a remembrance in the book." And, again in the book of Devarim (25:17): "Remember what Amalek did to you."

This, then, is step one: we must recognize evil as being evil and we must commit ourselves to waging war with evil and wiping it out. We must never forget that this is our responsibility as servants of God; we must take an active stand in the face of evil.

But step two takes an opposite approach. While the first thing we must do to rid ourselves of evil is reactive – we react to evil by waging war – the second thing we must do is proactive. Right after the Jewish people crossed the Yam Suf and went into the desert we are told that they complained about the bitter waters that they found there; they were unable to drink. So Hashem took a tree and threw it into the water and made the water sweet. The Torah (15:25) then states, "*Sham sam lo chok u-mishpat* – then God gave [to the Jewish people] laws and rulings."

This passage requires a deep understanding and many different approaches are taken to it. The most common approach is Rashi's, which states that Hashem took this opportunity to give the laws of Shabbat, the red heifer, and torts to the Jewish people.

But Ramban takes an entirely different approach. Ramban (Shemot 15:25) teaches that Hashem taught the Jewish people how to behave toward each other. Hashem was upset that the Jewish people complained about the lack of sweet water. It was bad manners to do so. After all, He had just led them through the sea and defeated the Egyptians, and this is how the Jewish people reacted? It is rude! So Hashem taught the Jewish people basic interpersonal skills. He taught them how to make a request without complaining (*lo derekh telunah*), how to get along with each other (*le'ehov ish et rei'eihu*), how to carry themselves modestly (*ve-hatzne'ah lekhet*), and how to interact with visiting nations (*ve-she-yinhagu shalom im ha-ba'im be-machaneh limkor bahem devarim*).

According to Ramban, Hashem taught these ideas to the Jewish people even prior to Sinai. Even before we could get the Torah we needed to have these basic interpersonal skills. This is the meaning of the famous rabbinic dictum "*Derekh eretz kadmah la-Torah*": before one can achieve Torah, one must have basic personal skills (Pirkei Avot 2:2).

In the context of our Torah portion, we are taught this law just prior to Amalek's appearance in order to teach us how to avoid future encounters with Amalek. This is a proactive way of defeating evil: we counteract evil by bringing love and sweetness into the world.

In fact, Ramban also writes that this is the very reason why Hashem throws the tree into the water. He says it wasn't even a miracle that the bitter water turned sweet. It was just that Hashem showed Moshe a special tree that had the natural ability to purify water – almost like a natural desalination plant. The water was bitter, and the tree came along and naturally sweetened the water.

Well, if it was all natural, then what is the point of the story? The Torah is teaching us that Hashem taught Moshe that there is a natural, non-miraculous quality of sweetness in the world and this sweetness has the ability to purify bitterness.

And this is the second way to conquer Amalek.

We must remember that this ability to remove bitterness exists in the natural world. We can take a sweet substance and add it to bitterness and then drink the water. The sweet substance that will defeat bitterness is the interpersonal skill set that Hashem teaches the Jewish people. This is the *chok u-mishpat* that they learn. It is what is necessary to guard the world against Amalek.

This is a proactive approach to defeating Amalek.

There is also a third step necessary in dealing with Amalek. The Torah tells us that when Yehoshua led the Jewish army into battle with Amalek, Moshe stood up on a mountain. When Moshe raised his hands the Jewish people prevailed in battle, but when he lowered his hands, the Amalekites got the upper hand. The Torah tells us:

וְאַהֲרֹן וְחוּר תָּמְכוּ בְיָדָיו מִזֶּה אֶחָד וּמִזֶּה אֶחָד וַיְהִי יָדָיו אֱמוּנָה עַד
בֹּא הַשָּׁמֶשׁ:

So Aharon and Chur each supported [Moshe's] arms
– one on this side and one on that side – and his arms
were steadfast until the sun came. (Shemot 17:12)

The word for "steadfast" is *emunah*. *Emunah* is also the word for "faith." One way to understand this verse is that Moshe remained steadfast in his faith until the sun or the dawn – i.e., the redemption – arrived.

When we encounter evil it is so easy to become disheartened and depressed. It is easy to give up on the world; it is easy to lose faith – faith in Hashem, but even more so, faith in the correctness of our mission and vision. That is why Moshe kept struggling to hold up his hands. He was doubting himself – am I on the right mission? – so he needed his friends and supporters to hold up his hands and strengthen his faith!

I was once visited by twenty-five Christian ministers from around the country who were in town for a scholarly seminar. Naturally, they wanted to visit the National Synagogue, so of course I hosted them. They asked me: what is the greatest challenge that spiritual leaders encounter? I answered that the single greatest challenge that spiritual leaders face is to maintain faith in their own ability to lead and inspire a community.

This is true for rabbis and it is true for all of us. Especially when we witness pure evil, we are so tempted to give up the fight and become cynical. Our hands waver, and we need our friends to support us. But the way to defeat Amalek is to remain steadfast in our belief in the Torah and in our mission; the way to defeat Amalek is to recognize that even though we have setbacks we can overpower them.

Alas, there is real evil that exists in the world. The war against Amalek is not yet finished. But we do have guidance from Hashem that teaches us how to respond to Amalek.

When we see evil we must reenergize ourselves by taking the three steps that are laid out in parashat Bashalach: recognize evil and wage battle against it; proactively defeat evil with the natural sweetness that exists in all of us; and do not allow our faith, the faith of our friends, or our faith in ourselves and the justness of our mission to waver.

And when we do that, then there isn't a bullet in the world that can stop us.

THOU SHALL NOT (BE AN ACCESSORY TO) MURDER

Yitro

Which of the Ten Commandments do you think you violate the most? Unfortunately, we all violate many of them far too often.

It is almost impossible to never violate the Shabbat – there are so many laws. But that is only once a week…. The commandment to honor your parents is also nearly impossible to get right. The commandment "Do not covet" is another one that is extremely difficult to observe properly. And how many of us can say that we never, ever steal, not even a little bit?

If there is one commandment where we might assume that we keep it perfectly, it is the sixth commandment: *"Lo tirtzach* – Do not murder."* Most of us feel pretty comfortable in the fact that we have never murdered anyone.

I am sorry to tell you that we should not feel so comfortable. Here is how the rabbis interpret the sixth commandment:

The medieval French commentator, Chizkuni, writes: *"Hein be-yad, hein be-lashon, hein be-shtikah."* The prohibition of murder can be violated through the hand by physically killing someone, through words, and through silence.

Hashem holds us accountable for murder if we cause someone's death through words and silence. To some extent, this goes beyond American law. For example, there was a case called the "MySpace

100

Suicide Hoax." In the MySpace suicide, a thirteen-year-old girl in Missouri committed suicide after she was emotionally manipulated by adult neighbors in her neighborhood. As a "prank" the adults and kids set up a fake boyfriend for this girl. They insulted her with words and manipulated her emotions. Some knew about it and kept silent; others actively participated in badgering the self-esteem of a young girl.[1]

As Chizkuni argues, those who were actively or passively involved in this so-called hoax are considered to have violated the commandment of *Lo tirtzach*. We see from this that our words can directly lead to murder. The power of words is overwhelming. Even though this young girl hanged herself, those who insulted her are morally – if not legally – held responsible for her murder by Jewish law. In this context we should realize that the Torah calls the commandments *"Aseret ha-Devarim"* – not the Ten Commandments, but the Ten Utterances (20:1). Words have the power to be the holiest sanctification of God's name and they have the power to destroy. Words or the lack of speaking out can literally lead to murder.

Most of us are still feeling pretty good about ourselves. We might think that while we occasionally gossip or insult someone, most of us have not incited a crowd to violence or egged someone on to the point of suicide. But the truth is that the threshold for the violation of this prohibition is even lower.

There was once a rabbi named Rabbi Yonah of Gerona who discussed a radical expansion of the prohibition *Lo tirtzach*.

Rabbeinu Yonah was a great Talmudist and a great moralist. But in order to understand who he was, we need to understand his background. In the year 1233, Rabbeinu Yonah was one of the leaders of the Maimonidean controversy. Rabbeinu Yonah and other leading rabbis signed a ban against people reading

---

1. See Lauren Collins, "Friend Game: Behind the Online Hoax that Led to a Girl's Suicide," *New Yorker Magazine*, January 21, 2008.

Rambam's great philosophical work, *Guide for the Perplexed*, and the first book of the *Mishneh Torah*, known as *Sefer ha-Madda*. Rabbeinu Yonah believed that the philosophical ideas in these works were too dangerous for the public. Indeed, he went even further. At his urging the Christian authorities publicly burned Rambam's works in Paris in 1233.

But once you give people the idea that it is okay to start burning books it is hard to put out the flame, and so in 1242, twenty-four wagonloads of the Talmud were burned exactly where Rambam's books were burned.

When Rabbeinu Yonah saw this he felt that it was divine retribution for his participation in the early burning of Rambam's writings, and he publicly admitted that he was wrong in front of his entire congregation. For the rest of his life he tried to repent for his behavior. He quoted Rambam frequently and he wrote different works on how to repent. The most famous of these is a masterpiece called *Sha'arei Teshuvah*, the Gates of Repentance, which offers a blueprint to repentance.

In the work *Sha'arei Teshuvah* (3:139), Rabbeinu Yonah reminds us that the Torah commands us to give up our lives rather than violate the big three prohibitions: idolatry, adultery, and murder. He then discusses a concept called *avizrayhu*, or an accessory to those prohibitions, and writes that we must give up our lives not only for directly violating those prohibitions but even if we are merely asked to violate an accessory to them.

According to Rabbeinu Yonah, therefore, we must be killed rather than commit an "accessory" to the prohibition of *Lo tirtzach* (20:13).[2] Here is what he considers to be an accessory to murder: "The accessory to murder is shaming someone so that his face turns white. His face turns white and its ruddiness disappears and this is like murder." In Rabbeinu Yonah's opinion, this is not just a nice moral teaching. This is a legal ruling. He writes that one

---

2. This point of Rabbeinu Yonah was shown to me by Rabbi Josh Hoffman.

should allow oneself to be killed rather than embarrass someone to the point where his or her face turns white. As the Talmud says (Ketubot 67b), and he takes literally, "A person should throw themselves into a fire rather than embarrass someone in public."

Since most of us – myself included – have violated this commandment, there are different ways we can approach such a radical ruling like Rabbeinu Yonah's. We can throw up our hands and say it is ridiculous – clearly, embarrassing someone is nowhere nearly as bad as murder. Or, we can ask ourselves if our society is correct in not equating hurting people's feelings with a physical infliction like murder.

Some might suggest that if we seriously equate embarrassing someone with murder then we are devaluing the prohibition of murder. There is that danger. But the alternative – of creating a society that is not sensitive to people's feelings – is perhaps worse.

You can choose to take the Talmud's teaching literally or you can choose to take it as a nice homily intended to inspire you to be more conscious of people's feelings. (Rambam happens to take the latter approach, whereas Tosafot's position in tractate Sotah [10b] accords with Rabbeinu Yonah's view.) But what we cannot afford to do is ignore it.

The story is told about the great Chafetz Chayim: Once a certain person came to purchase all of his scholarly writings. The Chafetz Chayim said to him, "I notice that you bought all my books except the ones that talk about *lashon hara* (gossip)." The customer said, "That one is pointless for me as it is too hard for me to keep." The Chafetz Chayim answered, "It is worth buying the book even if your only reaction at the end of reading the book is a sigh."

We can learn from this that it is our responsibility to work on ourselves in these areas of watching our words and refraining from causing people emotional damage, even if we sometimes feel that we are hopelessly doomed to keep on sinning. One of the ways we can improve is by studying the laws of interpersonal behavior. The more we have these laws in our mind, the less likely we are to violate them. Everyone should take it upon themselves to study these laws at least once a week – even if their only reaction at the end of the session is a sigh.

But really, we should demand much more of ourselves. Many of us are in professions where it is taken as the norm that the way to get ahead is by insulting the competition; by putting someone else down; by saying something bad about someone else. This is not the way of Hashem.

Think about the example of Rabbeinu Yonah. He was a great rabbi and he was completely convinced that he was correct and that Rambam was wrong. Indeed, he was convinced that Rambam was spreading heresy, and so he criticized Rambam. But he realized afterwards that his approach was the wrong way to go. If he realized that – and in his case he was a great rabbi concerned about a matter as serious as heresy – how much more so as it relates to all of us who are not on his spiritual level and are concerned with matters of lesser significance.

In all of our personal lives and in all of our professions, we should be pioneers in changing the culture of our society to become a society that does not tolerate "accessories" to murder.

THE *EVED IVRI* IN CULPEPPER, VIRGINIA

Mishpatim

On December 30, 2010, I got the following letter in the mail:

> *Shalom Aleichem*. Our Traditional Jewish Community desperately needs a volunteer one Saturday evening per month to lead our conclusion of Shabbat, Havdalah service. Without your assistance we will be unable to meet and experience the *oneg* [pleasure], *menuchah* [rest], and *kedushah* [holiness] of Shabbat. We thank you from the bottom of our hearts, *be-shalom*."

Be-shalom was written in Hebrew letters.

The letter was from the Coffeewood Correctional Center in Culpepper, Virginia. The prisoners were asking for volunteers to lead a Jewish prayer service once a month for their congregation, which is in a medium security prison.

I thought of this letter as I was studying parashat Mishpatim, which takes up the narrative after the Ten Commandments were given at Sinai. In this portion we are taught a series of civil laws and torts. Ramban explains that these laws are basically a continuation and a fuller explanation of the Ten Commandments.

The first law that we are taught in this week's portion is the law of an *eved Ivri* (21:2), which is usually mistranslated as a "Hebrew slave." By virtue of the fact that this law is the first law taught in this section of civil laws, the Torah is emphasizing how special and important is this concept of an *eved Ivri*. It would be accurate to say that the idea of an *eved Ivri* is the underpinning for the basis of all of our civil laws and torts. What is so special about this law?

First, some background information in an attempt to clear up some confusion: There are two major types of *avadim* discussed in the Torah, an *eved Ivri* and an *eved Kena'ani*. The word *eved* can mean slave, as in "we were slaves to Pharaoh in Egypt." But it can also mean a "trusted servant" as in the *eved*, or servant, of Avraham who found a wife for Yitzchak. Moshe himself is also called an "*eved Hashem*," a servant of God.

The difference between these two meanings for the word *eved* is reflected in the two different concepts of an *eved Kena'ani* and an *eved Ivri*.

An *eved Kena'ani* is translated as a Canaanite slave. Such a slave was usually captured in battle, and this type of slavery is comparable to the horrible concept of slavery that we know of from American history. A Canaanite slave was basically the property of his owner.

Slavery is a horrible institution. It removes the dignity of a human being and takes away his humanity. And so even though the Torah is divine and beautiful and good beyond words, I am personally unable to understand how the Torah allowed for this institution. Sometimes the ways of the Torah are beyond my human ability to comprehend.

The best I can do – and I admit that this is apologetics – is to say that the rabbis in another area of the Torah put forth the concept, "*Lo dibrah Torah ela ke-neged yetzer ha-ra*" (see Rashi on Devarim 21:11). This means that the Torah sometimes doesn't outlaw certain activity, even though it doesn't like the activity, because it knows that to outlaw the activity all at once would be too much for society to handle and thus the reform of society wouldn't be successful.

Here too, I believe that the Torah really despises the idea of an *eved Kena'ani*, but it cannot outlaw it all at once, as such legislation would be too much, too fast. Instead the Torah puts forth a series of reforms that are intended to lead eventually to the total abolition of slavery.

These biblical reforms are as follows: the Canaanite slave was given off one day a week, Shabbat; an owner who beats his Canaanite slave to death is liable for murder; the Canaanite slave cannot be sold to a non-Israelite; if a Canaanite slave fled he could not be turned in; and if an owner knocked out a slave's tooth or eye or twenty-two other limbs on his body, then the slave would go free (see Kiddushin 24a–b). Although the Torah doesn't abolish this type of slavery, these laws lay the framework for the basis that a slave is also a human being who needs to be treated with dignity. And such a basis that forces the owner to treat his slave as a human being will eventually lead to the abolition of slavery.

That is the concept of *eved Kena'ani*. But the *eved Kena'ani* is not discussed at the beginning of the portion of Mishpatim. It is only discussed in the middle of the portion. The beginning of our portion discusses an *eved Ivri*, which is a completely different concept. It is totally inaccurate to translate *eved Ivri* as a "Hebrew slave." Rather, we should leave this term without translation and just define the concept.

There are two ways one can become an *eved Ivri*: one can be short of money and need to raise cash and thus sell oneself as an *eved Ivri*; or if one steals an object then the court can sell the thief as an *eved Ivri*. The *eved Ivri* is then required to work for the person who "purchases" him.

But look at the rules regarding an *eved Ivri*. The Talmud in tractate Kiddushin (20a) says, "One who purchases a slave is really purchasing a master." The reason for this is that an *eved Ivri* is not treated as a slave, but as an equal.

The *eved Ivri* must eat what the boss eats. If the boss only has one pillow then it goes to the *eved Ivri* and not to the boss. One cannot assign to the *eved Ivri* work that the *eved* was unaccustomed to do beforehand. One must provide room and board for the *eved Ivri*, as well as for his wife and children. And after six years, the *eved Ivri* must be set free. Only if he chooses to remain as an *eved Ivri* can he do so, but this choice is very much discouraged by the Torah. And at the end of six years when the *eved Ivri* goes free his boss must give him a severance package.

Still, at the end of the day this person is called an *eved Ivri*, and so you might be saying: "Okay, it is enlightened servitude, but it is still servitude. And that is a terrible thing."

I was once quoted in a newspaper as saying that the Messiah will not be able to come as long as there is one *agunah* left in the world.[1] In that context, a person approached me and asked me if there will be slavery in the time of the Messiah.

My answer to that question was: "I hope not but one never knows...."

I hope there won't be the concept of Canaanite slavery. It is inconceivable to me that that concept will ever arise again. We have surpassed that point and are well beyond it.

But, on a strictly utopian level – and I admit that this is not currently realistic – we might stand to gain if we would see the concept of *eved Ivri* reinstituted. We should think of the *eved Ivri* as a type of personal rehabilitation program. Can you imagine if in response to a crime of theft we encouraged each family to open their home and enter into an *eved Ivri* type of relationship with the criminal? Instead of incarceration, we would be bringing the criminal into a warm, loving, and caring environment with the hope of cleaning up his past and changing his future. Instead of teaching the criminal how to be a better criminal, which is how prisoners today often leave prison, we would be teaching the criminal a trade and giving him a chance to succeed in life.

---

1. See Mark Oppenheimer, "Religious Divorce Dispute Leads to Secular Protest," *New York Times*, January 3, 2011.

Compare this approach, which at its core seeks to treat the criminal with dignity, to the way the United States currently treats its criminals. Currently we have almost three million people incarcerated. Admittedly, not all of those people are incarcerated for theft, but still that is more than any other country today. This is true both as it relates to the actual number of prisoners as well as the percentage of the population of people imprisoned. In 2007, the United States incarcerated more that 23 percent of the total prison population of the world.[2]

Now I am not advocating that we lobby to change the current prison system from one of incarceration into an *eved Ivri* system. Such an approach is currently unrealistic and can only be done if we are living in a utopian world, i.e., in the messianic era. But we can dream and say: wouldn't it be wonderful, if instead of incarcerating people who steal, we instead opened our homes to individuals and changed their lives for the better.

And it is important to dream about how we can help these criminals. There is a reason why the Torah places these laws first in parashat Mishpatim. Once a criminal has committed a crime of theft he is exposed to the tremendous power of society and is open to being abused. By putting these laws at the outset of Mishpatim, the Torah is reminding us that the test of a society is how we punish people for their wrongdoings. Do we warehouse them or do we elevate them and bring them into our own families? Make no mistake about it: the way we treat our criminals is a central element as to who we are as a society.

The Torah tells us that even before any plagues were brought upon Pharaoh, Moshe was given a specific law to teach the people.

וַיְדַבֵּר ה' אֶל מֹשֶׁה וְאֶל אַהֲרֹן וַיְצַוֵּם אֶל בְּנֵי יִשְׂרָאֵל....

And Hashem spoke to Moshe and Aharon and He commanded them to the children of Israel.... (Shemot 6:13)

---

2. See http://en.wikipedia.org/wiki/United_States_incarceration_rate.

This begs the question: What did He command them? Explains the Jerusalem Talmud (Rosh Hashanah 3:5): "He commanded them regarding the obligation to free their slaves."

In other words, the very first commandment the children of Israel received, even before they received their freedom, was to free their slaves.

This teaching of the Talmud is a reference to the law in parashat Mishpatim stating that they cannot keep a Hebrew slave for more than six years. This is seen from the words of the prophet Yirmeyahu, who tells us in the haftarah for Mishpatim that the reason the Jews were expelled from Eretz Yisrael and our Temple destroyed was because our ancestors refused to free their Hebrew slaves after six years. As the prophet says: "So says Hashem, God of Israel, I made a covenant with your forefathers *on the day* that they were led out of Egypt saying…after your brother works for you for six years you must send him away, so that he may be free from you. And your fathers did not listen to Me…so you should repent today…and do what is good in My eyes and call out for freedom (*deror*) each man to his friend" (Yirmeyahu 34:13–17). The prophet is teaching us that a prerequisite to our redemption is calling out for freedom for all those who are enslaved.

Today we might not be able to bring back the *eved Ivri* model of a personal involvement with each prisoner; we might not be able to abandon an approach that advocates large-scale incarceration for criminals. But what we can do in a very small way is try to bring some spirituality into the lives of criminals who are imprisoned.

All these prisoners are seeking from us is to recite some basic prayers with us as a community. And this is what we pray for every day when we say, "O Guardian of Israel, watch the remnant of Israel, who say '*Shema Yisrael*.'"

So I called the Christian chaplain of that prison and I said: please tell our friend that I will go once a month and lead a prayer service in Culpepper, Virginia.

Even if you can't make the time for monthly prison visits, I hope you will join me in remembering the fundamental message of Mishpatim, which must govern all our interpersonal relationships: the Torah mandates preservation of human dignity even when dealing with a society that permits slavery; so too, we must remember that we have a responsibility in all our deeds and institutions to preserve human dignity.

LEARNING TO GIVE
Terumah

I've been to lunch a few times with a friend of mine named Chaim. Chaim, being the generous and giving person that he is, always ended up paying for the lunch. Even though I genuinely tried to pay, he refused to let me. Finally I started to feel uncomfortable, so before he arrived for our next lunch I went to the waiter and asked if I could pay in advance. When the bill came, Chaim realized that he was unable to treat me that day as I had already paid. He seemed very disappointed, but I thought the matter was settled.

Little did I realize how much Chaim really wanted to treat me to lunch! Lo and behold, a few weeks later I received from him gift certificates to that restaurant for the equivalent of twenty more lunches. That is a gift from a person who wants to give more than anything.

Why does a person want to give to someone else that badly?

The first answer is because of the feeling you get when you give. Giving is contagious. Once you start to give to others, then you realize how much you love to give. You realize that when you give freely and unconditionally, you acquire for yourself a feeling of goodness that is literally priceless.

Parashat Terumah is about giving and the power of giving, and the great things that happen to you when you give with a generous heart.

Says the Torah:

וְיִקְחוּ לִי תְּרוּמָה מֵאֵת כָּל אִישׁ אֲשֶׁר יִדְּבֶנּוּ לִבּוֹ....

Take for Me a donation from every person according to what his heart desires…. (Shemot 25:2)

The great commentators wonder about this verse. Why does it say "take for Me" using a form of the Hebrew word *lakach*? Instead, it should say "give Me" a donation, not "take for Me" a donation.

The Beit ha-Levi (R. Yosef Dov Ber Soloveitchik, d. 1892) explains that the verb "to take" is used because "when one gives to charity he is really taking for himself." The act of giving is really an act of acquiring.

All the possessions we "own" in this world are not eternal; they are material possessions which disappear rapidly. Thus, we do not really own them. The only thing we truly own is what we can take with us to our next world – and the only thing we can take with us is what we give in this world. And so when we give *tzedakah* we are in essence acquiring a place in the World to Come.

So the first reason we like to give is because of what we acquire when we give. We acquire a great feeling and we acquire a share in the World to Come.

But there is a second reason why we like to give: the more we give the more we learn to love. Too often we focus on finding someone to love us, but it is just as hard to find someone to love unconditionally. Learning to give teaches us how to love.

When we give to Hashem we are acquiring a relationship with God. The verse says, *ve-yikchu* li – "take for Me" or "give to Me." Of course, Hashem doesn't need anything to be given to Him. Rather, it means: give to Me in order to be close to Me.

Psychologically, the more we give to a person the more we end up loving them. Think about a parent and a child. The more a parent gives to a child, the more love the parent feels. Think about the way a parent gives to a newborn baby; the parent gives everything and ends up loving the child unconditionally. For a marriage to be a success each spouse needs to give unconditionally with no expectations of return from the other. Or even think about a pet owner and an animal; the more you care for an animal, the more you end up loving that animal. The more you give, the more you love to give and the more you love the one to whom you give.

If this works on a human level where there are so many other factors clouding a relationship, it certainly works in our relationship with Hashem. The more we give to Hashem the closer we become to Him; the more we open ourselves up to Him, the more we feel His presence in our lives.

The Torah is telling us that if we want to truly be close to Hashem then we need to give freely and generously to charity from our money. The charity that we give is called *nedavat libo*, giving freely from the heart – an open, generous heart is the sign of a deep relationship with Hashem. In contrast (as a friend of mine, Rick Atkins, reminds me), a closed heart is the sign of Pharaoh, from whom we just fled in parashat Beshalach.

In order to truly love Hashem, we need to give what we most value. That is exactly why we need to give our money to Hashem. The more we give Him, the more we will love Him. And so, when the Torah refers to donations in the parashah (25:3), it directly refers to our monetary donations. "These are the donations that you shall give: *zahav, va-khesef, u-nechoshet* – gold, silver, and copper."

Sometimes we resent being givers. We feel: I am always giving, giving, and giving. But if that is how we are feeling, then we are not really giving. If we are really giving with an open heart, then we will love so much more the person we are giving to. When you give unconditionally, you get love – not in the sense of being loved, but in the sense of knowing what it is like to love. If you expect love in return, you might not get love, but if you give unconditionally then you will end up knowing what it feels like to love someone more than anything in the world.

Our responsibility as Jews is to love God – *Ve-ahavta et Hashem* (Devarim 6:5). We can love God by giving to God unconditionally. The more we give, the more we will love Hashem.

There is a third reason why we like to give. If we give, not only will we love the act of giving, and not only will we love the one we give to, but something else will happen as well. Perhaps the greatest benefit of all!

Parashat Terumah emphasizes that the more we give to Hashem, the more God will be there for us when we need Him.

Our synagogue is famous for its 16th Street entrance. Everyone who drives down 16th Street sees the beautiful steps leading up to our majestic building. Most people notice the steps but they miss the quotation that the builders of the synagogue (back in 1958) inscribed onto the façade of the building. The words that appear are a quotation from parashat Terumah (25:8). Hashem tells Moshe to tell the children of Israel: "Make for Me a sanctuary so that I may dwell amongst them." The word *ve-shakhanti* – "that I may dwell," is related to the word *shakhen*, meaning "neighbor." Hashem is telling Moshe to build a sanctuary so that He may be our neighbor.

Rav Herschel Schachter of Yeshiva University said in the name of Rav Soloveitchik that the purpose of the Mishkan (Sanctuary) is to allow God to be our neighbor. Rav Schachter even quoted Rav Soloveitchik as saying that he identified with the aspect of Christian theology that sees God as both the father and the son. On the one hand God is all-powerful and way above us. But on the other hand, the idea of "god the son" is to empower a close personal relationship with Hashem. We don't accept that aspect of Christian theology, but we do accept the notion that Hashem is our neighbor; wherever we go Hashem goes with us and holds our hand. As the psalm says about Hashem, "*Ki Atah imadi* – You are with me" (23:4).

The portability of the traveling Mishkan reinforces this idea: if we build a Mishkan, then wherever we travel, Hashem travels with us as our Neighbor. The ideal spiritual state is to feel this closeness with God; we should strive to have a relationship with God that gives us strength no matter the stage of life we are in, to feel God as though He is always standing next to us and holding our hands.

Without a Mishkan, how can we make God our Neighbor today?

We do so by giving. The more we give the more we will feel God hovering over our shoulders and holding our hands as we navigate life. When we give generously and without limit, we not only love the act of giving, and we not only love the one whom we give to, we achieve an unsurpassable friendship with the Holy One, Blessed be He.

HALAKHAH: THE SOURCE OF SPIRITUALITY

Tetzaveh

Parashat Tetzaveh should be the most exciting and romantic of all of our Torah readings. But all too often, people complain to me that it is plain old boring. They laugh at me when I tell them that it is my favorite parashah. How can that be? they wonder. Doesn't it seem so dry and technical?

I grant you that there are parts that seem at first glance to be less than riveting. Let me give you an example. At the end of the parashah we are told how we can consecrate the *mizbe'ach*, the altar of the Mishkan. This should be the most spiritual moment of all. We are being told how we can connect to God in the deepest of ways. And yet, this awesome phenomenon is described in the most tedious of fashions. For example:

וְעִשָּׂרֹן סֹלֶת בָּלוּל בְּשֶׁמֶן כָּתִית רֶבַע הַהִין וְנֵסֶךְ רְבִיעִת הַהִין יַיִן לַכֶּבֶשׂ הָאֶחָד:

You should offer 1/10 ephah of fine flour mixed with 1/4 *hin* pressed olive oil, and a libation of 1/4 *hin* wine, with the first sheep. (Shemot 29:40)

What in this description will allow us to touch God? This seems so mundane; there seems to be so much of an emphasis on minutiae. How does one find God through the maze of all the details?

Really this parashah is a microcosm of how to live a proper spiritual life. It is pointing us in the direction of a life committed

117

to details when it comes to serving God. The problem is the problem of ritual. In Judaism the goal is to constantly push toward encountering God, and the medium that our rabbis tell us to use to reach this goal is the vehicle of ritual. But today, for many people, ritual has become not the vehicle to God, but the barrier to feeling God's presence in our lives.

Look closely at our Jewish community. When we perform rituals, is there the sense of God being in our presence? Do we really feel that this ritual is the vehicle toward God's wonders? In fact many argue that too often, the rituals confine us and do not allow us to open up and flow freely in our soulful nature.

I remember sitting at a Seder once, where we were involved in the deepest of discussions about the meaning of the Exodus from Egypt, when a person at the table hurried us along and commanded us to end the discussion so that we could eat our matzah, as a strict reading of the halakhah requires the eating of the *afikoman* before midnight (*chatzot*). The person meant well, but it completely destroyed the soulful nature of our discussion. Does this emphasis on halakhah not distract us from our ultimate goal of cleaving to God?

Two of the greatest Jewish thinkers of the twentieth century deal with this question in a way that informs my own practice of halakhah.

In his *Ish ha-Halakhah* (Halakhic Man), Rabbi Soloveitchik describes a spiritual way of life that is molded through observance and knowledge of halakhah. For Rabbi Soloveitchik, halakhah is a system or structure that governs our lives in a way that allows us to bring God into our earthly lives. Other religions will confine God to a sanctuary and remove God from the mundane activities of the world. But they also remove God from the needs of the world – from the cries of the poor and the needy.

Halakhah declares that man stands before God not only in the synagogue but also in the public domain. Halakhah sees the beauty of a Godly life in every mundane experience that we encounter. With halakhah dictating our lives, the spiritual is not something that we have to cleave to because it is something that is always part of who we are.

A non-halakhic person will walk through life and at times be moved by the beauty of a sunset or the majesty of a mountain peak. But for the halakhic person these experiences take on new meaning; everything is suffused with halakhic meaning. "When halakhic man looks to the western horizon and sees the fading rays of the setting sun or to the eastern horizon and sees the first light of dawn and the glowing rays of the rising sun, he knows that this sunset or sunrise imposes upon him anew obligations and commandments…the recitation of the morning *shema, tzitzit, tefillin,* the morning prayer…and the like…. When halakhic man chances upon the mighty mountains, he utilizes the measurements, which determine a private domain (*reshut ha-yahid*): a sloping mound that attains a height of ten handbreadths within a distance of four cubits."[1]

Just like a physicist has a deep scientific understanding of the world, so too, one who follows halakhah, one who understands in great depth the beauty of the halakhot, will have a religious experience of profound intensity and consistency.

So, for Rabbi Soloveitchik, halakhah is the source of our spirituality. It is the way of life that guides us to God by allowing us to see God everywhere.

But there is a difficulty with the way of life suggested by *Ish ha-Halakhah*. Let's assume for a moment that the system works as a whole on a macro level and the halakhic lifestyle will truly aid us in living ethical lives that give us a deep, spiritual connection to

---

1. Rabbi Joseph B. Soloveitchik, *Halakhic Man*, translated by Lawrence Kaplan (Philadelphia: Jewish Publication Society, 1983), 20.

God. We still must understand how this works on a micro level: How does the performance of each and every mitzvah help us come closer to God?

For example, why is it prohibited to eat meat boiled in milk? Rambam suggests, "Perhaps such food was eaten at one of the ceremonies of the [idolatrous] cults" (*Guide for the Perplexed* 3:48). Well, if that is the case – if some mitzvot contain irrelevant moral and philosophical ideals – how does my performance of that mitzvah today bring me any closer to God?

So while there is great value in accepting the approach of Rabbi Soloveitchik toward halakhah, for most people it must be supplemented by a second approach. This second approach is in many ways the opposite approach.

The scholar of kabbalah, Gershom Scholem, describes a second approach in his classic work *Major Trends in Jewish Mysticism*.[2] Scholem suggests that the strongest support for the performance of halakhah comes not from the scholars of Talmud, but from the kabbalists. For the kabbalists, the halakhot are not presented as allegories of deeper ideas, but rather as the performance of a secret rite: *sodot*.

The kabbalists believed that the performance of each mitzvah can be a *tikkun*; it can have an effect upon the inner workings of the divine, an inner theurgic effect. If I in my own private house can perform the mitzvah of eating matzah correctly, that action may indeed forever alter the cosmic nature of the universe. One who believes this theology can never take lightly the performance of any mitzvah. Every mitzvah, regardless of its meaning, is of paramount importance. Every mitzvah, regardless of whether or not one understands it in its full complexity, must be performed.

One doesn't need to be a kabbalist to appreciate the beauty of the kabbalistic approach. It recognizes the supreme value of each mitzvah. It argues that each mitzvah, whether or not we

2. New York: Schocken Books, 1995, 29–30.

understand it fully, must be performed with a sacredness and seriousness. It suggests that the performance of each mitzvah has the ability to unite us with God.

Can this theology help us if we are not full believers in the kabbalistic approach? Can it help us even if we are unable to comprehend the notion of theurgy – the idea that the actions of human beings have the ability to affect the divine?

It can, because it reminds us that this is not just the approach of the kabbalists. As the Gemara in tractate Kiddushin (40b) says: When we perform each mitzvah we must view the world's fate as hanging in the balance. A single mitzvah could tip the balance and save the world. Ritual, when properly performed, has a deep romantic and mystical power.

And so we see two directly opposite approaches. One suggests that we have to understand the halakhic system in an intellectual manner: The mitzvot are a beautiful way of life that allows us to appreciate God's beauty in this world. Following the mitzvot is a way of bringing God into our world. It is a way of seeing God in every aspect of life.

The second approach sees the mitzvot as a romantic encounter with God. The mitzvot allow us to rise to God and touch Him. The mitzvot are the key to cracking the code to God's throne. When we perform the mitzvot properly, we can literally change the destiny of the world.

On its own, neither approach is sufficient. But when combined together the approaches work beautifully. The rituals of the mitzvot as a whole are a powerful system that allows us to see God in our daily lives. And when we perform each mitzvah, we must realize that we are about to perform an action whose essence is holy – so holy that it can directly affect the world.

In fact this is the way we try to perform mitzvot in our synagogue. For example when a *brit milah* is performed we never just rush into the circumcision. First we explain in a general way what the mitzvah is all about. Then we try to focus on the substance of the ritual through understanding its teaching and internalizing its message. And then, when the actual moment comes, when the baby cries...then we are reminded of the teaching that the baby's cries at a *brit* literally open the gates of heaven. That moment becomes an opportunity to reach up toward God, to touch God, to encounter God, and to pray for change in the world.

The way we focus properly before a *brit milah* should be precisely the way we prepare before each and every ritual act that we do. If we do that then we will realize that there is nothing boring or tedious about the commandments. Rather, they are an exciting portal into the divine world.

This for me is what the halakhah is about – it's about accepting a lifestyle that is a path to God. And it's about performing mitzvot that allow us to forever change the destiny of the world.

GROWING OUR CONGREGATION: THE NUMBERS GAME

Ki Tisa

There is an old Jewish joke that isn't so funny. A small town had ten Jewish men. For years they never missed a minyan. All ten came every day without fail. Then one day an eleventh Jew moved into town. The next day no one showed up at minyan.

There is a great danger to growth. Our congregation went from thirty families to over three hundred families in less than five years. This is incredible growth. And in our congregation we are all proud of such growth. It is a sign that the Torah-true vision that we are advocating is resonating with a growing number of people. But parashat Ki Tisa reminds us that we must ask the question: Is such quick and incredible growth helpful or harmful to the spiritual direction of our congregation?

Studies of churches show that there is often disagreement about growth between the pastor and members. The pastor might aggressively work to grow the congregation, while members resist growth and argue that it is best to remain a small and intimate group.[1] Likewise there are great advantages in having a

---

1. To read more on this topic, see Eddie Gibbs and Ryan K. Bolger, *Emerging Churches: Creating Christian Community in Postmodern Cultures* (Grand Rapids, MI: Baker Academic, 2005); and Jackson W. Carroll and Wade Clark Roof, *Bridging Divided Worlds: Generational Cultures in Congregations* (San Francisco, CA: Jossey-Bass, 2002).

large synagogue congregation. With more people there are more opportunities all around. Plus, the davening and Torah study can be even more beautiful, as the verse states, "*Be-rov am hadrat melekh* – With a multitude of people rests the glory of the King" (Mishlei 14:28).

However, the downside to a larger congregation is that it allows people to shirk their responsibility. Recent church research shows that there is a concern about the large mega-churches now popular, since some argue that when you increase the size of an organization you necessarily also decrease each individual's commitment. This is the reason why, long ago, Max Weber wrote that "only small congregations are appropriate."[2] Best-selling author Malcolm Gladwell made this idea famous in his book *The Tipping Point.*[3] He refers to the rule of 150 – when a congregation crosses over the number 150 it signals a great change in how things happen. He argues that 150 is the number at which any group is organizationally most effective, and that when churches grow larger they should reorganize according to this principle and make smaller groups within the larger church.

The beginning of parashat Ki Tisa offers us insight into this discussion. The Torah teaches us how to count our people. When and if we take a census we must do so with a half-shekel. Rich and poor alike should both submit a half-shekel, so when we count up the shekalim we will know exactly how many people participated in the census. If we count in this manner, the Torah tells us, "*Lo yehiyeh bahem negef* – There will not be a plague amongst [our people]" (Shemot 30:12).

Many of you are probably familiar with a Jewish custom that teaches us how to count people. When we count people we don't count, one, two, three... Rather we substitute a word for a number

---

2. *From Max Weber: Essays in Sociology*, translated by H.H. Gerth and C. Wright Mills (New York: Oxford University Press, 1946), 316.

3. New York: Back Bay Books, 2002.

and then count. This custom comes from Rashi's explanation of this commandment.

Rashi teaches that this commandment to count with a half-shekel doesn't only apply in the desert; it applies forever. He teaches that we do not count people by counting their heads, rather we count through a proxy – in this case, shekalim.

There was once a leader of the Jewish people who made a terrible mistake and counted his people improperly. In the last chapter of the book of Shmuel, we are told that David ha-Melekh counted his people. However, David didn't use the half-shekel method. Consequently, God considers David's count to be a great sin and He punishes David by bringing a terrible plague upon the people of Israel.

Is that fair? All because David ha-Melekh didn't count up his people in the proper manner? What is the big deal? What is the difference if you count with a half-shekel or if you count with a number?

Rashi explains: When one counts with a straight number, "the evil eye (ayin ha-ra) rests upon him" (Shemot 30:12).

The ayin ha-ra is usually translated to mean the evil eye. It refers to an action that you do that displays your arrogance. Arrogance is a great sin – one can even say that it is the source of all sin. Thus, on a deeper level, David ha-Melekh was punished for the sin of arrogance. In fact, as he began to count, his chief general, Yoav, said to him, "My king, why do you need this counting?" (I Divrei ha-Yamim 21:3). David ha-Melekh's counting had no purpose other than his own self-serving satisfaction. He counted his people in a way that displayed his great pride. He was saying to the world, look how large our nation is. Look how mighty we are. And so God visited him with a plague.

David's counting was a counting that went nowhere. It served no spiritual purpose. This is the reason why he was punished.

As the medieval Provençal scholar, Rabbi David Kimchi, explains: "As long as the Jewish people counted for a good reason, they did not sin. Where there was no reason, they did sin – like the case of David" (*Radak*, II Shmuel 24:1). Or as another medieval scholar, Ramban, points out: David counted only "to gladden his heart over the fact that he ruled over such a multitude of people" (Bamidbar 1:3).

In contrast, the counting of parashat Ki Tisa serves a great purpose. The shekalim that were collected were given as a donation to the Mishkan, the sanctuary of the Jewish people. The counting wasn't just about self-pride. It served God.

The Torah tells us where the money of the census went. It didn't just go into the sanctuary's coffers. It bought specific objects which had great symbolic meaning. At the end of Shemot (38:25–27) we are told that the silver from the census contributed to the *adanim* and the *vavim* of the sanctuary. The *adanim* are the silver bases that are used as a support for the walls of the sanctuary. The *vavim* are the hooks that are used to connect the walls for the enclosure around the sanctuary.

Support and connection.

The message of the shekalim and the counting is that it has value only if it serves a larger purpose; otherwise it is a great sin. The same message applies to growth of synagogues and specifically to our synagogue.

Support and connection.

This is the positive side to growth. When we look externally, growth is so important because it can serve as greater support and provide a network for greater connection. Through support and connection, we can better spread the Torah.

And when we look internally, we see that the shekalim provided the base and the glue – the support for the walls and the connecting hooks. The counting thus served to foster the core support for the sanctuary and the glue necessary to hold it all together. Everyone needed to contribute a half-shekel; so too, as growth happens, everyone needs to assume the responsibility of contributing their time and effort as they would do for a small congregation.

I believe with all my heart that it is very important for our synagogue to grow – but only if we grow the right way and for the right reasons. Our growth as a shul has to serve a larger purpose. Growth for growth's sake is not a good thing. If our growth is just about becoming financially solvent (for example), then our growth is of limited value and can even be a source of great spiritual distraction.

I remember a few years ago I visited a major North American city. As I drove into the city, I saw a sign that said: "Welcome, population..." and then the sign listed the exact population, a number that I have long since forgotten, but I remember that it was in the millions. At the time, I was impressed. But now, after thinking about it, I think it would be better if the city gave us a description on that sign, rather than a population number. Maybe, "Welcome to our city, a population trying hard to make our world more beautiful."

Our growth has to come because we see it as providing support and connection. Growth can help us both internally and externally. Growth can help us provide support for Jews throughout the entire DC area. Growth can help us be a source of connection for Jews throughout the world. Growth can help us be an entire congregation of teachers of Torah. Growth can help us better use our spiritual energy to support the spread of Torah and love of God. If we do so, then our growth has great meaning.

INSPIRATIONAL SNAPSHOTS FROM ERETZ YISRAEL

Vayakhel

A group from our congregation often travels on a spiritual mission to Eretz Yisrael. I like to think that we are like the pilgrims in the time of the Temple; like them we too need to recharge our spiritual energy by visiting the Holy Land.

One year there were twenty-seven of us who traveled. We arrived in Israel at ten o'clock at night. Some of the group had never been to Israel before and wanted to go straight to the Western Wall (Kotel). My son, Roey, was six years old at the time and it was also his first trip to Israel.

I said to Roey: "Do you want to go the Wall tonight or would you like to go early in the morning?" He immediately said, "Both."

I see this excitement and enthusiasm in the faces of so many people who travel on our pilgrimages to Israel. I will never forget the expression on Doug's face as he saw the Kotel for the first time in his life. Doug is a brilliant man who was severely limited by a brain-trauma injury when his car was hit by a drunk driver. When Doug saw the Kotel for the first time in his life, his whole body shone.

I see this same cleansing and renewal in the body language of the people on our trips who typically gather before dawn so we can daven *vatikin* (with sunrise) at the Kotel. The idea of praying at sunrise is to daven to Hashem at the very first moment that halakhah allows. It is always an amazing experience doing so at the Kotel. There is so much noise as people shout the prayers aloud, and then, as the entire plaza reaches the Amidah at sunrise…total silence. That silence overwhelms me.

This enthusiasm and excitement is the emotion we should try to have in our service of Hashem.

The paradigm of enthusiasm and excitement is a theme of parashat Vayakhel. Moshe called for volunteers to build and donate to the Mishkan. But almost immediately we are told:

וַיָּבֹאוּ כָּל הַחֲכָמִים הָעֹשִׂים אֵת כָּל מְלֶאכֶת הַקֹּדֶשׁ.... וַיֹּאמְרוּ אֶל מֹשֶׁה לֵּאמֹר מַרְבִּים הָעָם לְהָבִיא מִדֵּי הָעֲבֹדָה לַמְּלָאכָה....

All the contractors of the holy work came… And they told Moshe, "The people are bringing too many donations, more than enough for the service of the work…." (Shemot 36:4–5)

When the call came to build the Mishkan, the enthusiasm and excitement was overwhelming. That excitement is what we should all seek in our religious lives. Yet, sometimes, the excitement wanes and we need to be inspired. When I want to be inspired, I travel to Israel. On our trips over the years I have met so many inspiring people. Here are just three snapshots of people and places that inspire me in Israel.

Snapshot #1: Rav Yehudah Bohrer

I met Rav Bohrer one evening in DC. He stopped by my office in the summer and gave me some mezuzah scrolls. After his daughter, Techiyah, was killed by terrorists, his response was to give out tefillin and mezuzah scrolls in her memory. When he heard that we have the Tefillin Challenge in our congregation, he generously sent us some pairs of tefillin. (Our Tefillin Challenge is a program that our shul started: we will give you a free pair of tefillin if you pray in our morning minyan thirty times in sixty days.)

Walking in Israel with Rav Bohrer is an amazing experience. He sees a biblical verse under every rock and on top of every hill in the land.

When we drove by the Jordan River and saw the hills of Moab, we all burst into the song from Psalm 114: "*Mah lekhah ha-yam ki tanus, ha-Yarden tisov le-achor. He-harim tirkedu ke-eilim, geva'ot kivnei tzon* – What alarmed you, O sea, that you fled; Jordan, that you ran backward; mountains, that you skipped like rams; hills, like sheep?" (114:5–6).

We stopped in Beit El. We saw the stone where many people believe our forefather Yaakov rested his head when he dreamed of angels going up and down the ladder (Bereishit 28:12).

And we stopped in Shiloh where the Tabernacle, the Mishkan, which we read about in parashat Vayakhel, stayed for many years after entering Eretz Yisrael. As we climbed to the place where the Mishkan rested, I kept thinking that this was the exact same path that Channah, mother of Shmuel the prophet, walked as she courageously recited her famous prayer (II Shmuel 2:1–10).

We can never forget that the places of the Bible are real places that need to be visited in order to be understood properly. We noticed this at Shiloh when we saw that the place where the Mishkan rested was a natural amphitheatre, as it is surrounded on three sides by hills.

Rav Bohrer taught me this again when he showed me the mountain where the goat for Azazel (the scapegoat of Yom Kippur) was thrown off. The mountain directly faces the mountain of Rosh ha-Peor, which was the site of the idolatrous cult of Ba'al. It was only then that I finally understood the significance of throwing the goat of Azazel off the cliff on Yom Kippur. It was meant to directly repudiate the idolatry of Ba'al.

I could go on and on with all of the biblical insights I gained from Rav Bohrer. But this is not the place. The point is that the Torah is not just an academic book for him. It is his life and impacts his every action in Eretz Yisrael. What a merit he has to be able to live in a place where every step he takes reminds him of the steps of the children of Israel.

Snapshot #2: Rav Bohrer's Brother

Rav Bohrer mentioned that he had a brother in Bnei Brak who makes matzot for Pesach. I asked if he could take us to his brother so we could see how the matzot are made.

Bnei Brak is known for being an ultra-Orthodox neighborhood. It is not a place where tourists usually go. But I insisted that I wanted to go, so Rav Bohrer arranged it.

He told us the address –18 Rashbam – and said he would meet us there. Unfortunately, our driver had never been to Bnei Brak and had no idea how to get there. We kept asking people for directions. But no one had heard of Rashbam Street. So I called Rav Bohrer and he said: "Ask for the Steipler." The Steipler was a great rabbi who lived on Rashbam Street and his holy son, Rabbi Chaim Kanievsky, lives there as well.

I stopped someone and said: "The Steipler?" Immediately, we were given precise directions: "Left, right, left, and then right." The geography of Bnei Brak is the geography of great rabbis.

We came to Rav Bohrer's brother and saw his "factory." We saw a shack and inside this shack were three ultra-Orthodox Jews grinding the grain of the wheat by hand into flour. It required both immense force and concentration. Although one is allowed to use a machine to grind the matzah, they were grinding it by hand in order to beautify the mitzvah. This type of matzah is called RASHI matzah (*reichayim shel yad* – ground by hand). The men doing the grinding were working up a tremendous sweat and could not be spoken to as it might interrupt their focus on grinding the grain for the purpose of eating matzah on Pesach.

Rav Bohrer's brother assured me that his matzah was the only matzah that Rav Chaim Kanievsky would eat.

This matzah "factory" produces four and a half tons of matzah. I asked him if he would ship some matzah to me in America, but he only laughed. I don't think I have a chance of getting that matzah from him, so if anyone is around Bnei Brak and can ship me some of his matzah I would appreciate it greatly.

I was overwhelmed by the dedication of these men to performing the mitzvah. For months and months they would prepare in order to fulfill the mitzvah of eating matzah properly. What a merit to be standing with someone who cared so deeply about the performance of a mitzvah that it would take over his life months in advance!

I found this so inspiring that I immediately decided that we too would make our own *shmurah* matzah in Washington DC. Since that time, every year we make kosher for Pesach, *shmurah* matzah. It is one of the most inspiring projects of our shul and I owe the impetus for it to seeing Rav Bohrer's brother in action.

Snapshot #3: Sderot

One year our group traveled to Sderot, a town of twenty-five thousand that borders Gaza. Sderot was founded in 1951 (note that that is well before the Six-Day War) and is recognized by everyone as being inside the green line. Yet Sderot has often faced a barrage of Kassam rocket attacks. These rocket attacks intensified greatly after Israel withdrew from Gaza.

The first place we stopped in Sderot was at Hesder Yeshiva Sderot. This is a yeshivah where the men do army service combined with Torah study. The head rabbi of the yeshivah, Rav Fendel, married a woman who grew up one block from me, so I felt comfortable calling him up and asking for an appointment.

We called him fifteen minutes before arriving, and he told us that a rocket had literally just fallen. When we arrived he showed us a picture of how a rocket had fallen only ten feet away from him but had miraculously not exploded. He then showed us how many of the students in his yeshivah slept every night in a bomb shelter.

Here is the amazing thing. Imagine what he was doing in the face of these daily rockets? He was expanding. The more the rockets rained down, the quicker the yeshivah was building and expanding. The Torah of the yeshivah would provide the moral strength for the entire city of Sderot.

From the moment the "code red" siren sounds, the people of Sderot have sixteen seconds to get to shelter. I asked him if we could arrange something so that the "code red" also lights a signal in our synagogue so that during those sixteen seconds we can recite special prayers for the people of Sderot.

After meeting with Rav Fendel we went to meet with Chavah. Chavah is forty-two years old and the mother of three children, the youngest of whom is nine. One Friday night a Kassam hit her building during Shabbat dinner. She cried to us that her nine-year-old has suffered tremendously since the Kassams started intensifying. She said he is afraid to sleep by himself or even go to the bathroom by himself. He is afraid to go outside and play. When the Kassams are quiet for a few days he gets an A on his tests; then the Kassams return and he gets a D. We asked her why she doesn't move. She said she has no money to move and she added: "If I give up on Sderot, I am giving up on all of Israel."

We left her apartment feeling sad and shaken by her tremendous daily struggle. Suddenly we heard music coming from the main market of Sderot. Unbeknownst to us, on that day ten thousand people from all over Israel had descended upon Sderot in a show of unity with the besieged city. The idea was that they would do their Shabbat shopping in the markets of Sderot in order to help the city's devastated economy.

A festive feeling overcame the city as people were dancing in the streets and strangers were hugging each other. One person from our group took out his guitar and started to sing. We hurriedly emptied our pockets of all our money as we started to buy anything we could find.

I found a Kiddush cup, which our group bought for the shul. From that day on, whenever we recite Kiddush in our congregation, we use the cup from Sderot. In reciting our Kiddush we pray that our cup overflows with the courage and bravery of the people of Sderot. Their Torah and their moral strength will help sanctify us and inspire us. And when I answer amen to Kiddush in our congregation, I think about the people of Sderot and pray that Hashem may guard them and protect them.

Before we left Sderot I stopped at the Sderot police station. There they had hundreds of Kassam rockets that had been fired on the city. Our group managed to convince the police to let us take one of the rockets back to DC. We did so and displayed it proudly in our synagogue for several years as a symbol of Jewish resilience in the face of adversity. Then in June of 2011 our synagogue sealed a time capsule for the next fifty years, and we decided to put the Kassam rocket in the time capsule. In fifty years when this capsule is opened people will see the rocket and understand about the brave strength of the people of Sderot.

So the next time you need some inspiration and want to be as excited to serve God as the Jews of the desert, do what I do: visit with these amazing people in the Land of Israel. It works for me every time.

An Easier Way to Achieve Redemption

Pekudei

A friend gave me a beautiful present: a children's book by Mordecai Gerstein called *The Man Who Walked between the Towers*.[1]

This book tells the story of Philippe Petit and his daring, death-defying walk between the Twin Towers on August 7, 1974.

Many of you are probably familiar with this story. Some of you might have been in New York City then or read about it afterwards. Others may have seen the Oscar-winning film based upon this walk.

Here is a brief recap of the story. Philippe Petit was a street performer in Paris and an expert tightrope walker. Soon after the Twin Towers were built he snuck into the towers disguised as a construction worker and in the middle of the night carried up a five-hundred-pound cable. He shot an arrow between the towers with a rope attached to it. Using that rope he strung the cable, which was only 5/8 of an inch thick, in between the two buildings.

He walked onto the cable just as New Yorkers were coming to work that morning and spent nearly an hour on the cable where he walked, jumped, and danced before he walked off the cable and was arrested by police officers.

After reading this book, I became fascinated by the story. So I wrote Philippe a letter and I asked him: "What most fascinates me is how it felt for you spiritually. What did it feel like to be alone up on the wire?" He responded to my letter with a phone call and we

---

1. New York: Roaring Brook Press, 2003.

had a very meaningful discussion. Of course I also asked Philippe
if he would agree to string a wire between our shul and the one
across the street and walk across. He only laughed when I asked
him that.

After hearing Philippe's story, most people wonder why he
would do this.

But for this question I felt I had an answer already. Philippe has
said that when he was on the wire – as the crowds gathered below
him, the helicopters buzzed above him, and the police shouted at
him on their bullhorns – he simply lay down on the wire. "I felt
totally free. No one could touch me. I was with the birds."

That moment of freedom is what we search for our entire lives.
We live our lives seeking a sensation that we can call freedom or
redemption.

Philippe Petit found his freedom up on a wire in the middle of
the sky. But that is an approach to achieving redemption that is
definitely not recommended for most people.

Parashat Pekudei shows us an easier way to achieve redemption.
Pekudei is the last parashah in Sefer Shemot. In English, Sefer
Shemot is called Exodus, but the great Ramban calls this book
Sefer Geula, or the Book of Redemption.

This book from beginning to end is the blueprint for how to
achieve redemption. It starts with the children of Israel being
enslaved in Egypt and ends with the following scene, which is a
scene of total redemption:

וַיְכַס הֶעָנָן אֶת אֹהֶל מוֹעֵד וּכְבוֹד ה' מָלֵא אֶת הַמִּשְׁכָּן.... כִּי עֲנַן ה'
עַל הַמִּשְׁכָּן יוֹמָם וְאֵשׁ תִּהְיֶה לַיְלָה בּוֹ לְעֵינֵי כָל בֵּית יִשְׂרָאֵל בְּכָל
מַסְעֵיהֶם:

And the Cloud covered the tent of the meeting and the
Glory of God filled the Tabernacle…. For the Cloud of
Hashem was above the Tabernacle by day, and fire on
it at night, in front of the eyes of all of Israel in all their
journeys. (Shemot 40:34, 38)

Just like at Sinai, this moment was redemption for all of Israel; they all witnessed the Cloud and the Glory of God.

How did *bnei Yisrael* achieve this redemption? In answer to this question there are two points that I want to emphasize as keys to the redemption of *bnei Yisrael*, which are also keys to our own redemption.

Point number one: At the end of our portion we are told that Hashem told Moshe to erect the Mishkan on the first day of the month of Nissan. There is a dispute amongst the rabbis as to how exactly to interpret this command. But the common interpretation is as follows (see Ramban 40:2): The first day of Nissan, the day Moshe was told to put up the Mishkan, is also known as the eighth day of the *miluim*, the inauguration of the Temple. This means that when Moshe built the Mishkan on the eighth day of the inauguration, or the first day of Nissan, he was basically putting up a grand opening sign saying, "The Mishkan is now open for business."

Prior to this, for one week, beginning on 23 Adar, Moshe was inaugurating the Mishkan. For that entire seven-day period, Moshe was building the Mishkan and taking it down by himself every single day. According to one opinion in the Midrash he built it and took it down twice a day. But according to Rabbi Chaninah ha-Gadol, who is also quoted in the Midrash, Moshe built it and took it down three times a day (Bamidbar Rabbah 12:15).

So according to Rabbi Chaninah ha-Gadol, Moshe built and took down the Mishkan twenty-one times during the week of *miluim*. All of this was very time consuming and physically difficult. The beams were very heavy; the curtains were very hard. Just think about building your sukkah and how hard that is, and imagine something much, much more difficult to build, and now imagine doing that three times a day for seven days straight. This is what Moshe had to do before the Mishkan could be open for business.

What was the purpose of this? Why the need for him to do this over and over again? Moshe's goal was not just to build the Mishkan; it was to build the Mishkan in such a way that the

Glory of God would dwell within it. Moshe wanted to achieve a great spiritual connection with Hashem. By building the Mishkan three times a day, Moshe was teaching us a spiritual lesson that is axiomatic to Judaism: the path to great moments of redemption can only come through repetitive effort and consistent hard work. Spiritual success requires enormous commitment and effort.

If Moshe had just put up the Mishkan once on the first day of Nissan it would have been less effective; perhaps he wouldn't have the proper *kavanah* (focus) or he wouldn't insert the beams in the proper manner. He needed to fine-tune and prepare the Mishkan for that special moment on the first day of Nissan.

Think about our high-wire act person, Philippe Petit. He didn't show up and walk across the towers and feel free. He meticulously planned his daring deed for six years. He studied every aspect of the towers. He built a model of the towers. He rented helicopters to observe the space. He spoke with physicists. He planned and rehearsed for the moment with the recognition that his life depended on success.

This is the same approach we should take to spirituality. Some people – not ones who come to our shul – say, "Shul doesn't do anything for me. It doesn't move me spiritually." Well, yes, if you are going to show up for shul once a year and sit there for forty-five minutes, I totally agree that your spiritual experience will be of a limited value. What is required for spiritual success is constant, daily commitment and preparation, just like the commitment that Moshe had in building the Mishkan.

This is what Moshe required from himself, and this is what he was trying to teach *bnei Yisrael*. And this is what we should require of ourselves. We should challenge ourselves to commit to Hashem in a serious manner on multiple occasions throughout the day.

There is also a second path to redemption that is seen in parashat Pekudei.

Let's go back to the story of Philippe Petit. Although Philippe achieved his moment of freedom, and although his story seems harmless and fun, there is an element about what he did that I find disturbing: there is something narcissistic about Petit's behavior.

There are no videos of his walk between the towers. Just still photos. What happened was that a person carried the video cameras onto the roof of the building, but then he was too tired to video the walk. Can you imagine if this had been done today? His walk would have easily been recorded and it would have been on YouTube instantly. And then it would have gone viral in minutes.

Now on the one hand there is nothing wrong with that. But on the other hand, there is something immodest and anti-spiritual about our entire YouTube society today. We have become a YouTube culture with individuals constantly promoting themselves by performing outlandish acts and posting them to YouTube.

The YouTube culture is a culture that promotes the individual. And while it is possible for an individual to achieve redemption, parashat Pekudei tells us that there is a better path to redemption. It teaches us that the path to redemption of the individual comes not through a glorification of the individual, but through the individual's communal participation.

At the beginning of Shemot, Hashem tells Moshe go tell the Jewish people, "*Pakod pakadeti etkhem* – I will redeem you" (3:16). Here the word *pakod* means "to redeem." In fact, the Midrash tells us that this phrase "*pakod pakadeti*" was a secret phrase passed down through Serach bat Asher, and the tradition was that whatever prophet would come to the Israelites with this secret phrase, "*pakod pakadeti*," would be the true prophet (Yalkut Shimoni, Lekh Lekha 64). (Serach was the granddaughter of Yaakov, and the tradition is that she was blessed with a long life because she was the first one to inform Yaakov that Yosef was still alive.) That is a strange Midrash. I think it means that whoever understood the meaning of the words *pakod pakadeti* would be able to redeem the people. And Moshe understood the meaning of these words. He understood that *pakod* means a redemption that comes through a communal counting of the people.

This is the message of parashat Shekalim, which often coincides with parashat Pekudei, and is always read in synagogue in the weeks leading up to Purim. It states in parashat Shekalim that everyone must give a half-shekel coin in order to be counted, and the Hebrew word for "count" is *pakod*. But we can also read it as saying that everyone must give a half-shekel in order to be redeemed, and the Hebrew word for "redeem" is also *pakod*. In other words the redemption of the individual comes not through the glorification of the individual, but through the participation in the communal building of a meaningful entity, in being counted and redeemed via their communal participation.

When God told Moshe to say to the children of Israel, "*Pakod pakadeti etkhem* – I will redeem you," He is saying: tell them that I will redeem you when you commit to something much larger than each of you.

That is a fundamental message of redemption – the path to an individual's redemption is through a community.

And it carries with it an additional responsibility for us as a community. Since communal participation is an individual's path to redemption, we as a religious community must always strive to be as inclusive as possible and thereby help the individual join the community. The individual is best redeemed through the community; but true redemption for the community can only come when the community remembers to make space for the individual.

Right after he was arrested for performing his high-wire act, Petit was asked, "Why did you do it?" And he answered, "There is no why."

He is right. We should not ask why the soul seeks redemption. Instead, we should ask how we can achieve it.

And we can achieve it. All it takes is a constant commitment to the hard work of spirituality and a dedication to the recognition that our individual redemption will come through a communal redemption. And if we understand those two ideas, then the path to redemption is very much achievable.

VAYIKRA

THE CALLING

Vayikra

I remember talking with a rebbe of mine when I was in college and telling him that I wasn't sure what I should do with my life. I told him I enjoyed academia and I was thinking about pursuing that as a career. But I also enjoyed teaching Torah and I was thinking of entering the rabbinate. He asked me a very simple question, "For which one do you hear a calling?"

This sefer is often mistakenly called Leviticus, but it really is Vayikra, "He called." Or more specifically, *"Vayikra el Moshe –* God called to Moshe." Rashi explains that the call was a powerful call. It went straight from God to Moshe's ears. And it was a very personal call. *Bnei Yisrael* could not hear it; Aharon and Miriam could not hear it. Only Moshe could hear it.

The call was a summons. It was a summons by God to do the will of God. Lucky for us Moshe heard the call of Hashem.

As many commentators have noticed, the word *Vayikra* ("He called") appears with a little aleph. The last letter of the word, the aleph, is written much smaller than the other letters. Why?

It is often assumed that Jews believe that Moshe was the greatest prophet of all time. This is not exactly true. We say in the Yigdal prayer, *"Lo kam be-Yisrael ke-Moshe od –* no one will arise *from amongst the Jews* who will be a greater prophet than Moshe." And many understand that to mean that there was an even greater prophet than Moshe, but he was not from amongst the Jews. That greater prophet was Bilam (Sifrei Devarim 357 [end]; see also Talmud Berakhot 7a, and Bamidbar Rabbah 20:1). Bilam was the prophet who set out to curse the Jewish people, but ended up blessing them against his will. But if he was such a great prophet, then why don't we have his teachings as our guide in life? Bilam's problem was not his ability to prophesy but his inability to hear the call of God. When Bilam met with Hashem, it says, "*Va-yikar Elokim el Bilam* – And God appeared to Bilam" (Bamidbar 23:4).

Vayikar versus *Vayikra*. The only difference between the two words is a little, tiny aleph. The aleph is so small that it doesn't even have a sound. And its smallness is magnified by the Torah writing it even smaller.

Sometimes the difference between something "happening" and a "call" is so imperceptible that we do not even notice.

But we must notice. It is the difference between Moshe and Bilam. Moshe heard the call (*Vayikra*) and he understood he had a specific mission to lead the Jewish people. Bilam had a prophecy "happen" to him; he didn't have a specific mission. He didn't hear the call and so his talent was wasted.

Our responsibility is to listen for the call. We must ask ourselves, "Is this the voice of Hashem calling us in life?" The difference between the life of greatness (Moshe) and a wasted life (Bilam) depends only upon a small aleph – a calling versus a happening.

Let me give you a more modern example. The first *rosh yeshivah* and president of Yeshiva University was Rabbi Dr. Bernard Revel. His impact upon American Jewry and specifically on Modern Orthodoxy was enormous. He put Yeshiva University on a path that trained thousands of rabbis over the last century. Can you imagine if he had decided not to become a rabbi? Well, it almost happened. In 1906, a young Bernard Revel came to America, unsure of what he would do. There was no Yeshiva University then, and it was certainly far from clear that a person with his skills could have a home in the Jewish community. In 1909 he decided to enroll in law school. However, according to Wikipedia, he "eventually decided that law was not his calling." Instead he decided to pursue a doctorate in philosophy. In 1915 he was invited to head up what would eventually become Yeshiva University.[1]

I am sure he would have made a good lawyer – even a great lawyer. But I thank Hashem that he heard the call and pursued his calling.

Of course, that brings us to the obvious question: How do we know if the calling is correct? How can we be sure?

This is a very difficult question to answer, but I want to offer a suggestion. Let us look at the content of this specific call from Hashem to Moshe.

אָדָם כִּי יַקְרִיב מִכֶּם קָרְבָּן לַה'....

> When a person will offer from amongst you an offering
> to Hashem.... (Vayikra 1:2)

The world for "offering" or "sacrifice" is *korban*. The origin of this word is k-r-v, "to come close." As Ramban explains, the word *korban* connotes "drawing close to Hashem or uniting with Hashem."

When we analyze a feeling to see if it is indeed a calling, the question we should ask ourselves is, "Does this bring me closer to Hashem? Does this calling capitalize on the uniqueness of my talents? Is this what Hashem created me to do?" The purpose of the calling is to bring us closer to Hashem and to allow others to feel that closeness. The calling must be linked to *korban*.

The calling can come at any age and at any time. But one must listen for it intently. We must be willing to live our lives in response to that calling. And we must recognize that we should not tarry in our response.

There was another call in Jewish history, a famous call.

---

1. For more on the life of Bernard Revel, see Aaron Rakeffet-Rothkoff, *Bernard Revel: Builder of American Jewish Orthodoxy* (Philadelphia: JPS, 1972).

On the holiday of Pesach we read Shir ha-Shirim, the Song of Songs. It is the story of two lovers. It tells of their initial love and later on their longing for each other.

Perhaps the most dramatic scene occurs in chapter 5. The beautiful Shulamite lies in her bed, when she hears a sound from outside. It is the call of her beloved: *kol dodi dofek*, the sound of her beloved is knocking at the door (5:2). He wants to reunite with her. He beseeches her, "*Pitchi li*, open up the door for me, my beloved" (5:2).

And she hesitates. She says, "*Pashateti et kutanti* – I've just take off my coat. How can I now go and get dressed? *Rachatzti et raglai, eikhakha atanfem* – I have just washed my feet, how can I go and get them dirty?" (5:3).

When she finally decides to get up he has already left (5:6). The moment has passed, and she struggles to find him again. She wanders though the night looking for him. But she is beaten and scorned (5:7). She has lost a great opportunity and it will take enormous effort to regain what she once had.

She hesitated when she heard the call and thus she lost the moment.

We must hear the call – a call that brings us closer to Hashem – and when we do, we cannot hesitate.

A RESPONSE TO CATASTROPHE

Tzav

On March 11, 2011, there was a major nuclear disaster at the Fukushima Nuclear Reactor in Japan. This was the largest nuclear disaster since the accident at Chernobyl in 1986. When I hear of such tragedies in the news I find them overwhelming. The tragedies are all consuming, and I find it difficult to think of anything else. I want to share with you how we can respond to such horrible news.

One of the problems with a nuclear crisis is that we often don't even know the full effects for a long time. After the Fukushima disaster, the *Washington Post* ran an article highlighting another significant element of a nuclear tragedy: the psychological fears and social stigma that radiation exposure causes.

On a limited level, I have seen this with my own eyes. I am close friends with a couple who are now in their nineties, who were unable to have children because the man was exposed to radiation in World War II. Magnify this couple's case infinitely and we have some inkling into the personal anguish that millions of people in Japan are now feeling. In addition to their mourning for their friends and relatives who are now gone, they are also frightened about their exposure to radiation and possible future complications. In all likelihood we will not be able to comprehend the effects of this tragedy for decades to come.

What can we do when we hear of such horrible news or other horrible tragedies? It is not at all clear how we, as average Joes, can help or make a difference. We can contribute to relief efforts (and we absolutely should) and we can offer prayers for the wounded (and we absolutely should), but many of us are still left with a feeling of total helplessness in the face of this unfolding disaster.

After hearing about the Fukushima reactor, I reached out to a friend of mine who I knew was in Japan when the disaster occurred. He had arrived back in the US safely that week. So I told him that since he was in a dangerous place and he survived he should recite the blessing called *birkat ha-gomel*. The blessing of *birkat ha-gomel* is a blessing of thanksgiving that is recited when surviving a terrible danger. It is based upon an obligation in the time of the Temple to bring an offering of thanks to Hashem in certain cases.

According to the Talmud in tractate Berakhot (54b), four categories of people were required to offer a thanksgiving offering: *yordei ha-yam* (people who traveled over the sea); *holkhei mid-barot* (people who crossed the desert); *choleh u-nitrapeh* (one who recovered from an illness); and *chavush be-veit ha-asurim* (one who was released from captivity). Since we no longer are able to offer a thanksgiving offering, we now recite a *birkat ha-gomel* instead.

The text of the *birkat ha-gomel* translates as follows: "Blessed are You…Who bestows kindness even on the unworthy, for He has bestowed goodness on me." According to the rabbis this blessing must be recited communally, in the presence of a minyan, and ideally it should be recited after an *aliyah* to the Torah.

The source for this blessing and its customs is in parashat Tzav. We are taught the laws of a *korban todah*, a thanksgiving offering. The *korban todah* has some unique laws. First, the *todah* is brought along with forty loaves of bread, four of which are given to the *kohein* and the rest are eaten by the non-*kohein*. And whereas the normal *shelamim* offerings can be eaten over a period of two days and one night, a *todah* offering has only one day and night for consumption. This means that the person who brings the *todah* offering has a shorter amount of time to eat his animal and an additional thirty-six loaves of bread.

Rabbi Menachem Liebtag, a brilliant, contemporary commentator on the Torah, explains that the only way that this could be done was to share the *korban todah* communally with as many friends and family members as possible. This way it would be eaten within the allotted time. The *korban todah* was designed not just as a personal offering of thanksgiving, but to inspire others to share in a communal offering of thanks. This teaches us that we as a community must respond with prayer when we witness great danger.

The *korban todah* and *birkat ha-gomel* are not blessings of joy, but blessings of gratitude. The Torah is teaching us that when there is a life-threatening moment we must stop and express our gratitude to Hashem. We are not only expressing gratitude that He has saved our lives on this occasion, but also gratitude for what He does for us on a daily basis. We are expressing gratitude for all that He gives us even though we are not worthy and our deeds are small.

I know that when there is an unspeakable tragedy that occurs in the world, our instinctive response is to turn off. It is so much easier not to think of the horrible tragedy in the world and to focus just on the happy elements of life. But such an approach is not what the Torah asks from us. Instead, when we hear of a tragedy it should remind us to take greater efforts to think about our role in this world, to have gratitude to Hashem for what He has already given us, to express our gratitude, and to empathize with those who are in need.

The rabbis tell us that there is a concept of going to a great tzaddik and asking the tzaddik to pray to Hashem on your behalf. Some explain that the reason the tzaddik is able to pray successfully for you is in the merit of the tremendous empathy that he feels for you when he hears of your distress. Empathy for those in need is a great mitzvah and can arouse the mercy of Hashem.

This dual emotion of gratitude to Hashem and empathy for the victim is the cornerstone of what it means to be a religious person.

Proof of this is that the Midrash (Vayikra Rabbah 9:7) teaches that in the future, "All the sacrifices will be obsolete, except for the *korban todah*." This means that even though other sacrifices – like a sin-offering or a guilt-offering – might one day be rendered unnecessary, the *todah* offering will never be outdated. It will always be needed because what the *todah* represents is a core value of Judaism: the idea that we must always have gratitude toward Hashem and an awareness of the victims in our midst.

Today we no longer have the *korban todah*, but we do have a custom to recite the *birkat ha-gomel*, and in addition we have the daily custom (except for Shabbat and holidays) of reciting the Psalm of Thanksgiving, *Mizmor le-Todah* (psalm 100), which is the psalm that was recited as the *korban todah* was offered in the Temple.

While we search for ways to be able to physically help people after hearing of a tragedy, we must always remember that we all have another obligation as well: we have a religious obligation to set aside time each day to focus on our gratitude to Hashem for His daily gifts and empathy for the victims. If we fulfill this obligation then we will become more sensitive people. It might not offer direct help to the people undergoing the crisis, but it is a positive response to an unspeakable tragedy.

The message of the *korban todah* is that we must respond to life-threatening events and catastrophes by trying to arouse within ourselves a heightened sensitivity to the needs of the people of the world and to service of God.

DON'T DWELL ON IT

Shemini

There is a terrific book called *Moonwalking with Einstein*.[1] The book is about memory and it discusses how and why we remember certain things. One of the major points of the book is that if we really want to remember something, we have to put it in a context that makes sense. The book makes the overarching point that our memory is very selective and we can train it to remember what we want.

This got me thinking about the following question: Do you think we are naturally more likely to remember our successes or our failures? I posed this question to my Facebook friends, and according to them the answer is our failures.

Parashat Shemini discusses this question. The parashah deals with one of the high points in Jewish history: the eighth day of the *miluim*, the inauguration of the Mishkan – or in other words, the very first day that the Mishkan was open. This was the day the Jewish people had been working toward since they started building the Mishkan. It was the final day of preparation, and all that was required was for Aharon to bring a few more sacrifices and then the Presence of God would come down to the Jewish people.

There was only one problem. Aharon was afraid.

The Torah says:

---

1. Joshua Foer, *Moonwalking with Einstein: The Art and Science of Remembering Everything* (New York: Penguin Books, 2011).

וַיֹּאמֶר מֹשֶׁה זֶה הַדָּבָר אֲשֶׁר צִוָּה ה' תַּעֲשׂוּ וְיֵרָא אֲלֵיכֶם כְּבוֹד ה':
וַיֹּאמֶר מֹשֶׁה אֶל אַהֲרֹן קְרַב אֶל הַמִּזְבֵּחַ וַעֲשֵׂה אֶת חַטָּאתְךָ....

And Moshe said: "This is the thing that Hashem commanded you to do and then the Presence of Hashem will appear over you." And Moshe said to Aharon, "Go close to the altar and bring your sin offering...." (Vayikra 9:6–7)

Moshe was telling Aharon that in order to bring Hashem's Presence into the Mishkan he first had to bring a calf sin offering. Rashi explains that the purpose of this sin offering of Aharon's was in order to demonstrate that Hashem was forgiving Aharon for the sin of the golden calf.

But still Aharon was afraid. And the text reflects that fear.

Moshe doesn't just tell Aharon, "aseh," bring the offering. Rather, he tells him "kerav, go close" and then bring the offering. Rashi explains that this indicates that Aharon was afraid: "Aharon was embarrassed and afraid to come close to the altar." So Moshe had to turn to Aharon and say, "Why are you afraid? This is what you were selected for."

Ramban quotes a parable from the Midrash called Torat Kohanim (Vayikra 9:7) that elucidates Aharon's strange behavior.

There was once a king who married a woman and was expecting her to arrive on the wedding night. Lo and behold, on the wedding night, the bride was refusing to leave her room. She was too embarrassed to see the king. So her sister came to visit her and said: "My sister, why did you agree to marry the king? Is it not in order to visit him on the wedding night? Get yourself together and go and visit the king." So, too, Moshe said to Aharon: "My brother, why were you selected to be the high priest? Was it not in order to serve in the presence of God? Get yourself together and go and perform your service."

But still we are left with the question, why was Aharon so afraid?

Here too, Ramban helps us. He explains that when Aharon looked at the altar all he could see were the horns of an ox; all he could think about as he looked at the altar was the sin of the golden calf. As Ramban writes, "That sin was fixed upon his thought." So even though Aharon was standing on the threshold of the greatest moment in his life, all he could see was his greatest failure. Aharon had the vision of the golden calf before his eyes at all times and he couldn't see beyond it.

I once heard a lecture from a psychologist named Philip Zimbardo. He broke down the personalities of the world into six different categories connected to three time zones. There is past, present, and future. Within each of these time zones there is a negative and a positive. So a past negative person dwells on the mistakes of his past and a past positive person dwells on the successes.

Many of us are past negative people. We see our failures in life at all times. Like Aharon, when there is an altar in front of us, we don't see the altar. We only see the image of the golden calf.

The problem with being a past negative person is that when we keep looking at our failures we never see our destiny. We never see what we can accomplish in the world. All the data shows that past negative people tend to be, well, downright miserable. On the other hand, future positive people are happier and more successful.

So how do we change from being past negative personalities into becoming future positive people? This is the secret message of the riddle of the red heifer, the *parah adumah*.

In the weeks leading up to Pesach we also read the passage of the Torah that discusses the red heifer, parashat Parah (Bamidbar 19:1–22). In order to become spiritually purified so that we can partake in the *korban Pesach*, it is necessary to take a red heifer and bring it outside of the entire camp, slaughter it, burn it, and then mix it with cedar wood, hyssop, a crimson thread, and water, and sprinkle it on the person who is ritually impure. According to the Midrash, Shlomo ha-Melekh, who was the smartest person who ever lived, explained that this ritual was beyond his comprehension. As he said, "It is distant from me." (Bamidbar Rabbah 19:3, quoting Kohelet 7:23).

While the ritual in its entirety is difficult to understand, there are parts of it that we can explain. Thus, Rashi, quoting the Midrash, writes that the whole reason for this ritual is to atone for the sin of the golden calf. A parable is offered by Rashi: If there is a maid working in the king's palace and her son makes the palace dirty, they call the mother and ask her to clean up the mess of her son. Here, too, let the mother cow come and atone for the calf.

The verse states that we are supposed to keep the ashes of the red heifer as a *mishmeret,* as a remembrance. And Rashi explains that it is a "remembrance" in that it is comparable to the sin of the golden calf, which is remembered by Hashem for generations; so, too, for all eternity there is no punishment that we receive which does not on some level also contain within it the punishment for the sin of the golden calf.

This is the message of the *parah adumah.* It was a ritual performed by the *kohein* upon a ritually impure person in order to purify them. But at the same time it was a ritual specifically performed by a *kohein* in order to atone for Aharon's sin of the golden calf. On a spiritual level the sin of the golden calf contaminated us all. We were in a moment of spiritual bliss and then along came this tremendous sin. No one felt responsible for this sin more than Aharon.

In order to atone for this sin, Aharon's descendants need to grind up a cow and burn it outside the camp. The message for us is that we, too, need to grind up our failures and burn them in our minds in order to move on with our life and grow spiritually. This is another reason why the passage of the *parah adumah* is read in the days leading up to Pesach. In order to achieve spiritual redemption, our failures need to be burned.

There was once a great Russian mnemonist named Solomon Venaiminovitch Shereshevsky who remembered everything. But the problem with remembering everything is that sometimes we need to move beyond the past. So in order to forget, what this mnemonist did is imagine certain memories in his mind and burn the images in order to erase them.[2] Whether or not we literally want to partake in that exercise, the point is that if we want to achieve our destiny, we need to let go of our failures.

This idea of the necessity of becoming future positive people applies to every aspect of our personal lives. And nowhere does it apply more than in the spiritual realm. We all have it in ourselves to succeed spiritually. Yet so many of us dwell on our spiritual inadequacies and areas where we have fallen short, and miss the fact that our spiritual future can be so different than our spiritual past.

This is why parashat Parah is always read in the days leading up to Pesach. Pesach is a holiday about remembering the Exodus, but in order to remember the Exodus we must allow ourselves to forget our own failings. This is the symbolism of burning the *chametz* on the eve of Pesach. *Chametz* represents sin. And it is not only a mitzvah to eat matzah; it is also a mitzvah to burn the *chametz*. Before we can be redeemed we need to destroy our past mistakes.

Parashat Parah is a wake-up call for Pesach. It is a reminder that the time to prepare spiritually for Pesach has arrived; the time has come to take up our past spiritual shortcomings, grind them into ashes, and push forward. We just have to believe that we are capable of great spiritual heights and then we will be capable of achieving them. We just have to allow ourselves to draw closer to the altar.

---

2. See Jerome Bruner, *The Mind of a Mnemonist: A Little Book about a Vast Memory* (Cambridge: Harvard University Press), 1987.

PRAY FOR HEALTH

Tazria

In 1988 a doctor named Randolph Byrd conducted a study in the coronary-care unit of San Francisco General Hospital. He studied whether or not intercessory prayers on behalf of other people were effective. He took 393 patients and randomly assigned them to two groups. One group of 192 patients was prayed for by strangers (born-again Christians) from around the country, who were given the patients' clinical information and name. The other group of 201 patients did not receive prayers from these strangers. All the patients in the study knew they were participating in a study of prayer, but no patient knew to which group he or she had been assigned. The only person who knew was the research nurse administering the study. The study met the rigorous scientific criteria of double blind, placebo-controlled clinical trials.

The findings were amazing. They defied the laws of science. The patients who were not prayed for were nearly twice as likely to suffer complications than patients who were prayed for.[1] The study seems to indicate that prayers, even by a stranger for a stranger, can help in fighting disease.

This study has spawned a great deal of criticism by academic scientists who argue that it is not sufficiently rigorous or reliable. But I am more interested in the spiritual question. From a spiritual perspective, are prayers really that powerful? Is this how prayer works? Is this a Torah approach?

---

1. Dale A. Matthews, MD, and Connie Clark, *The Faith Factor: Proof of the Healing Power of Prayer* (New York: Penguin, 1999), 199–200.

In parashat Tazria, the Torah talks about a disease: *tzara'at*, which is a skin disease. While many commentators choose to allegorize this disease, the simple reading of the Torah is that it is a physical disease. The Torah refers to this disease as *fasah hanega* (13:5), the disease is malignant. It is a malignant tumor that appears on the body.

Even though it is a physical disease, the response is a spiritual one. The person with *tzara'at* comes to the *kohein*. The *kohein* decides if he is *tamei* or *tahor*. The *kohein* decides on the proper treatment. He might decide that the patient needs to be quarantined or that the patient is physically fine, or that the patient is *tamei*.

The response to this physical illness is to come to this *kohein*, a spiritual person – a spiritual healer. What is the logic behind this teaching of the Torah?

The *Sefer ha-Chinukh* (a work published anonymously in Spain in the thirteenth century) offers the following explanation: This commandment is teaching us that the reason the person with this disease is commanded to come to the *kohein* is that perhaps if he stands in the presence of the *kohein* – a spiritual man – the *kohein* will inspire him to meditate introspectively. This is also the concept behind the quarantine; it will allow the patient to consider his affairs unhurriedly and examine his deeds.

We have to read this source very carefully. The *Sefer ha-Chinukh* is not saying that all illness comes from sin. The most righteous people in the world can be afflicted with the most terrible illnesses. Instead, he is suggesting that one way to treat illness is through spiritual reflection. The patient comes to the *kohein*, who can guide him on a spiritual path to health. Perhaps the Torah is suggesting that the best way to treat sickness is with spirituality.

When I was in rabbinical school, we had classes on pastoral counseling. One time we had a class and the rabbi teaching the class gave us a situation. You walk into a hospital room and discover that the person has just been diagnosed with a terminal illness. What do you tell the person? The rabbi then went on to say, "I'll tell you what you don't say. Don't say, 'Now is the time for *tehillim* (psalms). You have to daven, get all your friends to daven. Daven to Hashem to cure you.'"

I understood my teacher's words to mean that he was suggesting that prayers don't work to change a situation. He was arguing that from a medical and psychological perspective, the prayers won't heal you. Instead patients would do better to focus their energy on other areas.

I have come to disagree with this teacher's approach. With the affliction of *tzara'at* the Torah is telling us that prayers can and do work. Spirituality can provide mental and physical health. Spirituality can be a legitimate response to illness. This is what the medical, scientific community is slowly beginning to realize. Study after study shows how increased religiosity directly correlates to increased physical health.

A study of 2,754 men and women in Tecumseh, Michigan, found that men and women who attend church more frequently live longer than those who attend less frequently. A study in Georgia shows that those who attend church more often have lower blood pressure – even if they are smokers – than those who attend less often. A study of 91,000 people in Maryland shows that people who attend church at least once a week had significantly lower risk for coronary disease.[2] All of these studies – and there are many more studies – look at how frequently people attend worship services to pray. The more often one attends worship service, the healthier you are likely to be.

There are scientific reasons for this. Prayer relaxes us. It reduces stress by reminding us to care for our bodies and to constantly seek renewal, by giving us a purpose in life, and by providing us with a sense of being loved.

But let's not ignore the spiritual possibilities as well. Let's not ignore the possibility that prayers simply work – that they actually heal the disease. When facing illness we should encourage a spiritual response, as well as a medical response. A spiritual

2. Matthews and Clark, *The Faith Factor*, 20.

response embraces the physical touch. A caregiver will sometimes wear gloves when touching a patient. A spiritual response will embrace physical contact. A spiritual response will encourage holding the patient's hand, hugging the patient, kissing the patient gently on the forehead.

The Mishnah (Negaim 3:2) teaches that if a *chatan* (bridegroom) has the discolorations of *tzara'at*, "*notnin lo shivat yemei ha-mishteh*," we give him the seven festive days of his wedding; in other words, we don't quarantine him or declare him *tamei* until after the wedding party has finished.

Here is a person who has a physical ailment and we are telling him to wait for treatment. Why not treat it right away? The point is that a *chatan* is already treating the illness. He is on a spiritual high; he is surrounded by his friends. Since the wedding is a spiritual moment he is certainly going through tremendous introspection. He can push off the treatment because he is already receiving his spiritual medication.

I will not bore you with miraculous stories about people who have been cured through faith and prayer. There are too many to tell. There are also too many stories of people who had tremendous faith and prayed incessantly and yet were not healed from their ailment. That's not the point. The point is that just like a medical approach does not always work, and yet we try it anyway, so too a spiritual approach does not always work and yet it should be tried.

A spiritual approach to our health uses the words of our prayers in order to ground us, strengthen us, and heal us. This is what faith is about. It should be something we embrace at all times in our life. God forbid, if one falls ill, the words of our prayers would offer comfort and healing as well.

Miriam the prophetess was stricken with *tzara'at*. When her brother Moshe saw this he cried out to Hashem, "*El nah, refah nah lah* – O God, please heal her" (Bamidbar 12:13). When seeing illness, we too have that power. We too can together cry out, "O God, heal the wounded."

HE LIVED TO TEACH

Metzora

On Tuesday at 10 p.m., I found myself on the phone with a Rabbi Ronald Koppelman of Roanoke, Virginia. Rabbi Koppelman had the honor of performing *shemirah* on the body of Liviu Librescu. It was his responsibility to remain with the body and recite psalms until the hearse came to drive the body to an airplane in New York, before eventually flying to Israel for burial.

On April 16, 2007, a man named Seung-Hui Cho went on a killing rampage on the Virginia Tech campus. Before he was done he ended up killing thirty-two people. He would have killed even more were it not for Liviu. At the age of seventy-six, Liviu managed to save the students in his Virginia Tech classroom by throwing himself in front of the door and taking the bullets in his own body while telling his students to run to safety.

Rabbi Koppelman was himself in great shock. He told me that his son had applied to Virginia Tech, but for some reason he had applied late and was told that he had to wait a year before attending the school. And so he waited. Rabbi Koppelman explained that his son's major is mechanical engineering and no doubt he would have been in that classroom with Liviu Librescu on Monday. And now, here he was guarding and protecting the body of this man – a Holocaust survivor – who had protected so many others.

I shared with Rabbi Koppelman that I wanted to organize a proper funeral procession for the hearse that would be carrying Liviu. Our entire community should have met and escorted that hearse as it drove to New York City. Liviu was a great man, worthy of us awaking at three in the morning as the hearse passed us on I-95 to escort him to the city limits.

The Talmud, tractate Avodah Zarah 10b, teaches, *"Yeish adam koneh olamo be-sha'ah achat* – A person can acquire the world in one moment." In one moment of heroism a person can show that he or she is worthy of ascending to the highest levels of heaven.

One never knows how he will act in a moment of intense pressure. The haftarah of Metzora tells us another story of immense pressure. The story from the Prophets (II Melakhim 7) tells of the Jewish people under siege from the Arameans. There was a great famine; everyone was expecting the worst. The Arameans were an incredibly powerful and rich army. Their power seemed unsurpassable. But then God made a miracle. The Aramean camp heard a sound; maybe it was an earthquake or maybe it was just a sound. And they all panicked. They said: "The King of Israel has hired the Hittites or the Egyptians to defeat us" (II Melakhim 7:6). And so they ran. In a moment, the entire camp was deserted. Under pressure, the Arameans ran. As the news came back to the Jewish people that the siege was lifted and that there was now food, a stampede occurred. As a result of the stampede, , the captain of the city was trampled to death.

Under intense pressure, many good people lose all perspective. We never know how we will act until that moment comes. How would we have acted under similar pressure?

When we read about the life of Liviu, we realize that there was a great man living in Blacksburg, Virginia. He responded to pressure with great honor.

During the Shoah, he was placed in a forced-labor camp, and then deported to a ghetto in the city of Focsani, Romania. He then worked at a government aerospace company. But his career was ended when he refused to swear allegiance to the Communist regime. He was fired when he requested permission to move to Israel. He survived the Shoah and then had the courage to risk his life by not swearing loyalty to Communism. He risked his life by declaring he was a Jew to the Romanian government and asking to move to Israel; and he gave his life so that all of his students could survive.

CNN showed a picture of him with a *kippah* and that was appropriate, since this was a man who gave his life *al kiddush Hashem*, sanctifying God's name.

After reading about his life, I felt the need to call his family and express my admiration for their father. I called his son Joe in Raanana, Israel. He was so grateful for my call. "*Kevod ha-Rav*," he said, "thank you for calling." I shared with him that our entire community was with him in his moments of pain. We admired his father's greatness and courage and were reciting prayers on his behalf.

I then said to Joe, "What would you like to tell our congregation?" He said to me, "Rabbi, I was going to ask you: What can I say at my father's funeral? Is there anything from our Jewish tradition that comes to mind?"

This is what I shared with him:

"Your father lived to teach. That was his life. He taught students. As you said, 'That's what woke him up in the morning.'

"But he didn't just live his life teaching. He also died teaching. The way he died was an act of teaching. By reacting under pressure with immense heroism, he taught millions of people what it means to be a teacher and what it means to live a life of dignity and service of Hashem. In the darkness of the tragedy, millions of people gained strength and inspiration from his actions. For millions of people, at a time when the world seemed so dark, he was a symbol of the goodness of humanity. At a time of darkness, he showed us how we can give light to the world.

"In our tradition, there was another great man who died while teaching. That man was Rabbi Akiva, perhaps the greatest rabbi of the Mishnah. Our tradition teaches that Rabbi Akiva was ordered by the Romans to stop teaching Torah. When he refused, they burned his body alive. As Rabbi Akiva died, he shouted the words '*Shema Yisrael, Hashem Elokeinu, Hashem Echad* – Hear O Israel, the

Lord our God, the Lord is One.' Like Rabbi Akiva, your father died teaching.

"The time of year in which parashat Metzora is read is called the Omer period. It is a time where we are in communal mourning for the twenty-four thousand students of Rabbi Akiva who died in this exact period. By acting with such heroism and dedication, your father demonstrated that he was a true student of Rabbi Akiva. Rabbi Akiva died but his teachings have lived on for two thousand years, offering comfort and strength to the Jewish people. This week at Virginia Tech, all of Rabbi Akiva's students lived! Like Rabbi Akiva, your father's actions – his teachings – will live on for many, many years. His actions will guide us and inspire all of us."

By this time, we were both crying. Even though we had never met and were thousands of miles away, we felt so connected. We couldn't get off the phone. We said "Good-bye" five or six times. Finally, as I hung up the phone, Joe said to me, "*Ten neshikot le-kulam*, give kisses to everyone."

At the Romanian university where Liviu originally graduated, his picture was put on a table, a candle was lit, and flowers were placed. A professor there said, "We remember him as a great specialist in aeronautics. He left behind hundreds of prestigious papers."

He surely did. But this is the inscription that I would write outside room 204 in Virginia Tech's Norris Hall:

"We rename this room the Liviu Librescu Room. He lived to teach and he died while teaching. Through his death he ensured that we can live on. Through his death he ensured that his teachings will never die."

May his soul be blessed!

THE CYCLES OF YOM KIPPUR

Acharei Mot

A few years after becoming a rabbi in DC I learned something new about our shul, something that both shocked me and excited me at the same time.

Sadly, an old-time synagogue family lost a loved one, and they came to visit me. I listened to their story and was absorbing the history of their connection to the shul. The man who was speaking said that his grandfather was the former president of the shul, and that he went to Hebrew school at Ohev Sholom. And then he said, "I even remember when we put the time capsule into the building."

"The WHAT?" I said.

"The time capsule," he repeated. Then he told me the story of our shul's time capsule.

Back in November of 1960, when the building was first dedicated, the shul members gathered for a *chanukat ha-bayit*, a dedication of the synagogue. You can still see the picture in our memorabilia room. They got an orchestra from the armed forces, closed down 16th Street, and had an elaborate ceremony. And at this ceremony they put a time capsule into the cornerstone of the building. I had never heard about this time capsule and I had a lot of questions about it. What's in it? He had forgotten. When are we supposed to open it? No one remembers the answer to that question. Whose idea was it? No one remembers. Did they put any bonds or bank notes in the capsule?

When I told this story to our daily minyan, someone suggested that we should open the capsule and put more stuff in it for fifty years from now. I asked the minyan, "What should we put in it?"

Ethan Steinberg, who had just turned thirteen, raised his hand and said, "I'll volunteer to go in the time capsule."

Time gets away from us. Sometimes we look back at the previous year and say, "Oh my gosh! Where did the year go? What did I do with my time?" Parashat Acharei Mot teaches us about the central rituals of the biblical holiday of Yom Kippur, and the ritual service of Yom Kippur teaches us this lesson of time.

In parashat Acharei Mot the Torah commands us to take a goat to the *kohein gadol*, the high priest on Yom Kippur. The *kohein gadol* first places his hands upon the goat and confesses over it for all of the sins of Israel. Then this goat, known as the *se'ir la-azazel* (or scapegoat in colloquial English), is sent off into the wilderness and, according to the Talmud, pushed off a cliff (Yoma 39a). Symbolically all of our sins are transferred to this goat, and its death atones for the Jewish people.

This goat had extremely powerful spiritual strength. Rambam says in reference to this goat: "The goat that was sent to Azazel atoned for all of the sins of the Torah, both stringent and minor, whether they were violated purposefully or accidentally. That is, provided one repents. But if one does not repent, the goat still atones for all of the minor sins" (*Hilkhot Teshuvah* 1:2). How is this possible? How can the goat wipe away our sins even without any contrition on our part?

With this goat, Hashem is teaching us about the essence of Yom Kippur. The scapegoat is a gift from Hashem, and it is a gift that we absolutely do not deserve. Yom Kippur is a holiday that comes at the end of a cycle of repentance. Ever since Rosh Chodesh Elul – for forty days – we have been urged to repent. This idea dominates our liturgy: repent because Yom Kippur is coming, the Day of Judgment is near. But routinely we ignore the warnings and we do not fully repent. We basically continue with our status-quo behavior.

Hashem has mercy upon us. He knows just how difficult it is for us to try something new. He knows that we get caught up in our unending cycles of behavior: cycles of sin; cycles of fights; and cycles of laziness and disappointment. Hashem knows that without His help we will never be able to break the cycles.

That is what Yom Kippur is all about. It is our opportunity to break the cycle.

Hashem gives us the scapegoat and tells us: Even though you have not repented fully, I will break the cycle. I will give you an opportunity to start over and wipe your sins clean on this day. And that is the power of Yom Kippur: Hashem allows us to break through our cycle of sin.

It is as though Hashem tells us: "I know it is hard for you, maybe even too hard. So I will take the first step and wipe your slate clean."

Today, without the existence of the Holy Temple, we no longer have the supernatural power of the goat. We no longer have this gift from Hashem. However, today, instead of the goat, we can still break the cycle of our sins through repentance and the awesomeness of the day of Yom Kippur. The rabbis say that the essence of the day of Yom Kippur is special. It has a unique power to atone. It is almost as if you get lucky and go before a judge on his birthday.

Yom Kippur is Hashem's gift to us to help us break the sinful cycles of our lives.

But it is not always so easy to get a gift. It is hard and it makes some of us uncomfortable.

After our baby daughter, Kolbi Aden, was born, we announced her birth and I wrote in an email "No gifts please." A friend of mine, a senior rabbi who is on my email list, gently told me that I was wrong. He told me that I should be including people in my celebration, and when I say "no gifts," I was shutting that door. He told me, "Take it on the chin and accept the gifts."

And I think he was right. Sometimes it is harder to accept the gift than to give the gift in the first place.

So we must be sure to accept this gift from Hashem; we should accept this gift of breaking the sinful cycles of our life. We can do so by committing ourselves to another cycle. We respond back to the gift of the scapegoat – the gift of Yom Kippur – by saying we will continue the cycle. Not the cycle of sin, but the holy cycles, the cycles of mitzvot, the sacred traditions of our ancestors.

This idea is contained in a special prayer that we say on Yom Kippur. Actually we say this prayer every day, but on Yom Kippur we say it differently.

Every day, four times a day, we recite the Shema: *Shema Yisrael, Hashem Elokeinu, Hashem Echad* – Hear O Israel, Hashem is Our God, Hashem is One. This verse and the ensuing paragraph that we recite come from Devarim, chapter 6. But we always insert a phrase following this verse, and this phrase does not come from the Bible. After reciting Shema, we say in a hushed tone, "*Barukh shem kevod malkhuto le-olam va-ed* – Blessed be the name of His glorious kingdom forever and ever."

There is only one time during the year when this phrase is not said quietly but rather in a loud and clear voice, and that time is Yom Kippur.

Why do we recite this phrase at all? It is very strange, since it is a statement inserted into the middle of a biblical passage.

Again we turn to Rambam to understand this. And here is his explanation (*Hilkhot Keriat Shema* 1:4):

It is a tradition that when Yaakov was about to die he gathered his children together in Egypt. Yaakov was worried that his children would not continue on his path, so he started preaching and exhorting them to understand the greatness of God and the fact that there is only one God in this world. He turned to his children and asked: "My children, is there perhaps a defective one amongst you? Do any of you not believe in one God?"

All of his sons turned to him and declared: "*Shema Yisrael,* listen Israel (our father): Hashem is our God, Hashem is One." When Yaakov heard this he was overwhelmed with emotion and appreciation, and he declared, "*Baruch shem kevod malkhuto le-olam va-ed.*"

This phrase – *Baruch shem kevod malkhuto le-olam va-ed* – is an affirmation of our belief in Hashem's unity. But in this story it represents more than that; it represents a commitment to pass this belief down through the generations. Just as Yaakov did to his own children, we must do to the next generation as well.

Hashem gives us the gift of Yom Kippur, of helping us break our sinful cycles. And we respond with a commitment to continue the cycles of our holy traditions through the generations.

It is no accident that we begin our service on Yom Kippur by reciting this phrase aloud during the recitation of Shema after Kol Nidre, and then we end the fast of Yom Kippur by literally shouting this phrase three times at the end of the Neila service. This special phrase uniquely bookends our sacred day and reminds us of our responsibility.

We have been given a gift from Hashem, but with that gift comes the responsibility symbolized within the meaning of *Baruch shem kevod malkhuto le-olam va-ed*.

As we read parashat Acharei Mot we should imagine ourselves receiving a tremendous gift from Hashem: a chance to start fresh. In return for this gift we should imagine that we are there with Yaakov our forefather, promising him that we will continue his traditions and teachings.

And then we should imagine we are promising our loved ones – first our great-grandparents, then our grandparents, then our own parents, and then our children, and then all the children of our congregation – that we too will not break the cycle.

And if we do that, then we are in essence always reciting that very powerful phrase, *Baruch shem kevod malkhuto le-olam va-ed* – Blessed be the name of His glorious kingdom forever and ever.

REMEMBERING THE BESHT

Kedoshim

Sometimes when we are sitting down to dinner in our house, the phone will ring or someone will ring the doorbell. It is often an annoying intrusion of somebody trying to sell us something. It can be aggravating. Well, the next time that happens to you, think about this story.[1]

One time the Ba'al Shem Tov was sitting in his house teaching his students when a knock was heard on the window. A poor man looked inside the Ba'al Shem Tov's house and said: "Does anything need to be repaired? Perhaps a chair, or a gutter, or a part of the roof?"

The students of the Ba'al Shem Tov were annoyed by this interruption. They wanted to continue their Torah studies. So they shouted back, "We are all fine. Everything is all set. There is no need for any repairs."

"Nothing at all?" said the poor man. "Surely something needs to be fixed inside your house. If you look hard enough you will find it."

"Indeed," said the Ba'al Shem Tov turning to his students, "nothing is by chance. How often do we think we are all fine and that everything is all set. But if we look inside our hearts and evaluate our lives, we will understand that we are in need of great repairs."

The *yahrtzeit* of the Ba'al Shem Tov is on the holiday of Shavuot, as he died on May 22, 1760, which translates into 7 Sivan, or Shavuot, 5520. The Ba'al Shem Tov, whose actual name was Rabbi

---

1. The full version of the story can be found at http://www.chabad.org/library/article_cdo/aid/53343/jewish/Pushcart-Prophet.htm.

Yisrael ben Eliezer, was one of the most influential rabbis of the last two thousand years, and his *yahrtzeit* always comes near parashat Kedoshim. The Ba'al Shem Tov, or the Besht, is the founder of Chasidut, a stream of Judaism that emphasizes pious behavior and attachment to a Rebbe. The movement has had a profound effect upon the entire Jewish people.

As important a figure as he is in Jewish history, the Ba'al Shem Tov as an actual historical figure is shrouded in mystery. There is so little in the way of contemporaneous sources about his life. The primary source for the life and teachings of the Besht is the *Shivchei ha-Besht*, which contains many of his anecdotes and teachings. But it was only published in 1815, two generations after his death. So as a historical source of the Besht's life, it is incomplete. A scholar named Moshe Rosman went through the tax records of the Besht's hometown and was able to glean some more personal and historical information. But still, so much of this great figure's life remains a mystery.

According to the legends told of the Besht, he was born (in what is now modern-day Ukraine) to two parents who were very old; they are described as "close to one hundred years old" at the time of his birth. He was orphaned as a young boy and the Jewish community enrolled him in the local *cheder*. Although he was a bright student, he had some unique habits that set him apart – like, for example, wandering off from school to spend time whistling and walking alone in the forest.

His first job in life was as a teacher's assistant. His task was to walk the children to and from school. Here, too, he was unusual. Instead of just walking them to school, he would sing to them as they walked, and thus his students would enter the classroom with great joy.

Later he moved to a new town where he got a job as a school teacher. He married a woman who was the daughter of a prominent rabbi, Avraham Gershon Kutover of Brody. But before the marriage could take place the rabbi died. The rabbi's son was horrified that the Besht – who appeared to be a simple Jew – would marry into his distinguished family, but nonetheless the marriage took place. However, the Besht and his new wife were given a horse and a wagon and told to leave town so as not to embarrass the prominent family.

The Besht and his new bride lived for seven years in an isolated village in the Carpathian Mountains. While living there, the Besht spent most of his time in the seclusion of the majestic mountains pondering the greatness of Hashem.

At the age of thirty-six the Besht finally decided to reveal his greatness to the world; he revealed to the world that he was, in fact, a *ba'al Shem*. *Ba'al Shem* literally means a "master of the Name." It refers to a person who has the possibility to use the Name of Hashem in a mystical manner, like through kabbalah, amulets, and special prayers.

Eventually word of the Besht's miracles and great holiness spread, and people began to approach him in his town of Medzhybizh for help. He would often respond by praying with great fervor for a miracle. We are told that when he prayed in a barn, he prayed with such *kavanah* that even the barrels around him would dance. Medzhybizh eventually became the center of a new movement, which was slowly formulating a revolutionary approach to Judaism.

The most important of the Besht's students was Rabbi Dov Ber of Mezeritch, also known as the Maggid of Mezeritch. It is primarily through the Maggid that many of the Besht's teachings were able to spread far and wide.

What was so revolutionary about Chasidut? A few things.

Chasidut popularized many of the secrets of kabbalah; it emphasized joy in the service of Judaism; it gave great importance to the soul of the uneducated Jew and turned away from the elitist Talmudic scholar; it frowned on asceticism; and it emphasized the role of the tzaddik, the greatness of the spiritual leader's connection to Hashem.

In order to get a small taste of the Besht's theology, let us examine one example of his teachings as it relates to parashat Kedoshim.

This Torah portion contains one of the most fundamental mitzvot of the entire Torah: *"Ve-ahavta le-rei'akha kamokha* – love your neighbor like you love yourself" (19:18). Rashi says about this verse: *Zeh klal gadol ba-Torah*, this verse is a central principle of the Torah. But how is this so? Traditionally this verse was explained in the Talmud by understanding the negative. As the Talmud says (Shabbat 31a): "Don't do unto others what you wouldn't want done unto yourself."

But the Ba'al Shem Tov took a new approach to this verse. The Besht compares the word *ve-ahavta* in the verse "Love your neighbor..." to the word *ve-ahavta* in the first paragraph of Shema. He explains that *Ve-ahavta le-rei'akha kamokha* is actually an interpretation of and commentary on *Ve-ahavta et Hashem Elokekha*. One who loves a fellow Jew loves Hashem, because every Jew has a part of Hashem within himself. When one loves a fellow Jew, he loves the Jew's inner essence, and thus loves Hashem.

The Maggid of Mezeritch reported about his teacher's love of his fellow Jew: "If only we could kiss a Torah scroll with the same love that my master kissed the children when he took them to school as a teacher's assistant."[2]

For the Besht, loving every Jew became a core of his theology – a way of actually loving God. When one looks at a fellow Jew one is supposed to see a reflection of God. For many of us today this might not seem like such a revolutionary idea. But that only proves the success of the Besht's revolution. The Besht took a culture in which many Jews were unlearned and illiterate and therefore despised and ridiculed by the rabbinic elite, and the Besht not only loved them, but he also elevated them. He taught them that even

---

2. This story is cited at: http://www.chabad.org/library/article_cdo/aid/
   1208507/jewish/Biography.htm.

though they were not Talmud scholars or towering intellects, they were essential to the redemption of the Jewish people.

He taught the Jewish community that the way to loving One God is by loving another Jew. And he taught the unlearned Jews that one could come close to God without knowing the Talmud. In order to do so, what he or she needed to work on was clinging to God through prayer and bringing holiness into the performance of their mitzvot.

Whereas the intellectual center of the Jewish community, like Lithuania, focused on Talmudic casuistry, which was completely inaccessible to the average Jew, the Besht taught that it was not about Talmud study. Instead it was about *deveikut,* or cleaving to Hashem. He said: "Cleaving to Hashem is the master key that opens all locks. Every Jew, including the most simple, possesses the ability to cleave to the words of Torah and prayer, thereby achieving the highest degrees of unity with Hashem."[3]

With this approach the Besht took the idea of *Ve-ahavta le-rei'akha kamokha* from a nice simple aphorism and transformed it into the central pillar of his theology. We must love every Jew, and thus we must teach them that they too can be spiritually connected to Hashem as long as they cleave to Him.

As we commemorate the Besht's *yahrtzeit* let us bear his teachings in mind. Let us recognize this fundamental teaching that we can fulfill the mitzvah of loving Hashem by loving our neighbor. And that loving our neighbors is essential to our redemption as a nation.

There is a famous story of the Ba'al Shem Tov that teaches us this lesson: we must strive for a holiness that is dependent upon all of us climbing on each other's backs. It is a holiness that can be found through prayer and performing the mitzvot with special *kedushah.*

The Baal Shem Tov used to daven at great length and with tremendous intensity, longing and yearning for his Creator. His

---

3. http://www.jewishhealing.com/besht.html.

students would finish their prayers much earlier and then wait, sometimes for hours, for the Rebbe to finish. Once the Baal Shem Tov extended his prayers even longer than usual, and the disciples grew weary of waiting. They decided that each one would attend to whatever he had to do and then they would gather again in the shul an hour later. After an hour, they had all returned, and they waited some more until the Baal Shem Tov finished his prayer.

He then turned to them and accused, "You've created a great disunification in that you went out to attend to your private needs and left me here alone!" Then he told them the following parable.

It is known that the nature of birds is to migrate to the warm countries during the winter months. Once, the inhabitants of one of those countries spotted an unusually beautiful and unusual bird with feathers of every color in the universe, and he was perched at the crest of a very high and mighty tree that was impossible to climb. When the king of the land heard about the bird, he decided that he must capture it. He ordered many, many people to be brought to the forest where the tree was located. One was to stand on the shoulders of the other until they were able to reach the perch of the beautiful bird, and then to bring it to the king.

The procedure of reaching the heights of the tree was very arduous and time consuming. Some of those at the bottom of the human ladder lost sight of the task at hand. Weary and disgruntled with the amount of time it was taking, they began to disperse. It goes without saying that the whole ladder toppled to the ground, injuring those in the highest sections. The king wanted his people to be banded together with a common purpose, but this time nothing was gained.

"It was good," concluded the Baal Shem Tov, "when you were bound together with me in my prayer. But when you disbanded, each going his own separate way, everything fell. What I had hoped to achieve was lost."

In memory of the Besht, whenever we pray let us always remember to bind ourselves together in prayer.

THE NATIONAL SYNAGOGUE: THE POWER OF A NAME

Emor

The notorious anti-Semite David Duke attacks me on his website.[1] He doesn't like my explanation for the holiday of Purim and accuses me of promoting genocide upon the gentiles. In his view, my mistakes are magnified because we are such an important congregation. He says: "Rabbi Herzfeld is no lightweight Jew. His synagogue is important enough to be referred to as the National Synagogue of the United States."

Finally, someone recognizes the importance of using the name "National Synagogue." In contrast to David Duke, there have been a couple of voices in the Jewish community critical of this name.

This reminds me of a joke. An old Jew is reading *The Protocols of the Elders of Zion* on a park bench, when his friend approaches him and asks him why he doesn't read something else. He says, "When I read the Jewish books, they keep telling me how badly we are doing. When I read the anti-Semites, they tell us that we own all the banks, we run the world. I am much happier reading the anti-Semites."

"National Synagogue" is a name that serves an important purpose. Let me share a story with you.

One Sunday, as we were davening our morning service, I noticed a middle-aged man wandering our hallways. We were chanting and singing in Hebrew, and he was looking at us in bewilderment. I left the davening to greet him. He told me that his

---

1. http://www.davidduke.com/general/1831_1831.html.

name was Michael, he was from Cincinnati, and he was stopping in DC to look at colleges for his son. While he was here he wanted to visit the National Synagogue. I immediately invited him to come in and daven with us. We rolled up his sleeve and prepared to put on tefillin. He told me he was (in his words) a "reformed Jew." He said, "We never put these things on in Cincinnati." After the davening, I taught Michael how to say Shema and told him how to get a pair of tzitzit. I told him to wear the tzitzit everyday and to hold on to the fringes if he thought he might sin.

We spoke and we really bonded. Michael was looking to reconnect with Judaism and felt he could come to our shul because we were the National Synagogue. To him it meant that everyone in the country could stop by; it was a shul for everyone.

Our connection was so strong, but we were also sad, because we knew he was just stopping through. On his way out, he mentioned that he was moving to Portland, Maine, on Tuesday.

When I heard that I almost fainted. The whole of southern Maine has a whopping total of five thousand Jews. That's it; just five thousand. However, as it happens, my brother is currently the rabbi of the Orthodox synagogue in Portland, Maine. I immediately put Michael in touch with my brother, Akiva, and that Shabbat Michael and his fiancée enjoyed Shabbat dinner in the Orthodox shul of Portland, Maine, with Rabbi Akiva Herzfeld.

The power of the name "National Synagogue" is that it allows everyone to feel that the shul belongs to them. Everyone should feel like they have a link to our shul.

In parashat Emor we are told of another story. There is a man who is the son of an Israelite woman and an Egyptian man (*ben ish Mitzri*). The Torah tells us that he got into a fight with a man who had two Israelite parents. As a result of the fight, the man with the Egyptian father did a terrible thing. He cursed the other man using the name of God (24:10–13).

What causes a person to curse with God's name, which is in effect cursing God Himself? How could someone do that? Rashi tells us what happened: This man had wanted to place his tent with his mother's tribe, the tribe of Dan. But they said to him, "You don't belong here. Membership in tribes follows the father, and your father wasn't one of us. Move your tent outside of the camp."

This man should not have cursed God. It was a great sin which cannot be excused.

At the same time, it is also fair to say that the actions of the tribe of Dan are what led him to curse God. They had a legal right to kick him out of their camp, but in doing so they didn't only kick him out of their tribe, they also kicked him out of all of the Jewish people. They turned him off forever. People curse God when they feel that they have no place in the community.

Sometimes when people join our shul they tell me the most heartbreaking stories. One person in our congregation told me that when she once went to another synagogue, she was told, "You're not Orthodox; we don't want you."

Our motto should be just the opposite. Our motto should be: "If you're not Orthodox, then we especially want you." How else can we show people the path of Torah if we don't allow them into our shul?

Right before the passage in the Torah about the *ben ish Mitzri* who cursed God there is another passage. The Torah tells us (24:2) that we have an obligation *"le-ha'alot ner tamid* – to raise up an eternal light." The ninth-century philosopher and biblical commentator Rabbi Saadiah Gaon explains in his commentary to that verse that the purpose of this is "to light the flames." We need an eternal light to light the other lights. Every person in our synagogue has an opportunity to be a *ner tamid*, a light to light other lights. This is a tremendous responsibility. It means when people walk through our doors we must realize that it is up to us to connect them to our synagogue and to Torah.

Somebody suggested to me that we should have a welcoming committee. I appreciated that suggestion a great deal. I was enthusiastic. But then someone else explained to me that *the whole synagogue* needs to be the welcoming committee. We all must take the personal responsibility of lighting the candle. This is a core value of who we are. Just like we don't have a davening committee, made up of people whose job it is to daven, so too we shouldn't have a welcoming committee. We all need to be welcoming.

The name "National Synagogue" has a lot of power. It is an accessible name. Even people who don't know basic words in Hebrew can feel linked to an opening and welcoming name like "National Synagogue."

Most importantly, the name means we are a synagogue with an embracing and accepting mission that is open to all. Everyone who lives and visits our area should feel that this synagogue belongs to them. In the National Synagogue, everyone has a seat with their name on it just waiting for them to occupy it.

When I go to visit my brother in Portland, Maine, I might see Michael. Who knows? When I walk into the shul for the first time, I also might be wandering the halls. And there to greet me will be Michael. He will stretch out his hand and say, "Shalom. I'm Michael. Welcome to our shul." By that time, he might even be the shul president.

ARE JEWS FREE TODAY?

Behar

When I was a rabbi in the Bronx, I remember attending a meeting between Jewish communal leaders of the Bronx and the man who was at that time the Bronx-borough president, Adolfo Carrion. At the meeting I expressed publicly my opinion that some Jews in New York are feeling vulnerable. I shared with the borough president my concern about a hate crime against a Jew in New York City, and I said that that hate crime should be a wake-up call for all of us.

As soon as the meeting ended, the head of a local Jewish organization approached me and expressed great upset with my comments. He told me that I was an alarmist giving a distorted picture of Jewish vulnerability to an influential gentile. He contended that Jews are perfectly safe in New York City – as proof, he offered that he feels no concern at all when walking to his own car.

This incident has replayed itself time and time again in my rabbinate. On numerous occasions I have raised public concern about the safety of the Jewish community. Whether it is danger on the streets of New York City, or threats facing the Jews living in Sderot, Israel, or the existential danger facing the Jewish community of Venezuela, I have tried to stir the consciousness of the world to the threats that Jewish communities might face.

So the question is, was that Jewish community leader correct in accusing me of being an alarmist? The answer to this question lies in what it means to say we're safe. What does "safe" mean?

An answer is suggested by one of the words used in parashat Behar. Every fiftieth year, the Torah commands us to celebrate a

Yovel, a Jubilee year. On this year all land remains uncultivated, all land goes back to its original owners, all debts are erased, and all slaves go free. It is a revolutionary year – a year of great freedom – a year when no one is more powerful than anyone else.

Says the Torah:

וְקִדַּשְׁתֶּם אֵת שְׁנַת הַחֲמִשִּׁים שָׁנָה וּקְרָאתֶם דְּרוֹר בָּאָרֶץ לְכָל יֹשְׁבֶיהָ....

You should sanctify the fiftieth year and put out a call of *deror* to all the people of the land.... (Vayikra 25:10)

A call for *deror*. *Deror* is usually translated as freedom – a call goes out into the entire land for freedom.

Yet, the word *deror* is actually a very rare word. In fact, this is the only place in the entire Five Books of Moses where the word *deror* appears. Whenever a word is so rare, our rabbis struggle to capture its precise meaning. What our rabbis sought to understand was what does the word *deror* really mean? Rashi quotes the Midrash (Torat Kohanim 2:2) and offers the following explanation: *Deror* derives from the Aramaic word *dar*, "to dwell" or "to live." *Deror* means, *she-dar bekol makom she-rotzeh*, that the person lives in any place that they desire.

The word *deror* thus means that one has the ability to live safely – peacefully and openly – in any place that he wants. That is what the very concept of *Yovel* is about, and that is what the word *deror* means. *Deror* means you are safe.

By such a definition Jews are hardly safe today. Today's war against the Jews is being waged in such a way that Jews are continually being told where it is acceptable for us to live. Let us look at Israel. At one time, it was considered dangerous to live in Chevron, but it wasn't perceived as dangerous to live in Sderot or in southern Israel. But then things change and Jews are implicitly and explicitly told where it is acceptable for them to live.

Our rabbis tell us in the Talmud, tractate Rosh Hashanah (9b), that when the laws of *Yovel* and safety apply to Eretz Yisrael, they also apply to lands outside of Israel, and when the laws of safety do not apply in the Land of Israel, then they also do not apply outside the Land of Israel. We are living this today. What began in Israel is now spreading throughout the world. First Jews were told in Israel where they can live and where they cannot live, and now Jews are being told throughout the world where they can practice their Judaism and where they cannot be Jewish.

It is often perceived as too dangerous for a Jew to wear a *kippah* on the streets of Europe. In the summer of 2011, one European country – Netherlands – passed a bill in one of its parliamentary houses outlawing *shechitah*, or slaughter of animals in accordance with Jewish law. In response to that I met with the Dutch ambassador to the United States and I told her that by outlawing *shechitah* she was in essence saying to the Jewish community: "The way you eat is barbaric." From there it is just a short logical leap to saying that Jews are barbaric as well and not welcome at all in the country.

So I do believe that according to the rabbis' definition of safety, Jews are not safe today. We cannot practice our Judaism however we want, and thus we are not safe. Not in Israel, not in Europe, and not in Venezuela.

But if the concept of *deror* teaches that we are not safe today, the Torah also shows us through the mitzvah of *Yovel* what is required from us in order to acquire a feeling of safety and security. *Yovel* is a blueprint of the path to safety; follow the guidelines of *Yovel* and safety will follow. The Torah lists many aspects to *Yovel*, but for now let's focus on just two.

The *Yovel* year follows upon a biblically commanded sabbatical year known as *shemittah*. In both of these years there was an obligation to let the land lie fallow. As a result, for two straight years no one could work the land. How were people to live? It took tremendous faith in God to believe that God would provide for two years without working. It was an almost superhuman faith in God. Yet, that was what the Torah required.

The Torah says, "If you ask: What will we eat?" The answer is *"ki Li ha-aretz* – for the land is Mine" (25:23). God will provide. True safety arises only when the individual demonstrates complete faith in God. Only then is one invulnerable.

There is another major factor that leads to freedom.

The *Yovel* year begins with sound of the shofar. But it is a different shofar than the one sounded on Rosh Hashanah. On Rosh Hashanah one shofar is sounded for the entire community. Not so on the *Yovel*; on the *Yovel* everyone must be personally and actively involved. *"Ta'aviru shofar be-khol artzekhem* – You should sound the shofar throughout your land" (25:9); the keywords are "throughout your land." Say our rabbis, every single individual is obligated to sound the call, to blast the siren for strength. The blast of the trumpet is a clarion call for safety. The shofar is the human input into the divine plan.

Safety from our enemies will arrive when each of us as individuals sounds our own shofar. The obligation to sound an individual shofar is what ushers in the year of safety. Perhaps this is because only if each of us as individuals feel free and bold enough to sound a personal shofar can we have the courage to live wherever we want.

To summarize: The mitzvah of *Yovel* shows two paths to safety. Each and every individual must submit in full faith to God. And each and every person must arise and proudly declare his or her freedom. This is how the Torah tells us we can accomplish *deror* – safety – which ultimately leads to true freedom. If you truly want to be safe, stand up and declare your personal sovereignty. And individually rely upon your faith in God.

Despite the fact that Jews today live with an appearance of physical safety and security, and despite the fact that we are more secure now than we were one hundred years ago, it is still not enough. If we scratch beneath the surface, we will notice that the truth is that Jews throughout the world are currently without an acceptable level of *deror*, without the security to act openly and proudly as Jews wherever we want.

Each of us must accept our individual responsibility to sound the shofar and fight for the safety of Jews throughout the world. And each of us must demonstrate an absolute faith in the correctness of our mission, our destiny, and our God. If we do, we will be on the path to true *deror*, true freedom.

IF YOU WANT
TO SLEEP AT NIGHT,
GIVE AWAY YOUR PILLOW
Bechukotai

Twice a year we read passages in the Torah that are described as *tokhachah*, or the curses that will befall the Jewish people if we do not obey the commandments of the Torah.

Different customs have arisen surrounding the actual reading of the *tokhachah*. Some congregations do not call anyone up by name to receive the *aliyah* for that portion of the Torah lest people think that the reason why he got this *aliyah* is because, God forbid, he is worthy of being cursed. Some have the custom of giving the *tokhachah aliyah* to the Torah reader himself, lest he have in mind to curse the person who got the *aliyah*. It is also a custom to read the curses in a quicker and lower voice than usual in hopes that the curses never be fulfilled.

But some people take these customs too far. Sometimes the *tokhachah* is read so low and so quickly that the words cannot even be heard. And some people even have the custom of leaving the room as the *tokhachah* is read so as not to be in the presence of the curses.

The great Chafetz Chayim was critical of these last two customs. He said that someone who leaves the room or slurs the words is comparable to a person who is warned not to walk down a certain path as it is full of thorns and dangerous animals. And after receiving the warning, this stubborn person not only does not listen to the warnings about traveling down that path, but he

184

goes so far as to place a blindfold over his face so he won't see the dangerous objects, enabling him to pretend that they don't exist!

So too, with the *tokhachah* in the Torah. We must not skip over these passages; we must internalize them and listen carefully to the Torah's warnings. We must remember that the Torah includes these curses in order to guide us properly so that we can avoid the thorns and dangerous animals in our lives.

Speaking of dangerous animals, before we are told the curses in parashat Bechukotai we are promised blessings if we keep the Torah. One of the blessings that the Torah promises us is that if we obey the mitzvot and we walk in the path of Hashem then we will not have to worry about dangerous animals. Says the Torah:

וְנָתַתִּי שָׁלוֹם בָּאָרֶץ, וּשְׁכַבְתֶּם וְאֵין מַחֲרִיד וְהִשְׁבַּתִּי חַיָּה רָעָה מִן הָאָרֶץ וְחֶרֶב לֹא תַעֲבֹר בְּאַרְצְכֶם:

> And I will place peace in the land, and you will sleep and not be afraid, and I will wipe away the dangerous animals from the earth, and a sword will not pass through your land. (Vayikra 26:6)

The fifteenth-century, Spanish commentator Isaac Abrabanel wonders about these blessings. One of the main ideas of Judaism is the belief in a non-material reward: a reward in the World to Come, or a spiritual reward. Why then does the Torah promise us that as a reward for keeping the Torah that we will be physically blessed? Why not promise us a reward in the World to Come or a messianic reward? The answer is that we need to understand whether or not these blessings are meant literally as external manifestations of our lives or metaphorically as internal changes in our own selves.

The great Ramban argues that these are external rewards, but they are not physical rewards as much as spiritual rewards. They are spiritual blessings that are in reality referring to a utopian messianic age. The proof of this is a Midrash that is cited by Ramban. The Midrash (Torat Kohanim 2:1) discusses the promise that Hashem will wipe out all the dangerous animals from the world. Says the Midrash, it means "*Mashbitin she-lo yaziku*," they will be destroyed in the sense that they will no longer attack and hurt any living creature. Writes Ramban: "This is the correct interpretation for when Israel observes the commandments; then the Land of Israel will be like the world was at its beginning, before the sin of the first man, when no wild beast or creeping thing would kill a man, as the sages say, 'It is not the wild donkey that kills, it is the sin that kills!'"

Ramban understands that the only reason why animals attack human beings today is because their nature changed as a result of the sin of Adam. Originally, all animals were peaceful; they never attacked another animal or ate the flesh of another creature. Only after we sinned did their nature change. Ramban argues that if we perform these mitzvot, then the nature of the animals will once again revert back to its original state. Right now they prey on us and other animals, but if we walk properly and fulfill all of the mitzvot, then we will change their nature.

What this means in the larger sense is that the blessings God promises us point to our ability to literally change the nature of the world. Ramban is arguing that there is an external manifestation to the blessings and curses, a drastic change in the nature of the world. That is, in the time of the Messiah, peace will return to the world and carnivorous animals and all dangerous beasts will cease to exist.

However, there is another way to approach the rewards and curses of the Torah. We might understand them as referring to a transformation that will occur inside us depending upon whether or not we obey the Torah.

Let us take as an example the promise that we will be able to sleep peacefully at night. The verse states: "You will sleep and not be afraid, and I will wipe away the dangerous animals from the earth" (26:6). Here, too, are we required to wait until the Messiah comes in order to get a good night's sleep, or is it possible to get a good sleep in even before the arrival of the Messiah?

Sleep disorders are very pervasive in our country. My wife, the neurologist Dr. Rhanni Herzfeld, told me that more than seventeen million people have a diagnosable sleep disorder, like sleep apnea, insomnia, or abnormal sleep movements. And as a rabbi I hear a lot about sleep disorders. Sometimes people tell me, I would love to come to minyan, but I need my sleep and I have a hard time falling asleep at night.

Now it might be that you have a medical condition, and in that case you will need a medical doctor to heal you. So you can go see a good neurologist, and he or she might even send you to the sleep center that my wife's medical practice owns and operates in Bethesda. But it is possible that it is not a medical condition as much as it is something that is bothering you emotionally and is thus preventing you from sleeping. In that case you should listen to the following story that I am going to tell you about the Ponovizher Rav (as I saw cited in a *shiur* by Rabbi Shalom Rosner[1]), for this story will teach us how to get a good night's sleep even before the *Mashiach* comes.

Parashat Bechukotai is usually read in conjunction with parashat Behar. The fact that they are often coupled teaches us that if we ignore the commandments of parashat Behar we might bring the *tokhachah* upon ourselves.

In parashat Behar we are given the following commandment:

וְכִי יָמוּךְ אָחִיךָ וּמָטָה יָדוֹ עִמָּךְ וְהֶחֱזַקְתָּ בּוֹ גֵּר וְתוֹשָׁב וָחַי עִמָּךְ:

If your brother becomes poor, then you shall strengthen him and cause him to live with you. (Vayikra 25:35)

---

1. http://www.yutorah.org/lectures/lecture.cfm/744742/Rabbi_Shalom_
Rosner/Behar_Bechukotai_5770.

The rabbis learn out from this verse that the poor person must live *with you* – *ve-chai achikha* imakh; that is, when you support the poor you yourself have to live and not die. The example for this is that if you are in the desert and you only have enough water for one person to survive, then you should not give the water to your friend, but you should drink it yourself, because your life takes precedence. (See Baba Metzia 60b.)

The Ponovizher Rav gave an extraordinary explanation of this teaching. The Ponovizher Rav was the rabbi in Bnei Brak, and in 1943 he heard that a large group of orphan refugees who had run away from the Nazis would be coming to live in a makeshift orphanage in Bnei Brak. But there was a problem. At that time in Israel, pillows were very scarce and it would not be possible to purchase pillows for these orphans.

No one knew what to do about this problem. How would they find pillows for the orphans?

Two days before the orphans were set to arrive, word spread that the Ponovizher Rav was going to give a special sermon for the entire city on Shabbat afternoon. So of course everyone gathered to hear what this great rabbi would discuss.

He posed the following question: There is a law in the Talmud that states that if a person has a Hebrew servant (*eved Ivri*) and there is only one pillow in the house, then the law is that the servant gets the pillow and not the master. As the Talmud in tractate Kiddushin (20a) says, "*Koneh eved koneh rabbo* – One who acquires a servant is really acquiring a master"; it is therefore necessary to give priority to the needs of the servant.

Asked the Ponovizher Rav, how can this be as we have another law that teaches us *ve-chai achikha imakh* – your life takes precedence? So according to this principle, why are you required to give your one and only pillow to your servant?

Answers the Ponovizher Rav, it must be that the law requiring a master to give his one and only pillow to his servant is part and parcel of the mitzvah of *ve-chai achikha imakh*. In other words, the Torah understands the very essence of the human soul and understands that if the master is sleeping on a pillow while his servant is sleeping on a hard floor, then the master will not have a restful sleep. Just the opposite: he will be tossing and turning all evening in distress as he thinks of the poor servant who lacks a pillow. Therefore, the Torah commands him – specifically because of the mitzvah of *ve-chai achikha imakh* – in order for you to have a good sleep at night you must give away your pillow to your servant.

That night, right after Shabbat, the Ponovizher Rav was told by the leaders of his community: Don't worry about getting pillows for the orphans. We will give them our pillows, because if we don't we won't be able to sleep.

The point is that if we want to sleep at night we need to give away our pillows.

This is what the Torah means when it says you will sleep and not be afraid. If you want to sleep, get rid of your pillow. That is also the blessing promised to us by the Torah.

I know so many people who have all the pillows they need and yet have trouble sleeping at night; they walk through their lives sleep deprived. What many don't realize is that the Torah already told them why they can't sleep. Deep down they are disturbed about their place in the world. How can they sleep while their friend is missing a pillow? How can they sleep while there is so much tragedy in the world?

The ultimate blessing and reward for keeping the mitzvot is in the promise of a World to Come and a pure messianic age, but we can achieve a blessing and reward in this world as well. It is the blessing of a good night's sleep. If we want to feel some sort of relief in this world then we need to spend our life giving to others. The more we give, the better we will sleep.

If we all do that then slowly we will also transform the nature of the world – both externally and internally. And the more we change internally, the more we can impact the world externally as well.

BAMIDBAR

WHY I WANT TO VISIT
SOUTH KOREA
Bamidbar

In March, 2011, I read an article on IsraelNationalNews.com about the fact that the people of South Korea are very interested in the Talmud and that millions of Koreans are reading and studying stories from the Talmud in the hopes of gleaning wisdom. After hearing about this I reached out to the South Korean ambassador to the US, and he invited me for a wonderful lunch. He too was very eager to learn more about Judaism and the Jewish community in America.

Now I know that these kinds of stories – about the love and admiration that different cultures have for the Jewish people – appear from time to time in the press and that they are often silly exaggerations and stereotypes. They also often reflect a crude idea that the Jews are a supersuccessful people worthy of admiration because of their success in business, government, and science.

Still, when I heard all this, I began to dream a little: What if one day we all went on a synagogue mission to South Korea?

I sometimes meet people who lack self-confidence. They are great people and super talented – after all, God created them – but sadly, deep down they feel that they lack any special talent. Moreover, I sometimes meet people who are embarrassed about their Judaism and don't think that there is anything special about their particular religion. Just imagine how that might change if all of these reports about the South Koreans' love for the Jews were true. In South Korea we would meet with people who would respect us and admire us. If we traveled around South Korea we would realize just how special an honor it is to be Jewish.

Of course, we would be well respected not because of anything we have done, but for who we are and what we represent. We would understand that we are not just Yankel Berel or Shmuel Herzfeld from Washington, DC. No! Who are we? We are the children of Avraham. What do we represent? The product of a great civilization that, based upon the teachings of the Torah, has produced a great community. Imagine how inspiring such a trip might be.

This message appears in parashat Bamidbar. The portion begins with Hashem commanding Moshe to count the Jewish people. Rashi points out that this is the third time in the last thirteen months that Hashem has counted the Jewish people. The Jewish people were counted when we left Egypt, and we were counted after the sin of the golden calf in the month of Tishrei. Now, just seven months later, we are again being counted in the month of Iyar after the Mishkan has been completed.

Rashi's explanation for this is that the frequent counting of the people represents just how much Hashem loves us: out of His great love for us, He counts us. This is like a little boy who loves his baseball cards and keeps counting the cards over and over. Not just to see how many cards he has, but because he simply loves his cards. So too, Hashem is counting us not to determine exactly how many people we are, but because of His great love for us.

I think that there is another lesson here as well.

This counting – the third counting – was done differently than the other countings. This time the Torah (1:18) uses a strange phrase: *va-yityaldu al mishpechotam le-veit avotam*, which roughly translates as "they were registered by family ancestry according to the house of their fathers."[1]

---

1. Translation according to Aryeh Kaplan, *The Living Torah* (New York: Moznaim, 1981).

The first two times we were not counted in this manner. We were counted in a more general sense. Each family brought its count to the leader of the tribe and the leader added it up and brought the total number to Moshe. But this time was different. Rashi (1:18) says that this time each person had to come forward with *sifrei yichuseihem*, their "books of lineage," and *eidei chezkat leidatam*, "witnesses to their birth." Rashi also says that as each person came forward to be counted they had to walk in front of the *nasi*, the prince of each tribe, and also in front of Moshe and Aharon.

Ramban (1:18) goes even further in his description of the event. He explains that the phrase *va-yityaldu al mishpechotam* means that each person came forward and said his own name: "Each man brought his half-shekel to Moshe and said, 'I, so-and-so, was born to such-and-such a person of such-and-such a family from the tribe of Reuven.'" The twelfth-century commentator Avraham ibn Ezra suggests that this means that each person actually had to state his birthday in front of Moshe and Aharon.

This is hardly an efficient way to conduct a census. Roughly six hundred thousand people had to literally walk in front of Moshe and Aharon and pronounce their name and birthday and declare their lineage. Why such an elaborate census process? What was the purpose in all of this? Can you imagine if everyone in DC had to do this in front of the mayor of DC the next time we took a census here?

The understanding of this process goes to the core reason of why we are being counted. Hashem doesn't want us just to know how many of us there are, but who we are and what we are about. This is why we are bringing *sifrei yichusim*, our documents of lineage. He wants us to know that we are not only the descendants of slaves who have just escaped from Egypt, but we are also the descendants of the great Avraham and Sarah, the founders of monotheism and leaders of the land of Canaan. We are the descendants of the holy Yitzchak, who willingly walked with his father up the mountain, and we are the descendants of Yaakov, who kept all the mitzvot even while he lived with Lavan (see Rashi on Bereishit 32:5).

This is why we were commanded to all say our names and our birthdays in front of Moshe and Aharon. Each of us needs to realize how special we are and how special our parents and ancestors are. Each of us needs to realize that it is worth the time of Moshe and Aharon to stop what they are doing and learn each of our names because each one of us is a great and worthy person.

This is how Ramban (1:45) explains it:

> One who comes before the father of the prophets [Moshe] and his brother, Aharon...and becomes known to them by name, receives thereby a *zekhut* [merit] and *chayim* [life], because he has come into the council and the register of the Jewish people, and he receives a part in the merits of the community by being included in their numbers. So, too, each of the people receives a special merit through being counted by a number before Moshe and Aharon, for they will set their eyes upon them for good and intercede on their behalf for mercy. Hashem told Moshe to count each one of them with respect and to treat each one of them with honor due to his greatness. Thus He said, "You shall not say to the head of the family: How many people are in your family? How many sons do you have? But they are each to pass before you with awe and respect and you are supposed to count them!"

Usually a common citizen is constantly being reminded of just how great his leader or his prophet is. But this time Hashem wanted to remind Moshe and Aharon of the greatness of all of the people of Israel. This time it is Moshe and Aharon who must treat the people with honor and respect on account of their greatness.

As each person walked in front of the greatest Jew in history, they realized that the great Moshe Rabbeinu was taking time out of his day to learn their name and their birthday and their history and to treat them – a person who a little more than a year ago was a mere slave – with great honor and respect. Wow! Imagine how special they would now feel. Each person would come away from that encounter with the recognition of just how great and important they really are.

And of course it is important for us to realize and understand how special and great we are, because if we don't think we are special and great then we will not be able to accomplish special and great things in this world. The Torah teaches us this idea through the passage about the census.

There are a few different words for counting in the Torah. One of those words is *pekod*. The Torah uses a form of the word *pekod* in this week's portion (1:49) when it says, "*Et matteh Levi lo tifkod* – Do not count the tribe of Levi amongst all the other tribes of Israel." The tribe of Levi was different. They had an even higher responsibility than the other tribes. They were to be counted in a unique manner because they had a special and unique task: to guard the Mishkan and to serve the Jewish people.

Right after the Torah tells us not to count the tribe of Levi, it commands Moshe: "*Ve-atah hafked et ha-Levi'im* – And you should appoint the Levi'im" (1:50). The word used is *hafked*, and though it is similar to *pekod*, it means something very different. Rashi (1:50) makes sure to teach us that it is not the same word. *Pekod* means "to count." But *hafked* means *minui*, "to be appointed for a task."

Hashem commanded Moshe to not only count the Levi'im but to appoint them to the task of guarding the Jewish people; to be the spiritual vanguard of our people.

But on another level, the relationship between *hafked* and *pekod* reminds us why we are counted in this manner: to give us respect and empower us and help us realize how special we are. We need to realize that we are being counted in order to be appointed for a task. We are all being told that we are worthy of being counted personally by Moshe and Aharon because we have a responsibility to become messengers of the Torah. The Levi'im guard us and teach us the Torah. But we are commanded to be the spiritual Levi'im to the world. If the Levi'im teach us the Torah, we then must bring the message of the Torah to the world. Even though the Levi'im were a special tribe, if we accept upon ourselves the responsibility of being teachers of Torah and messengers of Hashem, then we are all like the Levi'im and we are all appointed for a task.

We are *pakod*, counted, only in order to become *pekidim*, messengers of the Torah. This is what makes us special and unique and this is our responsibility in life.

Admittedly there are different ways we can live this message. We can travel to South Korea and share our knowledge of Judaism with an eager audience, or we can live our life here in a way that inspires others to better understand the message of the Torah.

We are a special people. Not because we personally have done anything, but because we have tremendous ancestors who have paved the way for us. But our ancestors have also given us a tremendous responsibility: to carry on their mission to the world and spread the message of the Torah. We need to be the Levi'im to the world.

NAZIR AND KOHEIN:
TWO MODELS OF SPIRITUALITY
Naso

We see it all the time in our communities. A kid goes through our Modern Orthodox Jewish day school system and then goes off to study for a year in an Israeli yeshivah. He becomes enamored and attracted to the pure spirituality of his yeshivah, and his response is a total rejection of his parents' community.

Typically he accepts the message of his yeshivah in its entirety and becomes much more right wing in his observance of Judaism. He replaces his knitted *kippah* for a black hat; he tells his parents that he doesn't want to go to Columbia or Harvard. The younger siblings say that their older brother or sister has "flipped out." In short, the student rejects the more modern lifestyle of his society in favor of a more demanding and ultra-strict lifestyle.

Why is this happening? Why are some kids rejecting Modern Orthodoxy in favor of more right-wing Judaism? These kids are rejecting the nuanced spirituality that Modern Orthodoxy offers for a form of spirituality that seeks to separate them entirely from the world around them. They are attracted to a more intense spiritual life, but is it really the ideal way of living as a Jew?

In parashat Naso the Torah discusses two models of spirituality. One model is that of the *nazir*. A *nazir* is a person who takes a vow not to drink wine, cut his or her hair, or come in contact with any dead person, even the body of a close relative.

The Torah discusses the *nazir* (6:1–21) immediately after the paragraph of the *sotah*, the woman who is accused of being unfaithful (5:11–31). Rashi (6:2) explains that the *nazir* saw the *sotah* in her embarrassment and as a result was disgusted. The *nazir* turns away from the world of the *sotah* and swears to cut himself off from living in the world that we know. The *nazir* stops drinking wine because he feels that wine led the *sotah* to sin; the *nazir* keeps his hair long because he doesn't want to focus his life on caring for his physical body.

The very word *nazir* means "to separate." And this is what the *nazir* does: he separates himself from the world. Indeed, he even separates himself from his own parents. He prohibits himself from even attending to their funerals.

This is one model of spirituality. It sees separation as the greatest path to spirituality. The world is filled with sinners and sinful attractions. The *nazir* looks at the world and runs away from his community in order to come closer to Hashem. But ultimately the *nazir* is an inadequate model of spirituality. The Torah tells us that when the *nazir* finishes his days of being a *nazir*, he must bring a sin offering (6:1–14). He is bringing a sin offering because there is something fundamentally wrong about being a *nazir*.

In order to achieve his spiritual high the *nazir* leaves society. But the Torah wants us to live in the real world. As the prophet states (Yeshayahu 45:18), "the world was created for us to live in and inhabit." Hashem created the universe for us to develop it within the context of society and not to live the lives of loners seeking our own spiritual perfection.

Moreover, the more one separates himself in the service of Hashem, the more mitzvot he will end up missing out on. Rabbi Meir Simcha of Dvinsk (1843–1926) in his commentary the *Meshekh Chokhmah* (6:14), explains that this is the reason the *nazir* brings a sin offering: because he misses out on the opportunity to do many mitzvot as a result of his *nezirut*. For example, because he does not drink wine, he misses out on the proper way to recite Kiddush; because he does not attend to his parents at their funeral, he misses out on the mitzvah of honoring his parents.

So *nezirut*, according to some commentators, is a flawed spiritual model because it causes the person to separate from society, in contrast to the Torah's teaching that God wants us to serve Him within a communal context. Also, even though he is separating himself with the express intent of coming closer to God, the *nazir* actually moves further away from God as he loses out on the ability to perform basic mitzvot.[1]

But there is another spiritual model described in this week's portion. This is the model of the *kohein*, the priest. The *kohein* is an example of a figure who lives the life of a spiritual leader by being involved in the nitty-gritty of the community.

Here are three examples of this from parashat Naso.

First, we see that the *kohein* became directly involved in the matter of the *sotah*. The *sotah* and her husband are involved in a bitter marital dispute. In the midst of this dispute the *kohein* plays a vital role: "The man and his wife come before the *kohein*" (5:15). There is no community involvement that is stickier than working with a couple that is going through a marital dispute. The *kohein* does not retreat to make an offering in the Temple. Instead he steps into this situation with the ultimate goal of making *shalom bayit*, peace in the house.

A second example of the *kohein's* spiritual life being immersed in the welfare of the community arises from his relationship with the *ger*, the convert. Parashat Naso tells us of a scenario of *gezel hager* – where a person steals from a convert and then the convert dies without any relatives at all (see Rashi's comments on 5:8). To whom does the thief repay the money? If someone dies in DC without any relatives and without any will, the money goes to the mayor's discretionary fund. But the Torah has other plans. The Torah tells us that the money goes to the *kohein*. The reason why the *kohein* receives these funds is because the *kohein* is responsible

---

1. We see that the Torah sometimes allows specific acts even though they are not the ideal. For another example, see Devarim 21:10–14, a captive woman in battle.

for the protection of the convert. When the convert joins the Jewish people and is a vulnerable member of society, the *kohein* must step up as a spiritual leader of the Jewish people and offer him protection.

And now we turn to a third example of the *kohein's* involvement in society. The Torah tells us that there were three circles of camps within the Jewish people. The outer circle was where everyone lived, except for the lepers and those who needed to be placed outside that camp. The second circle was called *machaneh leviyah*, or the camp of the tribe of Levi. This circle was open to people who had gone to the *mikveh* and purified themselves from *tumah* (ritual impurity) that was excreted from the body. The third level was the *machaneh Shekhinah*, the camp of the Divine Presence. One could not enter this camp if he were *tamei* through encountering a dead body. (See 4:2, and Rashi's comments there.)

The *kohein gadol* was not allowed to attend to a dead body of even a close relative. The *kohein gadol* had to always be ready to enter the *machaneh Shekhinah*. But a regular *kohein* did not face this level of prohibition. He was required to become ritually impure or *tamei* when his own relatives died. The regular *kohein* was required to be a member of society.

The *kohein* contrasts with the *nazir*. If the *nazir* is the person who is removed from the world in order to gain his spirituality, the *kohein's* spirituality increases as he involves himself in social concerns of the community.

I believe that it is the model of the *kohein*, and not the *nazir*, that the Torah wants us to follow. Sure, the spiritual model of a community is an imperfect model. There will always be issues and people in a communal setting that force even the most gentle souls to turn away and have a reaction similar to a *nazir*. But the *kohein* is the best model that we have; and it is the model that the Torah teaches will bring us closest to Hashem.

As spiritual Jews our spirituality needs to bring us in greater contact with the world around us. A retreat from that world is also a retreat from the paradigm of the *kohein* as taught in the Torah.

FATHER'S DAY

Beha'alotkha

The poet Wordsworth once said (*The Borderers*, Act I), "Father! – to God himself we cannot give a holier name." Referring to God as "Father" is commonplace in the Jewish liturgy. We say often *Avinu she-ba-shamayim*, our Father in heaven, or *Avinu Malkeinu*, our Father our King.

I like to remember that idea as the daily grind of fatherhood challenges me. One recent day (as I changed my fifth diaper of the day), I thought to myself that I must have changed more than two thousand diapers over an eight-year period. Of course, being a father is a great privilege and an honor. It is also a task of enormous responsibility and unending energy. No one ever said that being a father was easy.

Sometimes a parent will work really hard on preparing food for his or her children. Instead of devouring the food and saying thank you, the child will just look at the food and refuse even to taste it. Trust me when I tell you that that can be very frustrating.

Moshe experiences that as well in parashat Beha'alotkha. Hashem, through the vehicle of Moshe, provides manna to *bnei Yisrael*, and rather than saying "thank you," they complain; it is too dry, they cry out (11:5–6).

Moshe is frustrated so he cries to Hashem (11:12), "*Im anokhi yelidtihu* – Was I the woman who was pregnant with these people?" Throughout history, in moments of frustration, many fathers have turned to their wives and said, "Was this my idea?" Moshe continues, "But You said that I must carry them in my bosom just like a nurse carries an infant."

Moshe says: the task is too hard for me to do by myself. There were three million Jews with Moshe in the desert. Can you imagine nursing three million people? It felt impossible to him. *"Lo uchal anokhi levadi* – I cannot do this by myself"* (11:14). There then comes a line from the Torah that is probably the most quoted line of the Bible by Jewish parents. Moshe says, "If you are going to do this to me, just do me a favor and kill me, *hargeini na harog!"* The ultimate guilt trip – invented by Moshe!

Moshe is struggling with a question that many fathers struggle with today. How can he have the wisdom and energy to nourish his whole community? After all, he is just one person. So Hashem steps in and gives two answers to Moshe. These two answers are the two keys to fatherhood.

The first responsibility of being a father is to teach your children to follow your path. By this I do not mean your career path or your choice of personal preferences, but the path of following Hashem. This takes enormous dedication and effort, but it has to be the goal.

Hashem says to Moshe: you must spread your ability to be a prophet. Hashem tells him to take seventy elders and gather them around the *ohel moed*, the tent of meeting, and Hashem takes the spirit of Moshe and places it upon the elders. As a friend of mine, Rabbi Joshua Hoffman, pointed out to me, Rabbi Avraham ibn Ezra (Bamidbar 11:17) explains that the process was akin to lighting many flames from a single flame. When we take the energy from a candle, we are able to light another flame without diminishing the first flame. And we keep the new flame lit until it burns strongly.

As it says at the beginning of this week's portion, *Beha'alotkha et ha-nerot*, when you kindle the candles, but more literally, when you "lift up the candles." Rashi explains (8:2) that you need to light them until the flames are strong enough to stay lit on their own. This is one of the two major goals of fatherhood: light the flame until it can stay lit on its own. The more we light the flame for the children to follow our path, the more energy we produce.

We know that even though prophetic ability was taken from Moshe to make the elders into prophets, Moshe's own prophetic talents were not diminished. At the end of the portion (12:7–9), we are told that Moshe is the greatest prophet of all. Thus, the Torah promises that even though we give, it will not detract from our own energy. Just the opposite, the more energy we give off, the more we get additional energy. We are energized by giving off energy.

This is one key to fatherhood that Hashem teaches Moshe: focus on lighting the flame until the child's flame is steady and strong.

But there is a second lesson taught through Moshe, and it is almost a contradictory lesson. There were two elders – Eldad and Meidad – who did not follow Moshe's direction. Moshe told them to come around *his* tent, the *ohel moed*, but instead they stayed in their *own* tent. Moshe told them to take from *his* prophecy, but instead they took from their *own*. The other elders prophesy only once (according to Rashi, 11:25), but according to the Talmud, tractate Sanhedrin (17a), they continued to prophesy.

Eldad and Meidad appeared to be rebellious. What where they prophesying about? One anonymous opinion in the Talmud (Sanhedrin 17a) is that they were saying, "Moshe will die and Yehoshua will lead us into the land." What an enormous challenge they were presenting to Moshe's leadership!

These two prophets were not following Moshe's path. They were doing it on their own. Their prophecy was independent and, at first glance, rebellious. How was Moshe to react to such a challenge?

The Torah says that a boy ran to tell Moshe (11:27). Rashi says that this boy was Gershom, Moshe's son. He was worried about the disrespect being shown to his father. Moshe's assistant, Yehoshua, shouts out, "My master, Moshe, destroy them!" (11:28).

But we now learn the second key lesson for fatherhood, and this is a much more difficult lesson to live by. When our children exhibit independence it can be seen either as a threat to our parenting or

as the fulfillment of our parenting. Moshe realizes that if he wants
to nourish all of his three million children then he should not view
Eldad and Meidad's independence as a threat.

Independence can be frustrating. A silly example: when a two-
year-old insists on pouring milk on his own. This is frustrating as
I know the milk will spill. But there are scarier examples as well.
For example, when a child insists on being more or less religious
than a parent.... This can be very scary to a parent. As parents, our
first reaction is to view independence of mind and spirit as a direct
challenge to our authority, but Moshe teaches that in some cases it
should really be seen as a fulfillment of our parenting.

One model of parenting is to light the flame of children until
it goes up on its own. A second model is to allow children to
light their own independent flame. We can guide, but we must
recognize their independent flame.

Moshe now recognizes the need for the second approach
when he says, "If only Hashem would allow all his people to be
prophets" (11:29). Independence does not scare us – it is what
we need. Moshe could not light three million candles; he needed
many to do it on their own. That is the only way the people of
Israel could flourish.

I note that this independence still flourishes today. On June
8, 2008, a columnist in the *New York Times* noted that in the first
quarter of 2008, the top four economies after America in attracting
venture capital for start-ups were: Europe $1.53 billion, China
$719 million, Israel $572 million, and India $99 million. Israel, with
seven million people, attracted almost as much as China, with 1.3
billion people.[1]

Baruch Hashem the independent spirit of Eldad and Meidad lives
on strongly in our people.

---

1. See Thomas L. Friedman, "People vs. Dinasours," *New York Times*, June 8.
   2008, http://www.nytimes.com/2008/06/08/opinion/08friedman.html?_r=1
   &scp=1&sq=people+vs.+dinosaurs&st=nyt.

As fathers, parents, teachers, or mentors we can offer these two models. Try to light the flame, or allow for an independent flame to go up. Of course, each child requires a unique approach (plus a lot of hard work and a lot of luck and help from Hashem). It is not easy to be a father, and to know which way is the best approach, and to have the energy to provide for our children. But the truth is that the Torah promises us that we will have the strength.

Moshe said to Hashem (11:12–13), "Did I carry them in my womb?... Where can I get the meat to feed them?" Moshe wasn't their actual father. He was their leader, but not their father. A father never asks that question. He knows that he will get the strength. He knows that he will provide. He knows that no matter what, he will find it within himself to serve his children, to do anything for them. This is the greatness of fathers everywhere. For this we must be eternally grateful, always.

Finding Happiness
in Front of Us
Shelach

Have you ever tried arguing with a three-year-old? It is definitely a no-win situation. Let me give you an example. A certain three-year-old I know might say to me: "I want chocolate milk in a sippy cup." I will then pour the milk into the sippy cup and add the chocolate syrup. No sooner will I add the syrup than I will be told, "Actually, I want plain milk, or strawberry milk, and I want it in a plain cup, not a sippy cup. Wait. Don't shake it. Wait, I want the powdered chocolate not the syrup." Just try convincing the three-year-old that he just asked for the exact opposite of what he now wants.

But how different is this psychology of the average three-year-old from that of many of us vis-à-vis the choices we ourselves make in life?

There is a very telling example from the Talmud. Tractate Ta'anit (23b) tells us the following story – but brace yourself. This is a very unusual story and at first glance it might seem chauvinistic to us. But if we listen closely to the story, we will understand that it is actually a rebuke of a man. Here is the story:

Rav Mani came to R. Yitzchak ben Elyashiv because he needed help with a problem. He wasn't happy with his wife. Rav Mani said: "My wife is not pretty enough."

R. Yitzchak ben Elyashiv knew how to solve this problem. He responded: "What is her name?" Rav Mani said, "Channah." So R. Yitzchak ben Elyashiv said: "*Tityafi Channah*, let Channah become beautiful."

And just like that, poof! Channah became beautiful!

But then Rav Mani returned to the same rabbi. He still wasn't happy. He said: "*Ka migandra alai* – she has become overbearing upon me." Now that Channah was so beautiful she had become unbearable; she wasn't the same Channah who he had fallen in love with. So Rav Mani begged R. Yitzchak to return her to the way she once was. Says the Gemara, *chazrah Channah* – R. Yitzchak ben Elyashiv prayed and Channah returned to her plainness.

Rav Mani in this story makes the mistake that so many of us make in our lives. We think that we will achieve happiness if only we can achieve a certain goal or acquire something or change something about our lives. We think that happiness is right around the corner. Sadly, since we are always seeking happiness, we never find it.

This in a nutshell is the sin of the Jewish people in parashat Shelach.

The portion begins by Moshe sending scouts, or *meraglim*, to tour Canaan (13:2). But the people are not happy with the report of the *meraglim* and a series of catastrophic sins occur.

First, *bnei Yisrael* sinned by choosing not to enter into Eretz Yisrael. Even though Hashem had given them Eretz Yisrael as an inheritance, and even though the land was flowing with milk and honey and was filled with large fruits, still they rejected it. When they heard a report about the land, they said, "It is better for us to return to Egypt" (14:3).

But then, when Hashem essentially grants them their wish by saying that they will indeed not enter into the land, they still aren't happy. Hashem's "punishment" for them is to give them essentially what they asked for. He tells them that they will not enter the Land of Israel. When they hear this, suddenly they now want to enter the land, as it says, "They woke up in the morning saying, 'We want to go up to the Land of Israel'" (14:40).

So at first they complain that they don't want to go into the land, and then when they are told that they can't go in, that is when they want to go in. How rational is that?

In a nutshell this is the sin of the generation of the desert. They are constantly unhappy with what Hashem has given them in life. And when Hashem gives them what they thought they wanted, then they are suddenly unhappy with that as well. Their rationale and decision making is comparable to a three-year-old and to Rav Mani's unhappiness with his wife.

Through these examples of their sins and through the story of Rav Mani, the underlying message of the Torah is that we should not define happiness by what we don't have, but by what we do have. And what we have in front of us is the path of God: the Torah and its commandments. We should find happiness through what we already have in front of us at all times.

The Torah doesn't just show us how not to behave by sharing with us the story of the *meraglim*. It also shows us what we need to do in order to internalize this lesson. The Torah teaches us that the happiness we seek is literally right in front of our eyes.

The same Torah portion that begins with the sin of the *meraglim* ends with the third paragraph of the Shema that we recite twice a day. The message of the third paragraph of the Shema is the antidote to the mentality of the *meraglim*. This paragraph tells us, *"Lo taturu acharei levavkhem ve-acharei eineikhem* – Do not follow after your hearts or after your eyes" (15:39).

Rashi notices that the portion ends with the same word that it begins with, *latur*, "to tour" or "to wander." The *meraglim* are told to wander (*va-yaturu* and *mitur ha-aretz* 13:25) in the land. And we are commanded not to allow ourselves to wander after our eyes (15:39).

Rashi makes this connection explicit by writing: "The heart and the eyes are the spies of the body" (15:39). In other words, it is the heart and the eyes that betray the body. The body would be on the straight path following the ways of Hashem, but we become diverted when we desire something that we have no need for. This is what we should have in mind when we say those words from the Shema: "Do not follow after your hearts or after your eyes."

We must not desire and long for what we don't need. We shouldn't be fooled into thinking that one more thing will make us happy.

But as so many of us know all too well, this message is easier said than done. So in this very paragraph of the Shema, the Torah gives us help to keep us from wandering. The third paragraph of the Shema commands us to attach fringes – tzitzit – to the corners of our garments. There are two ways in which the mitzvah of tzitzit is essentially a reminder to us to avoid seeking happiness in the wrong places.

First, there is a famous story in the Talmud, tractate Menachot (44a), that teaches us that the tzitzit are a reminder for us to keep us from sinning – but first, brace yourself again. If you thought the last story was shocking, this is even more so.

> There was a man who was very careful to observe the mitzvah of tzitzit. He heard about a harlot in a faraway city who charged four hundred gold talents for her services. He sent her this exorbitant fee and set an appointed time to meet her. When he arrived at the appointed time...she prepared for him seven beds, one atop the other – six of silver and the highest one was made of gold. Six silver ladders led to the six silver beds, and a golden ladder led to the uppermost one. As he was about to sin with her, the four fringes of his tzitzit slapped him in his face. He immediately slid off the bed on to the floor, where he was quickly joined by the woman.

The story ends with the harlot being so impressed by this man's devotion to Hashem that not only did she give up her trade, but she herself converted to Judaism.

This is the idea of tzitzit – that we have the greatness of Hashem and His teachings upon us at all times. We don't need to look elsewhere. The answer is always with us.

There is another way in which the mitzvah of tzitzit teaches this very basic and simple message. This passage of Shema also contains a biblical commandment to place upon the tzitzit a *petil tekhelet*, a blue fringe, a thread dyed with the color blue (15:38). This color blue was a very special color: in ancient and medieval times it was the color of royalty.

But there is an interesting halakhah about this blue dye. According to the rabbis (Menachot 44a) this blue dye had to come from a creature of the sea called a *chilazon*. There was, however, an identical color blue from an indigo plant that is called *kala ilan* (ibid. 40a). (This is possibly related to the Chinese word for indigo which is *lan*.) At first glance, the Talmud (ibid. 43a) tells us, the two colors of blue look exactly the same. But only the blue of the *chilazon* is considered acceptable.

So how does one tell the two blues apart? The Talmud says that one must do an experiment, for the blue of the *chilazon* creature will not fade, but the indigo blue will fade. The Talmud recommends taking the dyed thread and soaking it in alum, sap of fenugreek, and urine that is forty days old. If the thread fades, it is indigo, and thus invalid. If it doesn't fade then it is the acceptable *chilazon*.

Recently we have used this technique to identify the modern *tekhelet* that more and more Jews are beginning to wear.

From the close of the Talmudic period through the nineteenth century the blue dye of the *chilazon* was considered lost. But then in the nineteenth century, Rav Gershon Henoch Leiner, the Radziner Rebbe (the grandson of the author of the *Mei ha-Shiloach*, the Izbicer Rebbe) argued that the black/blue dye that shot out of a squid was the *tekhelet* dye (see his *Petil Tekhelet*, 1888). The only problem with his theory was that this dye would fade. So a chemist added a Prussian Blue (the equivalent of *kala ilan*) to this dye and it didn't fade anymore. The Radziner Rebbe didn't realize that it was the Prussian Blue that prevented the fading.

The former chief rabbi of Israel (from 1937–1959), Dr. Yitzchak Isaac ha-Levi Herzog, said that this cannot be the *tekhelet* because the dye of the *tekhelet* doesn't fade.[1]

But recently – in the past twenty years – it was discovered that the Murex snail is actually the creature that the ancient rabbis were referring to. This snail will produce a blue dye. To prove that this is the real *tekhelet*, Rabbi Dr. Moshe Tendler, who is both a *rosh yeshivah* at Yeshiva University's rabbinical school and a scientist in their college, took the *tekhelet* and soaked it in bleach for a week. Even after one week in bleach, its color did not fade.[2] This is one of the ways that we know that the Murex snail is actually the *chilazon*, and its dye is the true and valid *tekhelet*.

The true *tekhelet* never fades. Not in urine or in bleach. The difference between *tekhelet* and *kala ilan* is like the difference between the true happiness of life that the Torah represents and the ephemeral nature of materialistic pleasure.

The Torah's path in life remains constant. It reminds us to cling to the Eternal One, to Hashem, and not to wander after the fleeting pleasures of our eyes and attempt to seek happiness elsewhere. True happiness can be found in what we already have in our lives by realizing that everything we have is a gift from Hashem. Authentic happiness, like the *tekhelet*, will never fade.

When we recite the third paragraph of Shema morning and evening, and when we look at the *tekhelet*, we are reminding ourselves not to wander after a false happiness. And if we don't wander after a false happiness then our happiness will be like the authentic *tekhelet*.

---

1. See Ehud Spanier, *The Royal Purple and Biblical Blue* (Jerusalem: Keter Publishing, 1987).

2. See Rabbi Moshe Tendler, "Identifying Tekhelet: *Masoret* and *Yediyah*," in *Tekhelet: Renaissance of a Mitzvah*, ed. Alfred Cohen (New York: YU Press, 1996).

This is what the promise of following the path of the Torah offers. Its message is so beautiful and rewarding and joyous and happy...and it will never fade.

EMPOWERMENT THROUGH KNOWLEDGE AND COMMITMENT

Korach

One of the great mysteries of the Torah is whatever happened to Ohn Ben Pelet? The verse states, "And Korach, the son of Yitzhar… took Datan and Aviram…and Ohn ben Pelet, the sons of Reuven" (16:1). Korach's rebellion begins with Datan and Aviram and Ohn. We know what ends up happening to Datan and Aviram – they die in the rebellion; but Ohn seems to disappear from the text without a trace. Where did he go?

The Talmud fills in the gap. According to tractate Sanhedrin (109b), Ohn was saved by his wife, even though there is no mention of her at all in the text. Ohn came home and told his wife that he was joining Korach in a rebellion. His wife said to him, "What [benefit] are you going to get out of joining this rebellion?" So he said, "What can I do, as I have already sworn allegiance to Korach?" She said, "Leave it to me." That night she fed him wine and made him sleepy. She then sat by the opening of the tent and combed her hair immodestly. When Korach and his followers came to pick up Ohn, they were embarrassed to walk into the tent as she was sitting there grooming herself. Meanwhile Ohn overslept and missed the revolution, and so he was saved from death.

The Talmud contrasts Mrs. Ohn with Mrs. Korach, who it blames for needling Korach and convincing him to revolt against Moshe. Although the text of the Torah does not record such a conversation, the Talmud (Sanhedrin 109b) has Mrs. Korach saying

216

to Korach, "Look what Moshe is doing. He is taking all the power for himself, and his brother, and his nephews!"

These two stories reflect the fact that wives have tremendous influence over their husbands. They also reflect the idea that in biblical times, women were often not direct actors in the political leadership of society. Instead they had to act in a behind-the-scenes fashion. They were influential in a private manner that was not seen by the public.

This was, of course, the case for much of world history. Even in the United States, women did not get to vote until 1920.

In our own synagogue, the matter was not much different. When I arrived in Ohev Sholom in 2004, women had the right to vote on synagogue matters only if they had written consent from their husbands. This is not to say that women didn't have a voice in synagogue matters, but it was a behind-the-scenes, indirect voice. This matter changed when our bylaws were rewritten in 2006. Now women can vote as full members of the synagogue in the same way that men can vote.

I mention these stories from the Talmud and from our synagogue history, because I want to talk today about how women can have a direct involvement, as opposed to an indirect involvement, in the spiritual life of our synagogue.

From a traditional Orthodox perspective our synagogue is relatively progressive as it relates to women's direct spiritual involvement in the synagogue in areas traditionally reserved for men. For example, women carry the Torah in the women's section, there is a regular women's prayer service that meets, our *mechitzah* is down the middle of the sanctuary so that men and women share the space equally, women regularly deliver *divrei Torah* from the pulpit – this includes our *makom shabbaton*, which features girls teaching Torah in the shul over Shabbat – and women have leadership positions within the congregation in both a lay and a professional manner.

With all that, we do not have an egalitarian prayer service. We are an Orthodox synagogue and we must always be an Orthodox synagogue. Being an Orthodox synagogue means that we embrace halakhah, Jewish law, for we believe it must be a guidepost to our lives. This guidepost can be strict, and sometimes we may not understand its ways. But we submit ourselves to the tradition and to the law.

Let me give you a prosaic example. Every week, I teach a class downtown from 12:30 to 1:30 p.m. There are one-hour meters in front of the building where I teach the class. Last week I parked at 12:24 and put the money in the meter. I came down at 1:30 and saw that I got a ticket at 1:25 p.m. I was complaining to a friend that this was very unfair, and he put me in my place. He said: "Rabbi, you are Orthodox. Can I eat a hot dog that is just a little bit non-kosher? You either follow the law or you don't."

So too, sometimes we must struggle with halakhah. Sometimes we wonder, what if we are just a little bit off, does it really matter? But, the answer is that it does matter. With respect to halakhah, we cannot veer at all.

I know that there are some men and women in our congregation who struggle with this aspect of Orthodoxy. They struggle with a differentiation in rituals between men and women and with the fact that the traditional prayer service is dominated by men.

We once had a meeting in our synagogue about women's spiritual involvement in our congregation. It was one of the most powerful moments of my rabbinate. Around thirty of us gathered and sat in a circle and we shared our feelings. Some women and men shared that they were very happy with how this synagogue represented where they wanted to be spiritually. Others shared their concerns that because we are a non-egalitarian Orthodox synagogue their sons and daughters might grow up thinking that girls and women are less important spiritually. As a father of both boys and girls I can say that that is certainly a scary thought.

It was a powerful evening, because everyone in the room that night spoke from the heart and from a place of real spiritual depth. Many of the people in that room were extremely close friends and yet they had conflicting feelings about the proper spiritual path. One person's spiritual answer was another's spiritual betrayal. Together we were exploring a delicate but important issue that is at the center of the spiritual lives of many of us. Some of us openly wept with emotion and I can tell you that I was very proud that evening to be the rabbi of this shul.

That conversation was not a one-time event but a point on the spiritual journey that our congregation is taking. Since that night, I was shown a college thesis that was written by my good friend, Rachel Lieberman. Rachel graduated from Princeton in 2010, and she wrote a senior paper entitled "Reaching across the Mechitza: Feminism's Impact on Orthodox Judaism." Rachel taught me a conceptual model that I want to share with you today because I think it can help us as we move forward.

She explained that there are two primary models of feminism today that women feel strongly about. There is *difference feminism* and there is *equality feminism*. Those women who pursue equality feminism are trying to say that men and women need to be equal in every aspect of their lives. Whatever men do, women can and should do. The rallying cry for this approach is "equal opportunity and equal access." In contrast, difference feminism argues that men and women have different roles and women should not try to mimic the roles of men. It argues that a woman who does not desire to live like a man is no less a feminist.

From the perspective of Orthodox Judaism, Rachel writes in her thesis that Orthodox men and women, especially in Israel, are experimenting with new rituals and prayers to try and create a niche for Orthodox women that does not violate halakhah and at the same time does not compromise their spiritual desires.

I believe that a rabbinic consensus is emerging in the Orthodox world that Orthodox congregations should follow a third path, which is to use halakhah as the guide for understanding when it is appropriate to follow difference feminism versus equality feminism.

For example, in relationship to Torah study we follow equality feminism. Women's Talmud study and Torah scholarship has become widespread. And, as Rachel points out, it is important to note that even though Orthodoxy is often criticized for being the least progressive of the Jewish denominations, there is nothing in Reform or Conservative Judaism that can rival the advanced and rigorous opportunities for Talmud study currently available to women in the Orthodox world.

However, when it comes to prayer services and traditional rituals we should be more restrained and embrace a tradition that emphasizes difference feminism. Women's spirituality is no less important, but the tradition emphasizes that it must express itself differently. I can't tell you exactly why this consensus emerged from the rabbis and sociologically, but perhaps it has something to do with the difference between prayer and Torah study.

Torah study is an empowering activity. It is the acquisition of knowledge, and the more one knows the more power one has. Some women are already becoming halakhic experts for their communities. The more women study Torah, the more they will be empowered through knowledge.

Prayer service as a whole is generally not viewed in the same way; it is typically not seen as an empowering activity. Still, a prayer service can be empowering. It can give us the strength we need to live our lives and to overcome our struggles. And if difference feminism can help women better connect to a prayer service – and in that sense become more empowered in their daily lives and relationship with God – then I see a great value in our synagogue in advancing and amplifying aspects of difference feminism vis-à-vis prayer.

Why do I say that in our synagogue and community we should amplify aspects of difference feminism, as opposed to equality feminism, in our prayer services? The simple answer is that our synagogue is part of the larger world of halakhah – and the halakhic community, in my opinion, has not embraced equality feminism as part of a prayer service. It is possible that this will change in the future. Our history does recognize that changes have occurred in halakhah. But at this time, the state of the halakhic world is for the most part to reject equality feminism for prayer rituals.

For those men and women who feel rejected by my analysis, I want to share with you a thought I once heard from a teacher of mine at Yeshiva University, Professor Haym Soloveitchik. He pointed out that two competing groups, the chasidim and the *mitnagdim*, were engaged in vicious polemics at the start of the Chasidic movement. The *mitnagdim* were very upset at certain aspects of the highly radical and revolutionary Chasidic platform, but eventually their anger dissipated and was transformed into respect.

Professor Soloveitchik suggested that the change resulted from the admiration the *mitnagdim* gained for the chasidim when they saw them spending hours upon hours in prayer and other aspects of spirituality. When they saw their level of commitment and how deep and consistent it was, their opposition faded away and turned into respect.

I think we are seeing such a development as it relates to women's involvement in Torah study, but we are not yet seeing that on a broad and consistent level as it relates to women's involvement in Orthodox communal prayer rituals. Some rabbis have attacked those men and women who speak out on behalf of a more progressive approach by Orthodoxy toward women's spiritual involvement. We must never do such a thing.

Even though we are not always all on the same page, there is usually a common spirituality that we are seeking. My experience with people I have encountered who are seeking equality feminism in prayer is that they are often very impressive and personally inspiring.

Instead of viewing our differences as polarizing, we should applaud our common spiritual goals, for this common spirituality is exactly what we will need to help us each find our spiritual compass both as individuals and as a community as we move forward and grow together.

Homosexuality and Orthodox Jews

Chukat

I once had the very meaningful experience of being on an interdenominational rabbinic retreat. The retreat brought together rabbis from across the different denominations of Judaism, and we spent a week studying together in Newport, Rhode Island.

There is one moment in particular that happened on that retreat that will stick with me for a very long time. On the last night of the retreat, we saw the film *Trembling before God*, which movingly and emotionally portrays the conflicted and torn lives of individuals who come from a background of Orthodox Judaism – and in many cases still wish to remain within the Orthodox Jewish community – and yet have publicly announced that they are gay.

The director of this movie did a wonderful job of contrasting the views of rabbis whom he interviewed for the film, with those of the Jewish community and the families of gay individuals. The rabbis interviewed uniformly responded that a gay Jew is someone we must love, but is also someone who is entirely violating halakhah. The community, and more particularly the families of these individuals, generally ostracized the open homosexuals and made them feel unwelcome in our Godly community.

As powerful as this film was, what made the moment unforgettable was what happened after the film. I found myself in front of thirty-five other rabbis – some of whom were openly gay. They asked me how I, as an Orthodox rabbi, could advocate living in a society whose laws inflict pain on individuals who are innocent.

And so I sat there and openly wept for the pain of these individuals and their families. These people are in many ways real heroes. They are engaged in an extremely serious struggle. The concepts of *kedushah* and Torah are ideas that are a constant force in their lives. And I cried for the tragedy that they faced such a terrible conflict in their spiritual lives.

But when I finally found the words to speak I actually pointed to a text that we read in parashat Chukat, and I thought of Rashi's commentary on that text. We read of the mitzvah of *parah adumah*, the red heifer, about which the Torah states, "*Zot chukat ha-Torah* – This is the law of the Torah" (19:2). And Rashi, commenting on this verse and explaining the concept of *chok*, says, "For when the Satan and other nations will throw arguments at you and say, 'What is the meaning of this law and what reason is there for it?'" We should respond, *chok hi*, it is a *chok*, "it is a decree before Me, *ve-ein lekha reshut leharher acharehah* – and you have no permission to second-guess it."

And according to the Midrash, it is about the mitzvah of *parah adumah* that Shlomo ha-Melekh states in Kohelet, "I said that I would understand it, but *hi rechokah mimeni*, it is distant from me" (Bamidbar Rabbah 19:3, quoting Kohelet 7:23). Why is it that Rashi and Shlomo say that there are no explanations for this mitzvah? In fact, over the years I have heard many suggestions that quite rationally explain the mitzvah of *parah adumah*. The reason is because they felt that no single suggestion fully justified the commandment in their eyes.

And so, at that moment, I personally turned toward these texts, and I said *chok hi, ve-hi rechokah mimeni* – it is my law, and it is distant from me. I know that the Torah uses the word *to'evah* – usually translated as abomination – about this prohibition, but I also know that the word *to'evah* also appears in other contexts throughout the Torah that are not necessarily morally charged, like bringing an animal sacrifice that has a blemish on it (Devarim 17:1) and the prohibition of eating certain animals (ibid. 14:3).

So I cited the concept of *chok* as an explanation for this prohibition. Not because there are no explanations, but because all of the explanations are distant from me.

And yet as I sat there listening to the tearful words of an openly gay Conservative rabbi, I felt new insight into the depth of the pain of this community. For someone who is gay and yet loves the richness of an otherwise Orthodox Jewish lifestyle, there are basically three responses. This person can subdue their homosexuality, which they usually believe is given to them by God, and live an Orthodox Jewish life. Or they can leave the Orthodox lifestyle entirely. But to do that is often exceedingly difficult, because, as this gay rabbi said to me, "I am not defined by sexual identity."

And the third possible option is to live a life, like we all do, on different levels, full of conflict and internal pain. And then it becomes our responsibility to rise as a community to a level – and this film showed that our wider community is not yet on such a level – where we are able to say: your actions violate our laws, and yet we will not ostracize you; we will love you the same way we love all of our brothers and sisters.

However, there is a flip side to this analysis. We do not just read in our Torah about the mitzvah of *parah adumah*; we also read about the sin of the *egel ha-zahav*, the golden calf. And the closeness of these two concepts is very apparent. Both are the same types of animals – cows; both are similar colors – red and gold. In fact, Rashi (19:22) quotes the Midrash that comments on this close relationship and says, "The mother comes and atones for the son," meaning that the mitzvah of *parah adumah* is an atonement for the sin of the golden calf.

Why does the Torah select a *chok* to atone for this sin of idolatry? Perhaps the reason is because when people are unable to accept the obligations of a *chok* upon themselves their actions can very easily turn into idolatry. The rejection of the *parah adumah* can very easily turn into the acceptance of the *egel ha-zahav*.

The danger for this is certainly great when people feel rejected. Once they feel rejected, people often feel the need to defend themselves to the hilt. And since our sexuality is such an important part of us, homosexuality can thus more easily and even understandably become the centerpiece of their lives. But when anything other than God is the center of someone's life, then we have entered the realm of idolatry. And so when homosexuality becomes someone's primary identity – when the axis of God has been replaced as central in someone's life – then it is idolatrous.

My response to the film *Trembling before God* is that we as a community have to formulate a better response to someone who appreciates the beauty of Torah and halakhah and yet lives as a homosexual. Our response should be to create an environment where we as a family can sit together with such a person and say *chok hi*, it is a law of the Torah, but *hi rechokah mimeni*, it is distant and I do not understand it, *ve-ein li reshut leharher ach-arehah*, and I have no permission to reject the prohibition. For it is only by sitting and embracing such individuals that we as a community can prevent someone who loves Torah from turning their homosexuality into an idolatry, moving from a rejection of the *parah adumah* to an acceptance of idolatry.

INTERGENERATIONAL
SPARRING

Balak

Our shul once hosted a great Jewish boxer by the name of Dmitri Salita. Dmitri is a Golden Gloves champion boxer. He told us how he emigrated from Odessa as a young boy and took up boxing. Later, he became a very committed, devout Jew. Dmitri's punch is as fierce as his devotion to Orthodox Judaism is serious. He shared with us his unique and inspiring story.

Since we invited Dmitri to speak in our shul, people thought I was a big boxing fan. That isn't true at all, although I am a big admirer of Dmitri. I am also appreciative of the anonymous person who once left on my desk a biography of Barney Ross, written by Douglas Century.[1] Although some parts of Barney Ross's life should not be emulated or admired – for instance, he lost all of his money to gambling – I found his story as a whole extremely inspiring.

When Jews first arrived in America many of our ancestors became successful boxers. Names like Benny Leonard, Kingfish Levinsky, Abe Attel, Ruby Goldstein, Lew Tendler, and Barney Ross were household names throughout the country. Several people in our own congregation have told me that their fathers or grandfathers were serious boxers.

Barney Ross grew up in the toughest neighborhood of Chicago. He used to get into multiple fights every single day of his life walking to and from school. His father, an immigrant, was a

---

1. *Barney Ross: The Life of a Jewish Fighter* (New York: Schocken / Nextbook Press, 2009).

devout Orthodox Jew and a teacher of Talmud, who barely made a living running a small grocery. When Barney was fourteen his father was murdered by two people attempting to rob his shop. Soon after, Barney's mother fell to pieces and Barney's younger siblings were dispatched to an orphanage. Barney vowed to make enough money to get them out of the orphanage.

Barney worked on the street (possibly for Al Capone) and did odd jobs here and there until one day he entered a boxing gym. He wanted to fight. But he was told that he had zero talent. To make a long story short, he put his whole heart into it and ended up being a Hall of Fame boxer who held the title in two weight divisions simultaneously.

Barney was on top of the world. He fought in packed stadiums in front of celebrities and politicians. His fights were carried on the front pages of newspapers and he was even given a ticker tape parade in Chicago. Although at times in his life he drifted a little from his faith, he always wore his tzitzit under his shirt. And he was always proud and very public about his Judaism.

On December 7, 1941, the Japanese attacked the US at Pearl Harbor. Barney, a thirty-three-year-old retired boxing champion, immediately enlisted in the Marines and requested to serve on the front lines. He fought heroically and even earned a Silver Medal for bravery. One night Barney and his unit were ambushed by Japanese forces in the forest. His friends were severely wounded, but Barney did not surrender. He single-handedly killed twenty-two Japanese soldiers who had surrounded him.

Barney returned to the US as a wounded war hero, and he traveled the country and inspired people at large rallies with Eleanor Roosevelt. But as he grew even more and more famous he also became completely addicted to morphine. He voluntarily checked into a detox program, and from that point on he devoted his life to going around the country and educating children about the dangers of drugs. He would speak anywhere for free on the topic. He was a missionary for the cause.

Barney entered one more fight in his life. When Israel was founded, Barney fought passionately for the new state and did whatever he could to help. He was probably involved in running guns from the docks of New York to the new State of Israel.

In all the fights that he fought, Barney Ross was literally never knocked out. He fought against long odds and gave everything he had to the cause.

After I read this biography, I thought to myself: that was one tough Jew. He was strong in a way that most of our generation is not. He had a toughness that one can only acquire by literally being beaten every day of your life. It is no accident that for a Jew to be a boxer in Barney's era was normal, but in our area it is eyebrow raising. Barney's generation fought for every inch that they got. They were the first generation of immigrants, while our generation was given everything that our parents and grandparents worked so hard to give us. Let's face it: Barney's generation was tougher than ours.

Sometimes you see an interaction between two different generations, and you see that there is a great difficulty relating to and understanding each other. The older generation looks with disdain upon the softness and sense of entitlement of the younger generation, and the younger generation simply has no comprehension of what the older generation went through.

This is the story of the end of *bnei Yisrael*'s journey in the desert. After Miriam dies in parashat Chukat, the children of Israel come to Moshe and complain that there is no water (20:1–2). You might be excused for thinking that there is nothing new about this complaint. After all, the Jews have been complaining throughout the desert. And in fact they have already complained about a lack of water, right after they crossed the sea. But there is one major difference this time. Miriam's death takes place thirty-eight years after the previous story, the revolt of Korach. For the previous thirty-eight years, there have been no complaints at all. But when she dies, the complaints resume again.

Rashi (20:1) teaches that this generation that was complaining about the lack of water was an entirely new generation – a younger generation. They were not the generation that had lived in Egypt; those people had all died out in the wilderness. When Moshe heard their complaints he was disgusted. Standing before him was a group of ingrates. They were never enslaved to Pharaoh; they didn't lead a daring revolution out of Egypt; they didn't fight the Amalekites. They never fought for anything! They had their manna and water handed to them every morning and now they had the audacity to bring a complaint to Moshe!

Ibn Ezra (20:8) argues that Moshe was so upset about this complaint – even more so than all the complaints he had received from the earlier generation – that *ibed kavanato*, he lost his ability to concentrate properly on the command of Hashem. Because he lost his concentration, he had trouble getting water from the rock.

God had instructed Moshe to speak to a rock (20:8) and draw out water. But Moshe lost his concentration and hit a rock twice. If God said to speak to the rock, why would Moshe hit the rock?

Two reasons: First, he remembered that thirty-nine years earlier when the people asked for water, he hit a rock and water came out (Shemot 17:6). And second, he lost his focus. Rambam (*Shemonah Perakim* 4) says he grew angry and frustrated and so he hit the rock twice in his anger. Moshe wanted to hit the rock because that is what he knew how to do. That is the way he had taught the generation that came out of Egypt. That is the way he had communicated effectively with them: through physical acts of strength, through fire and brimstone. But Hashem didn't want Moshe to hit the rock. Hashem wanted him to speak to the rock.

The two generations were not the same. The generation that left Egypt, the older generation, was tough; and the new generation, thirty-nine years later, was still soft. The new generation needed a softer educational approach, talking, as opposed to hitting. Moshe tried to bring his old, forceful approach to the soft generation, and in doing so he failed miserably. Because Moshe hit the rock, he was not permitted to enter Eretz Yisrael, for he could not effectively educate the new generation.

The Torah emphasizes Moshe's mistake by telling the story of Bilam soon after the story of Moshe hitting the rock. According to some, Bilam was a prophet whose natural prophetic abilities even surpassed Moshe's. But in parashat Balak his actions look ridiculous. When his donkey disobeys him, he strikes the donkey with his staff three times. This prompts the donkey to speak: "What have I done to you that you have hit me now three times?" (22:28).

To a certain degree Bilam and Moshe were making the same mistake. These great prophets – by definition the greatest communicators in the world – were miserably failing to communicate. They were both hitting when a different method was called for.

How do we ourselves avoid this mistake of Moshe and Bilam in our own lives?

It is fashionable for every generation that accomplishes something to look down on the younger generation and scoff. But, of course, that is not helpful. The older generation needs to recognize that the younger generation will have its own challenges, which in retrospect will seem unfathomable and insurmountable.

It is significant that this sin of Moshe happened immediately after the death of Miriam. Right after Miriam died, we are told that there was no water and the Jewish people complained to Moshe. The rabbis in tractate Ta'anit (9a) say that the reason why there was no water after Miriam died is because the well of water existed in her merit.

But perhaps something else is going on here as well. Miriam understood how to communicate. She understood that sometimes it was necessary to communicate in a different way than Moshe. She knew how to convince Pharaoh's daughter to let her bring in a Hebrew nurse for baby Moshe. She knew how to convince the women to follow her and sing with her at the splitting of the sea, as it states, "All the women followed after Miriam" (Shemot 15:20). If Moshe operated with spice, she operated with sugar.

I believe that forty years earlier, it was Miriam who knew how to convince the people that the bitter waters around them were really sweet. Sometimes the difference between bitter waters and sweet waters is just a matter of perspective and communication. The rabbis hint at this when they say that the well existed in Miriam's merit. And the Torah itself hints at this, since the Torah calls the bitter waters *marim*, which is spelled the same way as "Miriam" (Shemot 15:23).

Through her communication skills and intuition, Miriam knew that the younger generation needed a message of sweetness. They weren't the hardened revolutionaries that their parents were. She never would have let Moshe hit the rock, let alone hit it twice! (Indeed, before Moshe hits the rock he cries out: "*Shimu na ha-morim*, listen now you rebels" (20:10). The word *morim* is spelled exactly like 'Miriam,' so Moshe could also be seen as summoning Miriam's name at that moment!)

She knew that the younger generation would be the ones to enter the land of the Canaan. They would indeed eventually surpass the feats of the older generation. And isn't that the goal, after all? As the Talmud states in tractate Sanhedrin (105b), "Everyone is jealous of everyone else, except for their child or student."

Bilam, too, understood this, and toward the end of his story he turned from hitting his donkey into blessing the Jewish people. It is Bilam's blessing for the Jewish people that we use to open our daily prayers: "How goodly are your tents, O Yaakov, and your dwelling places, Yisrael" (24:5).

When we look back at what our American Jewish ancestors did when they came to this country penniless, it is extraordinary – a true fulfillment of Bilam's blessing. In a short period of time they managed to build one of the most dynamic, successful, educated, and philanthropic Jewish communities in history.

But the message of Moshe's sin and Bilam's foolishness is also a cautionary reminder. No matter how great the older generations were, no matter how much they accomplished, we all must remember that the new generation will need to be educated differently, with newer methods, more patience, and with a unique style; perhaps with sweetness instead of spice. And if we remember that, then, God willing, our children will also be a true fulfillment of another blessing Bilam gave to the Jewish people: "He has not seen evildoers in Yaakov, and He has seen no transgression in Yisrael; Hashem, his God, is with him, and he has the King's friendship" (23:21).

THREE EDUCATIONAL LESSONS
Pinchas

I am really grateful for the great education I received from my rabbis, my teachers, and most of all, from my parents.

Parashat Pinchas gives us wonderful insight into how to communicate educationally. I want to focus on three educational lessons we learn.

First Lesson

After God tells Moshe that he is not going to lead the people into Eretz Yisrael, Moshe appeals to God, asking God to pick a successor for him. Hashem selects Yehoshua – Moshe's assistant – to be Moshe's successor.

Rashi (27:16) brings the Midrash Tanchuma, which imagines the following conversation taking place between Moshe and Hashem. Moshe turns to Hashem and says, "Hashem, isn't it now the appropriate time for my son to take over my position?" Hashem answers Moshe, "That isn't My plan." Moshe had intended that his son would take over the leadership role. Like so many parents and teachers, he had a plan for his son. But that wasn't God's plan.

This is a lesson for all of us. We try to educate and make plans and pigeonhole someone into a role. But that might not be their role.

I remember paying a shivah visit to one of the most famous Jewish artists in the world, who had lost his mother. Today his art hangs in the finest museums around the world and sells for many thousands of dollars. I asked him about his mother. He said,

234

"It was very unusual for a young Jewish boy who grew up in my community to want to be an artist. But my mother never tried to dissuade me from being an artist. People would come up to her in the pizza store and say the most terrible and mean things about what she was allowing me to do, and she would just ignore them. She always encouraged me to follow my own path."

As Rashi says, "That isn't My plan." When we educate we must try to see God's plan, not our plan. It is not about what we want our students to accomplish; it is about what God wants our students to accomplish.

Second Lesson

When God tells Moshe to appoint Yehoshua as the next leader, the words the Torah uses are "*Ve-samakhta et yadkha alav* – You should place your hand upon him" (27:18). The word "hand" is in the singular. But then we are told (27:23) Moshe places "*yadav*" both of his hands on Yehoshua.

God told him to only put one hand on Yehoshua, but Moshe put two. Rashi (27:23) explains: "Moshe did even more than he was commanded."

When we are teaching something our goal must be to give of ourselves completely to the one whom we are teaching. We must want our student to succeed as badly as we want ourselves to succeed, perhaps even more.

The Talmud, tractate Sanhedrin (105b), says, "Everyone is jealous of everyone else, except for their child or student." This means that on some level we feel a jealousy for all other human beings. How do we counteract this jealousy? We counteract it by teaching others what we know. We counteract it by giving ourselves completely over to our students. If we teach someone, then we won't be jealous of him since we will see ourselves as part of his success. Thus, if we spend our life teaching others then we won't be jealous of others.

The greatest teachers I had in school are the ones who gave themselves completely over to me. In a true sense they were like Moshe, and they viewed all their students as their Yehoshuas. They placed both their hands on the students and tried to teach everything they knew.

I remember one incident that happened when I was studying with Dr. Haym Soloveitchik, who is known as the premier scholar of medieval Jewish history. He is a man of towering intelligence and fastidious devotion to his research, and many students have been intimidated by his presence. He once mentioned that he gets secondhand books at a severe discount. I casually said to him, "Well, if you ever see a good purchase, please pick it up for me." The next night he called me up and said, "Do you have a car?" I said, "What do you mean, 'Do I have a car?'" I was very confused and we kept going back forth talking about whether or not I had a car. Finally, he grew frustrated with me and said, "Never mind. Just meet me in the faculty parking lot tomorrow at noon." When I showed up, I saw why he had asked if I had a car. He had taken it upon himself to purchase books for me. He had spent hours going to all the used bookstores in New York City and had bought four large boxes of used books. This world-renowned scholar had spent the entire day shopping for his student. That is an example of placing two hands on a student.

This is the second lesson of the Torah portion: When we teach we must give everything to our students. We must not settle for a simple hand – two hands are required.

Third Lesson

This week we read of the division of the land of Canaan into an inheritance amongst the tribes of Israel. The Torah tells us that only sons inherit the land. But then the daughters of Tzelofechad appear before Moshe and they say, "Our father had no sons. Why should our father be diminished?... Give us a portion" (27:3–4).

Moshe goes to Hashem with their request and Hashem tells Moshe, "The daughters of Tzelofechad are speaking correctly" (27:7). Thus the law is established that if a father has no sons, the daughters, too, inherit the land.

But we wonder why is it that the Torah did not teach this law to begin with? Why must we wait for the daughters of Tzelofechad to approach Moshe?

We must conclude that the Torah wants to give space for *bnei Yisrael* to learn this lesson on their own. The Torah could have simply stated this position, but it allows us the space to learn it ourselves. This is like a child who is learning to walk. One parent will never let the child walk for fear that the child might fall, while the other parent will give the child the space to fall in order that the child may one day become a stronger walker.

As we teach our own students, we must remember to leave space for the students to learn on their own.

I remember learning this lesson from one of my *roshei yeshivah* in Israel, Rav David Bigman. We would sometimes come to him expecting him to tell us exactly what we should do, and he wouldn't give us a direct answer. It wasn't because he didn't have an answer; rather it was because he wanted us to discover it on our own.

Many people think that a great rabbi should always tell you what to do. I disagree. I think that a great rabbi will allow you to discover on your own what the Torah wants you to do.

These are the three fundamental educational lessons:

As a teacher, follow God's plan, not your own plan.

Put everything you have into the success of your students.

Allow your students the space to learn on their own.

In order to be a truly great spiritual community we all need to be students of the Torah. But the truth is that we also all need to be teachers. It is through teaching one another in the proper way that we can all grow together.

WOMEN AND TALLIT

Mattot

In parashat Mattot, the tribes of Reuven and Gad (later they are joined by a part of Menashe) approach Moshe and ask him if they can remain on the "other side of the Jordan River" (32:5). They do not desire to live in the land of Canaan, as the other side of the Jordan is more favorable for their cattle. Moshe responds angrily and accuses them of abandoning their brothers in battle. They therefore agree to fight as the vanguard for the Jewish people and lead them into battle, and only then would they return to their cattle on the other side of the Jordan.

This teaches us the extreme importance of Jewish unity. Moshe was not willing to allow for the fracturing of our nation. Reuven and Gad took upon themselves to lead the fight for a land that they would end up not living in. Such is the importance of Jewish unity.

Unfortunately, our people are today heading down the opposite path. Today we are seeking more and more to isolate and marginalize those with whom we disagree, and this is a tragedy. It is often the case that those we have isolated for their "radical" positions might have different positions that are also well grounded in Jewish law. For the sake of unity our community needs to make room for conflicting positions.

In this context let us analyze a horrible situation in Israel that I fear is only getting worse.

On November 18, 2009, a woman was arrested for the crime of wearing a tallit – a prayer shawl – at the Western Wall.[1] Can you even imagine? Let's repeat that sentence: A woman is arrested for wearing a tallit at the Kotel!

The Western Wall is considered holy because it is directly adjacent to the Temple Mount in Jerusalem. The Temple Mount is considered to be the holiest spot in Judaism.

Before delving into the issue of whether or not a woman may wear a tallit according to halakhah, we must take note of the fact that there is another related issue here as well. That is the question of whether or not Israeli police should enforce Jewish law at the Western Wall. Should the Kotel be a specifically sacred place in strict accordance with Jewish law or should it be a place where people can worship and act as they please? However, we are not focusing on that issue here.

Here we are discussing how women were denied the right by the Israeli government to practice Jewish law in a manner that is permitted by many great traditional rabbinic authorities. In essence, the Jewish state denied them their right to practice Judaism. The reason the government and the police felt the imprimatur to arrest this woman is partly because of remarks attributed to an elderly, revered, Torah scholar named Rav Ovadia Yosef. Rav Yosef is reported to have called this practice "deviant," thus implying that it is prohibited.[2]

If Rav Ovadia Yosef really said that, and if his remarks were not taken out of context, then I think his remarks are very unfortunate.

Let us delve deeper into the nitty-gritty of this law.

---

1. See Nir Hasson and Liel Kyzer, "Police Arrest Woman for Wearing Prayer Shawl at Wall," *Haaretz*, November 18, 2009.

2. See http://blogs.forward.com/sisterhood-blog/118725/

The topic of women wearing a tallit was discussed by Rabbi Avi Weiss in his book *Women at Prayer*,[3] and it was also discussed by Aviva Cayam in an article published in *Jewish Legal Writings by Women*.[4] And we will draw upon their writings in our study of the topic.

The mitzvah to wear a tallit is found in the Torah. In the third paragraph of Shema, we are commanded: "Speak to the children of Israel and command them to make fringes [also known as tzitzit] on the corner of their garments" (15:38).

In the Talmud, a debate is recorded as to whether or not this law applies to men and women or just to men. According to Menachot (43a): "The rabbis taught: all are obligated in the laws of tzitzit: priests, Levi'im, and Israelites, converts, women, and slaves. Rabbi Shimon exempts women because it is a positive commandment limited by time, and from all positive commandments limited by time women are exempt. What is the reasoning of Rabbi Shimon? It has been taught 'and when you see it' – this excludes clothing worn at night." In general women are exempt from time-bound, positive commandments. According to Rabbi Shimon, the obligation to wear tzitzit is a time-bound, positive commandment and thus women are exempt. So whether or not women are obligated to wear tzitzit is a debate in the Talmud between Rabbi Shimon and the anonymous position of the text.

In Talmudic times we learn of two different sages who attached tzitzit to the garments of the women of their houses. We are told in tractate Sukkah (11a) that both Rabbi Yehudah and Rabbi Amram the Pious would attach tzitzit to the women's aprons.

Even though Rabbi Shimon does not obligate women to wear tzitzit, does he allow them to participate in this mitzvah if they so

---

3. *Women at Prayer: A Halakhic Analysis of Women's Prayer Groups* (Hoboken, NJ: KTAV, 2001).

4. "Fringe Benefits: Women and Tzitzit," in *Jewish Legal Writings by Women*, ed. Micah Halperin and Chana Safrai (Jerusalem: Urim Publications, 1998), 119–142.

desire? And if they voluntarily want to participate in this mitzvah may they recite a blessing? After all, it is a great mitzvah to wear tzitzit. The Talmud teaches that the mitzvah of tzitzit is equal to all the other commandments of the Torah. (See Rashi, 16:39, and Berakhot 12a.) The tzitzit are also symbolic of the holiness of the Jewish people. The very word "tzitzit" reminds us of the high priest's *tzitz*, which says upon it *Kodesh la-Hashem* (Shemot 28:36).

This issue is taken up in the three major halakhic cultures of the medieval period. The three major cultures are Spain-Egypt, southern France, and northern Europe. In all three places the ruling is very clear that woman may absolutely wear the tallit. The only dispute is whether or not she may recite a blessing when she wears this tallit.

In Egypt we see that the great Rambam ruled (*Hilkhot Tzitzit* 3:9): "Women are exempt from the biblical law of tzitzit. Women who want to wear tzitzit wrap themselves in it without a blessing. And this is the case regarding other positive commandments from which women are exempt. If they want to perform them without a blessing they are not prevented."

Rambam had a fierce and brilliant critic whose name is Rabad of Posquierre. He was a leading authority of Provencal halakhic literature. In response to Rambam's teaching, he wrote (ad loc.): "There are those who disagree and say that these laws can be done even with a blessing, and they say that even the voluntary recitation of a blessing is possible."

So too, we see that the leading rabbis of northern Europe allowed women to wear a tallit and recite a blessing when doing so. Here is what Tosafot write (commentary to Rosh Hashanah 33a):

> We rule like Rabbi Yose [that even though women are not obligated to blow the shofar they are not prevented from doing so]. And Michal the daughter of Shaul would lay tefillin, and the wife of Yonah the prophet went up to the Temple for the pilgrimage festivals, where she was brought into the courtyard of the

Temple and permitted to lay her hands on the animal in order to give women spiritual strength (*nachat ruach*). And it is permissible for them to make a blessing on time-bound positive commandments even though they are not required to perform those mitzvot...and if we would not let them make a blessing they would lose out on the mitzvah of tzitzit, *lulav*, tefillin, Megillah, Chanukah lights, sukkah, Havdalah, Kiddush, and the blessings of Shema. And we learn that anyone who wants to be pious should recite all the blessings!

Tosafot compare the mitzvah of tallit with other time-bound, positive commandments and rule that just like a woman can recite the blessing on other mitzvot – like shaking a *lulav* and sitting in a sukkah – so too can she recite the blessing on a tallit. To this day the Ashkenazic community follows this ruling of Tosafot. We thus rule that when a woman sits in a sukkah or shakes a *lulav* she should recite the blessing.

Regardless of whether or not a woman recites a blessing, it is clear that the leading rabbis of medieval Jewry all rule that a woman may wear a tallit.

There is only one cause for hesitation. This is the comment of Targum Yonatan (Devarim 22:5), an Aramaic commentary on the Torah, which states that a tallit is a man's garment – with the implication that a woman should wear it. But these medieval authorities all came after Targum Yonatan and none of them cited Targum Yonatan as a reason for a woman not to wear a tallit.

In the early modern period we see more cause for concern. We see the idea introduced by some that if a woman wears a tallit she is considered arrogant. This is because hardly any women are doing it, and if she does it, then she is standing out from the crowd with her piety. This concept is called *yoharah*, and it is the idea that one should not act in a way that appears excessively pious.

Accordingly one respected scholar, Rabbi Mordechai Yaffe, writes in the sixteenth century: "[It is legally permitted for women to wear tzitzit] but it is still foolish and arrogant to do so. Despite the fact that with other time-bound, positive commandments women have been accustomed to observing them and reciting the blessing, what they are used to doing, they do; what they are not used to doing, they do not do. And with tzitzit, we do not find it, except for one in a thousand, like Michal the daughter of Shaul and others; therefore, they should not wear tzitzit" (Levush, *Hilkhot Tzitzit* 17:2).

Modern codes of Jewish law debate whether or not a woman can wear a tallit. All agree that technically she can wear a tallit; the only question is whether or not it is arrogant for her to do so. Thus, one great work known as the *Arukh ha-Shulchan* of Rabbi Yechiel Michel Epstein (published from 1884–1893), states: "Yet in reality we have not heard of this and we do not permit her to wear a tallit, even more so to say the blessing. This is not like sukkah and *lulav*, which happen once a year and are a precept for that moment. But the law of tzitzit lasts all year and it is not nice for women.... This is the meaning of what Rema meant when he wrote, 'In any case, if women want...it appears arrogant and therefore women should not wear tzitzit, since it is not an obligation of the person.'"

Another classic work, the *Chayyei Adam* of Rabbi Avraham Danzig (1748–1820), takes the opposite position: "In any case, if they want to wear tzitzit and make the blessing, they may recite the blessing. That is the law with regard to all time-limited positive commandments, like *lulav* and sukkah and others...."

This issue was also directly addressed by one of the great contemporary authorities, Rabbi Moshe Feinstein. In 1976, he was asked the question whether or not a woman can wear a tallit. From the language of his responsum we see that he was right in the middle of the feminist battles of the time. And he felt that the motivation to wear a tallit was not stemming from a desire to come closer to Hashem, but to score another notch in the battle for feminist equality:

Thus he ruled as follows:

> It is clear that all women have the right to perform those commandments that the Torah did not obligate them in, and they are fulfilling a mitzvah and receiving a reward for doing it. According to the opinion of Tosafot, they are permitted to recite the blessing, and it is our custom that women observe the law of shofar and *lulav* and also say the blessing. Therefore, even tzitzit are allowed for a woman who wants to wear a garment which is distinguishable from men's clothing, yet has four corners on which she is able to attach fringes and fulfill the commandment…. However clearly this only applies when the woman desires to observe the law although she was not commanded; yet when it is not due to this intention, but rather stems from her resentment toward God and His Torah, then it is not a precept. On the contrary, it is a forbidden act of denial when she thinks that there will be any change in the laws of Torah that she took on. (*Iggrot Moshe*, Orach Chayim 4:49)

Rav Moshe was responding to a certain situation: a situation where he saw the world of feminism trying to destroy the walls of Orthodoxy.

Today we are living in a different world. It is a world where most women who desire to wear a tallit come from more liberal streams of Judaism and are very much accustomed to wearing a tallit. They have grown up wearing a tallit and it is entirely natural and spiritual for them. We should not see a woman wearing a tallit as part of a larger attempt to destroy Orthodox tenets.

Moreover, we must be exceedingly careful against impugning someone's motives. We cannot know what a woman or a man is thinking when they come to pray. We must give them the benefit of the doubt and assume that a woman who wears a tallit is doing so because she wants to take a mitzvah upon herself that will allow her to feel closer to Hashem. We must assume that she wants to wear a tallit for the same reason she wants to sit in the sukkah and hear the sounds of the shofar.

Finally, we see from this whole discussion that there is clearly a mainstream halakhic position permitting women to wear a tallit and recite a blessing upon it. The woman who was arrested for wearing a tallit woke up that morning at 4:30 a.m. for the purpose of praying at the Kotel. In the manner in which she prayed she was following the teachings of Rambam, Rabad, Tosafot, and the Chayyei Adam, and for doing so she was arrested. This is a colossal disgrace. And the government of Israel owes her an apology.

The legacy of Reuven and Gad reminds us that we must seek unity for our people. Even if want to end up living in different parts of the land, we all must work together on the core issues. Otherwise there may be a permanent disruption to the Jewish people, and that would be the greatest tragedy of all.

RETHINKING OUR JUSTICE SYSTEM

Masei

I once asked a federal judge what the most difficult part of his job was, and without pausing he said to me, "Taking away a person's liberty. That is the most difficult thing to do."

In America the most common treatment of convicted criminals is incarceration for lengthy periods of time. Our country has a higher proportion of people in prison than any other country in the world and at any other time in US history. Some evidence suggests that the fastest growing business in America is the prison business. The rate of incarceration has quadrupled in the last three decades. Those who are incarcerated can expect serious hardships. Prison rape is a very serious and real problem.[1] For those who are freed from incarceration nearly 70 percent will be arrested again within three years.[2]

As a rabbi, I occasionally have found myself visiting lost souls in prison, and I never fail to be disheartened by the current state of our prison system.

In parashat Masei the Torah commands *bnei Yisrael* to set up their own criminal justice system. Admittedly, it was a different world in the time of the giving of the Torah and to compare our world

---

1. See http://www.hrw.org/news/2007/12/15/us-federal-statistics-show-widespread-prison-rape.

2. See http://www.washingtonpost.com/wp-dyn/content/discussion/2008/02/28/DI2008022802960.html.

to the biblical world is worse than comparing apples to oranges. Neither the Torah nor the Talmud ever discusses anything even remotely close to our current prison system. But a comparison is still helpful as it can show us what our attitude toward criminals should be and perhaps we can allow this to influence us in our current lives.

There are three main points about the justice system that we can derive from this parashah.

The first is the message of personal responsibility in bringing a criminal to justice. This is the idea of the *goel ha-dam*, the blood redeemer. If one has a relative who is killed it is the responsibility of the deceased's relative to make sure that justice happens. Says the Torah in parashat Masei: "The blood redeemer must kill the murderer when he comes upon him" (35:21). That is, the responsibility of justice belongs to the closest relative. But the rabbis expand that idea. If there is no relative or if the relative is unable to bring him to justice, Ramban (in his *Hasagot al Sefer ha-Mitzvot*) says that the obligation then moves to society as a whole: "The court must appoint a person whose job it is to catch the criminal and fill the role of the blood relative."

If there is no blood relative, the community must assume the responsibility of that relative. The community's responsibility to bring a criminal to justice is only an extension of a relative's personal responsibility. All of society must feel the same obligation as the relative of the one who died. We must personally make sure that the criminal is brought to justice.

In our country today we no longer have this idea of personal responsibility of bringing someone to justice. The responsibility belongs to the police. To some degree, this is an improvement. But by placing the responsibility on the police we should be aware of what we are losing. We are losing a personal feeling of obligation to pursue justice in the world.

As one who has been victimized by crime on multiple occasions, I am sensitive to the fact that our society can improve in this area.

When something is stolen from me today I call the police, not because I expect them to catch the criminal but because I have to file an insurance claim! Too many of our criminals are not caught because there is a lack of personal responsibility in tracking down the criminal. The responsibility of the biblical *goel ha-dam* has not been transferred adequately to the modern-day police force.

However, the obligation of bringing the criminal to justice is balanced by a contrasting obligation of the criminal and the criminal's responsibility.

This leads us to point number two: Before the Jewish people cross over the Jordan, God tells them to set up cities called *arei miklat*. There were to be six of these cities, three on each side of the Jordan (35:9–15), plus forty-two Levitical cities that also served as cities of refuge (35:1–8). If a person killed someone without premeditation then he was sentenced to live in such a city. He was exiled for having committed the crime.

Once the killer was ordered to be exiled he could not buy his way out of the punishment. The verse says, *"Ve-lo tikchu kofer la-nus el ir miklato"* (35:32). Rashi explains this to mean that he could not give money in exchange for exile. The key word here is *kofer*, which is the same word as *kaparah*, atonement. The reason that the criminal could not buy his way out of the punishment is because he needed the exile as an atonement. As much as the exile was a punishment it was also obligatory in order to teach the criminal that it is his responsibility to repent.

In his *Hilkhot Teshuvah* (2:4), Rambam teaches that if one desires to repent he must go into exile and wander. The idea of exile is that it humbles us and leads to introspection. In our modern society we do a good job of punishing the criminal but we do a very poor job of teaching the criminal about introspection and of how to accept responsibility for his actions. Ultimately it is society that pays the price for the prisoner's failure to change his actions.

So far we have discussed the community's responsibility for justice and the criminal's responsibility for repentance.

There is another way to look at the *arei miklat*. One way is to call them cities of exile; but another way is to call them cities of refuge. These cities were literally places of refuge since if the criminal did not run to them, then the relative of the victim could legally kill him. So the city physically protected the criminal.

However, the city was also a refuge for another reason. The city was administered by the tribe of Levi. The Levi'im were spiritual leaders and teachers of Torah. They lived in close proximity with the criminals and taught them Torah. So the city was a *spiritual* refuge.

Another interesting aspect of the *arei miklat* was that the criminal would go free upon the death of the *kohein gadol*, the high priest. The Talmud, tractate Makkot (11a), teaches that as a consequence of this law the mother of the *kohein gadol* was concerned that the prisoners might hope and pray for the death of her son. "Therefore the *kohein gadol*'s mother would bring gifts of food and clothing to the killers living in the refuge cities, so they would not pray that her son should die!"

Was the mother of the *kohein gadol* really trying to bribe these prisoners? Wouldn't they prefer freedom from exile to a meal every now and then?

Here, too, we see the concept of city of refuge, rather than exile. The mother of the *kohein gadol* was expressing love and care for the killers in the hopes that she could turn them from killers into caring people. If she taught them to care then maybe they would not desire the death of her son. Maybe they would learn to love.

I once met a man who was sergeant major for the US Marine Corps. In his capacity as sergeant major he often was the chief drill instructor for the entire base and then for the entire Marines, and then sergeant major for NATO.

The Marines are known for being the toughest people around. So I asked him, "When you line your recruits up for the first time and you want to whip them into shape, what do you say to them? Do you put the fear of God into them?"

He said: "Just the opposite! The first thing I tell them is a message that I learned from a rabbi, 'You must love yourself completely, so that you can love others adequately.'"

This is the message that the Levi'im and the mother of the *kohein gadol* were teaching their criminals. They were teaching them that even though they had committed a crime they were still loved by God. If these criminals realized how much God loved them then they wouldn't give up on themselves. Believing that God created you for a great reason is the first step toward changing your ways. In short: the Levi'im were teaching the criminals to love themselves completely so that they can love others adequately.

Society must feel a personal responsibility when it comes to pursuing justice.

A criminal must go through a period of introspection in order to achieve atonement.

We must teach criminals to love themselves completely so that they can love others adequately.

There are no easy answers to the problems facing our society. But the powerful spirituality of the Torah must be our guide and our conscience.

DEVARIM

THE UPLIFTING MESSAGE OF TISHAH B'AV

Devarim

Parashat Devarim is always read right before the saddest day in the Jewish calendar, Tishah b'Av. It is important to understand what the message of this unique day is. What and why are we mourning? And how does this day, which commemorates the destruction of the Temple almost two thousand years ago, still have relevance for us today?

On Tishah b'Av night we read the book of Eikhah (Lamentations). The title of this book comes from the first word of the book: *eikhah*. The word *eikhah* is an exclamatory cry; it means "how." And while that is its literal meaning, depending on the context in which it appears it can carry with it entirely different meanings. Let's compare the way two different prophets used this word *eikhah*.

First, in parashat Devarim Moshe recounts how at Sinai he faced the reality that the Jewish people had grown too large for him to rule alone. This reality was astonishing: just a short time before, the Jewish people were slaves to Pharaoh in Egypt, and now from out of nowhere Moshe sees a nation that is large and great. And the nation was not only large in numbers, but also in their spiritual status. It was a nation about to reach the highest spiritual levels in receiving the Torah at Sinai.

Overwhelmed by the development of his dream so fast and so successfully, Moshe cries out to the Jewish people, "*Eikhah esah levadi tarchakhem, u-masakhem, ve-rivkhem* – How can I bear the burden, responsibility, and conflict that you present?!*" (1:12). In

253

this sense *eikhah* is almost a happy term, expressing overwhelming joy and astonishment.

The term *eikhah* is again used by a prophet at the beginning of the work called Eikhah, which is traditionally attributed to Yirmeyahu. Yirmeyahu writes this prophecy after seeing the destruction of Jerusalem. His whole life – the Temple and Jerusalem – has gone up in smoke. Yirmeyahu sees a city that was once a metropolis – a city that stood at the center of the everyday lives of the Jewish people – and is no more. Upon seeing this, he weeps and groans, *"Eikhah yashvah badad ha-ir rabati am* – How does this city, which once was so full of life and had so many people, now lie desolate and abandoned?!"

The same word, *eikhah*, appears in both these contexts: once in reference to the greatest joy with Moshe, and once to greatest grief with Yirmeyahu. The *Duda'ei Reuven*, a work authored by Reuven Katz – the chief rabbi of Petach Tikvah in the middle of the twentieth century – discusses in his essay on parashat Devarim the common denominator between these two occurrences.

What binds these two occasions together is they both describe extreme situations. Moshe's situation was an extreme. The people were preparing for Sinai. They were at the high point in their history; their joy and success would never be greater. In contrast, Yirmeyahu's situation was the nadir of Jewish existence. Their whole existence was no more; without the Temple, who knew what would become of Judaism? They had reached an all-time low.

So why is it that our Tanakh chose to use the same term to describe extreme sadness and extreme joy? Would we not think to completely disassociate these two ideas? Why are our prophets intentionally drawing them close together?

The idea is – and this is the central idea of Tishah b'Av – that in our greatest moments of joy, in our greatest moments of success, we must realize that in an instant our lives can turn and descend.

After all, wasn't this what really happened with the destruction of the Beit ha-Mikdash? The Temple was a place full of the finest ornaments, the finest technology. The description of Shlomo's Temple in Sefer Melakhim (I, chapter 7) is intended to show that the Jewish people had built for themselves the most impressive Temple in the entire world. The Jews were on top of the world, materially and spiritually.

And yet, Yirmeyahu witnessed it all literally going up in smoke. It vanished as if it had never been. This is the message of Tishah b'Av: Realize and understand that our glorious achievements, our great successes, nationally and individually, can all vanish in an instant. If the greatest achievement of all could go up in smoke – the Temple – then surely our own achievements, which are much more ephemeral, can disappear into thin air.

This is the sober reality of our lives that Tishah b'Av forces us to focus on. However, Tishah b'Av is called a *moed*, a holiday, which means it also carries an uplifting message. That is because the word *eikhah* teaches us that the reverse is also true.

Moshe used the word *eikhah* to express his overwhelming joy. The joy was like the sadness of Yirmeyahu, which came about in an instant and was built on preceding success. This joy, conversely, was also created in an instant and built on preceding tragedies. The Jewish people moved in almost the blink of an eye from being a tortured, battered, and enslaved people to being an exalted nation – people chosen before God and able to receive the Torah at Sinai.

This is what the word *eikhah* teaches us: that we can move in an instant from the greatest joy to the greatest sadness and from the greatest sadness to the greatest joy. And this is the central message of Tishah b'Av: realize that our lives can change in an instant.

No wonder that Tishah b'Av is sandwiched in the Jewish calendar between the two greatest moments of exhilaration, the two times Moshe received the *luchot* (set of tablets). Just sixty days after the exhilaration of Shavuot, the celebration of Sinai, we are mourning the destruction of the Temple. And nearly sixty days later this is reversed when on Yom Kippur we celebrate the giving of the second *luchot* to Moshe. The message of this calendar is a reminder of how even (or especially) when we feel we are on top we need to recall the potential for sadness, and even in sadness we retain the potential for great joy.

It's a message for all of us to remember on an individual level, that no matter how dark the world may seem, we should prepare ourselves for the possibility of an overflowing of brightness – brightness unimaginable in our darkness.

The same message applies to us on a national level. For example, following the Six-Day War, the mood in Israel was one of exhilaration and invincibility; there was a surety to the belief that now was the time that God was shining His Providence upon us. And just a few years later, that mood of invincibility vanished into a feeling of vulnerability, when Israel's very existence was threatened during the Yom Kippur War. There was that switch from extreme joy to deep concern.

So the observance of Tishah b'Av is a reminder to always place our lives in a spiritual context. Even when things are at their darkest, we have to be alive for the possibility of a new *eikhah*, for the possibility that our deep despair can again turn into great elation and exultation. So that once again, like the prophets before us, we may shout out *eikhah*…this time not in sadness and grief, but in complete and total joy.

DID MOSHE SIN?

Va'etchanan

Moshe Rabbeinu dedicated his life to the children of Israel. He led them out of slavery, he led them through the desert, he faced down rebellions and false accusations, and all he asked for was one thing from Hashem: he wanted to lead the people into the land. *"Va'etchanan el Hashem"* (3:23) – he beseeches God, again and again, to allow him to lead the people and fulfill his dream. But God says no. God does not allow Moshe to fulfill his life in this respect.

It seems unfair and almost cruel. Why does Hashem deny Moshe the fulfillment of his dream of settling the land? This is one of the great questions of the Torah: why does Hashem not allow Moshe to lead the Jewish people into the Land of Israel?

In parashat Chukat we read that Hashem tells Moshe:

> יַעַן לֹא הֶאֱמַנְתֶּם בִּי לְהַקְדִּישֵׁנִי לְעֵינֵי בְּנֵי יִשְׂרָאֵל לָכֵן לֹא תָבִיאוּ אֶת הַקָּהָל הַזֶּה אֶל הָאָרֶץ אֲשֶׁר נָתַתִּי לָהֶם:

> Because you did not believe in Me to sanctify Me in the eyes of the children of Israel, therefore you will not bring this congregation into the land that I shall give to them. (Bamidbar 20:12)

This verse directly follows an incident where Hashem told Moshe to speak to a rock in order to get water. Most commentators understand that the two paragraphs are related and that Moshe's sin occurred in this previous incident.

Here is the setting: At the end of the forty years in the desert, Miriam dies and the well that had nourished the people for the previous forty years dries up. The people being affected by this drought are an entirely new generation. Rashi says (Bamidbar 20:1), "The generation that had sinned in the desert had entirely died out."

This new generation now comes to Moshe and complains about the lack of water. They say to Moshe, "Why did you bring us up to die in the desert?" Moshe then falls on his face, presumably in prayer. Hashem comes to the rescue and tells Moshe what to do. Hashem says, "Gather the people, you and your brother, Aharon, and speak to the rock, and water the congregation and their people" (20:8). But instead Moshe takes his staff and says to the people, "*Shimu na ha-morim* – Listen now, you rebels" (20:10). He then hits the rock twice and water comes flowing out.

What was Moshe's great sin that was so deserving of this harsh punishment of not entering the land? Rashi argues that the sin was that Moshe hit the rock instead of speaking to the rock. If he had only spoken to the rock it would have been a greater sanctification of God's name. We wonder about Rashi's answer. Why is drawing water from a rock by hitting it is any less a miracle than drawing water by speaking to it?

The eleventh-century North African scholar Rabbeinu Channanel says that the sin was that Moshe said, "Should *we* draw water from the rock?" (This opinion is cited by Ramban to Bamidbar 20:8.) This implies that Moshe caused the miracle to happen when really it was *Ha-Kadosh Baruch Hu* who brought about the miracle.

Rambam writes (*Shemonah Perakim* 4) that the sin was that Moshe lost his temper when he said, "Listen now, you rebels." According to Rambam, the sin of losing one's temper is so great it is deserving of this punishment. It was, in Rambam's words, a great *chillul Hashem*, desecration of God.

There are many more approaches but I would like to suggest another path of understanding. Why is it that Moshe did not listen to Hashem? Hashem told him to speak to the rock. Why would he hit it? Moshe never directly disobeyed God, so why did he not listen here?

A very similar incident to this one had happened forty years earlier when the children of Israel first left Egypt. This first incident happened in Midbar Sin and the second incident happened in Midbar Tzin (Shemot 16:1). So the Torah definitely wants us to compare the two stories.

After crossing the sea, that generation too complained about water. But notice the difference in the two accounts. Here is what happened the first time (Shemot 17:5–7): After the people complained to Moshe, he cried out to Hashem. Hashem said, "Pass before the people and take with you the elders of Israel. *Ve-hikita va-tzur* – and you should hit the rock, and then water will flow out." And Moshe did exactly that, and as a result they called the place Masah u-Merivah to remind themselves of the place where they tested Hashem.

The first time Moshe was told to hit the rock. The second time Moshe was told to speak to the rock. The problem was that when Moshe was told to speak to the rock he thought he could hit the rock and it would be just as effective. He thought the two situations were the same.

But they weren't. They might have looked the same and felt the same to Moshe, but forty years later it was a new generation. A new approach and technique were needed. Moshe was sticking with the old approach and didn't hear that God was telling him to do something new. If you look closely at the second incident you will notice that God wasn't telling only Moshe to speak to the rock. The word is *ve-dibartem*, "speak," but in the plural! Moshe was not to do it on his own. He was supposed to do the speaking along with others, perhaps with Aharon, or perhaps as a community with the people.

The first incident ends with a teaching moment. The people named the place Masah u-Merivah: the place where we tested God, the place where we learned our lesson not to test God. Notice that the second time, the place where the incident happens is not named. The teaching moment is lost.

At that point Hashem decrees that Moshe should not enter the land. He was unwilling to adapt as a leader. He was trying to impose his techniques from forty years ago on this new generation. Because he could not adapt at this point in his life, it was time for new ideas and a fresh approach.

We should not look at Moshe's dismissal as a punishment so much as a necessary adaptation to the needs of a new generation and a new environment. At the beginning of Moshe's career he led a revolution and now it was time for him to step aside.

The great leaders and the great communities are the ones that recognize when it is necessary to evolve and adapt. They are the ones that are constantly retooling themselves and are creative enough to try new ideas and new approaches. I once read a biography of Rabbi Joseph Soloveitchik by Rabbi Aaron Rakeffet-Rothkoff, and that helped me better understand why he was such a successful leader. He had this attribute of creativity and willingness to adapt, and this is one of the qualities that made him such a great leader.

Rabbi Soloveitchik was born in Pruzhana, Poland, and spent the formative years of his youth growing up in Khaslavichy, Belarus. These are hardly metropolises, and they are very distant from American culture. Yet, this rabbi understood, in a way similar to the Lubavitcher Rebbe and very few others, that the United States was not Poland or Russia. In order for the Jewish community to thrive, new methods were needed.

He was able to recognize this and adapt to it, and that is what made him special. Just as an example, in 1937 he founded the Maimonides School in Boston. It began with six students and it often met in his home. When he started it, most of the people of Boston opposed it because they felt it was a return to the ghetto. But soon the idea of Jewish day schools became commonplace and the norm. Even when he was a great *rosh yeshivah* he would still make the time to visit the nursery and speak in the classrooms on Friday mornings. He understood that this school was necessary to the future of the Jewish people in America.

Years later he wrote: "When a new idea is thrust upon the world, it generally passes through three stages. First, it is scorned, then it is fought, and finally it is accepted as self-evident. The scorn has long since been overcome. The struggle for survival has been gloriously won, and the concept of the Hebrew Day School as a vital force on the American Jewish scene has become dramatically self-evident."[1]

As another example, he ordained over two thousand rabbis (an overwhelming number) and sent them around America. He recognized that American society needed a new type of rabbi; it needed a more modern rabbi who could relate to the "customs of America."

The willingness to always create new ideas and not transplant old ideas into a forced situation is what is necessary to make a great community. That entrepreneurial spirit is what made America great. American society loves entrepreneurs and encourages such activity. This creativity is the key to success.

As a community this should be our motto: We are Orthodox and we strictly keep halakhah and follow tradition. And yet at the same time we need to encourage as many ideas as possible. We need to be willing to change and willing to adapt. And we need to recognize when the age of hitting the rock has passed and when it is the time to speak.

1. Aaron Rakeffet-Rothkoff, *The Rav: The World of Rabbi Joseph B. Soloveitchik*, vol. 1 (Hoboken, NJ: KTAV, 1999), 28.

THE FRAGILE RELATIONSHIP
Eikev

How many days was Moshe up on Mount Sinai? Parashat Eikev teaches that Moshe was up on Mount Sinai for a total of 120 days.

First, he goes up the mountain right after the Ten Commandments were given. The verse states:

וָאֵשֵׁב בָּהָר אַרְבָּעִים יוֹם וְאַרְבָּעִים לַיְלָה לֶחֶם לֹא אָכַלְתִּי וּמַיִם לֹא שָׁתִיתִי:

> And I dwelt on the mountain for forty days and forty nights; I did not eat bread nor did I drink water. (Devarim 9:9)

Moshe comes down forty days later, on the seventeenth of Tamuz. On that day, he sees the children of Israel worshiping the golden calf and he immediately breaks the tablets.

The very next day – the eighteenth of Tamuz – Moshe goes up the mountain to plead with Hashem not to kill the Jewish people (Rashi, 9:18). We see this from a verse in our portion that states:

וָאֶתְנַפַּל לִפְנֵי ה' כָּרִאשׁנָה אַרְבָּעִים יוֹם וְאַרְבָּעִים לַיְלָה לֶחֶם לֹא אָכַלְתִּי וּמַיִם לֹא שָׁתִיתִי....

> And I fell down before God like the first time for forty days and forty nights; I did not eat bread or drink water.... (Devarim 9:18)

We know that this second set of forty days was also on a mountain top because of a verse in Shemot right after the story of the golden calf (32:30), which states: "And it was the next day and Moshe

262

said, 'You have sinned a great sin, and *I will go up* to Hashem and perhaps I will achieve atonement for your sin.'"

After this second set of forty days Moshe again comes down from the mountain. The date is the twenty-ninth of Av. The next day is Rosh Chodesh Elul, and this time Hashem tells him:

פְּסָל לְךָ שְׁנֵי לוּחֹת אֲבָנִים כָּרִאשֹׁנִים וַעֲלֵה אֵלַי הָהָרָה וְעָשִׂיתָ לְךָ
אֲרוֹן עֵץ:

Engrave for yourself two tablets of stone just like the first ones, and ascend to Me up the mountain and make for yourself an ark of wood. (Devarim 10:1)

Again Moshe goes up and down the mountain but this time it is different. This time the forty days end on Yom Kippur and the Jewish people are forgiven for their sin, as Hashem says to Moshe, "*Salachti kidvarekha* – I have forgiven, according to your words." (This is the language Rashi uses and it reflects Bamidbar 14:20.)

This is the chronology of the events as explained by Rashi (9:18). He writes that the first forty days were *be-ratzon*, in a manner pleasing to Hashem, and the last forty days were also *be-ratzon* and with *simchah*, great joy. However, the middle forty days were *be-ka'as*, "in anger." Hashem did not even forgive the Jewish people until Moshe went up the mountain for the third time on Rosh Chodesh Elul.

Why is that the case? Why did Hashem keep Moshe up on the mountain for those middle forty days and not forgive the Jewish people?

It seems that the middle forty days were a necessary prelude to the final forgiveness of the last forty days. In the middle forty days, Hashem was still angry with the Jewish people. He had decided not to kill them, but still He had not yet decided to forgive them. It was only after He decided not to kill them that He could totally forgive them.

Before He could forgive, He had to decide not to kill.

Obviously, God could have forgiven instantly, but through His behavior He was teaching us a very important lesson: in order to develop a positive relationship one needs to work very hard over an extended period of time. We can't just instantaneously expect a perfect relationship; it takes effort. Hashem wanted to teach us that we just can't transition into a perfect relationship of joy with God – especially if we are coming from a place of real anger and disappointment. A relationship of pure joy takes time and effort.

The Tanakh uses different metaphors to help us understand our relationship with God. But perhaps the most powerful imagery in the Bible of an intimate relationship with God is the spousal relationship and spousal love.

I feel like I have some insight into spousal love, since on August 6, 2011, Rhanni and I celebrated our fifteenth wedding anniversary. I am profoundly grateful to Hashem for the wonderful blessing of these fifteen years. The Torah way of life views marriage as something greater than a mere union of a man and a woman. Marriage is such an important relationship that it is understood as a shared spiritual destiny and is seen as the symbol of how God relates to the Jewish people. When we obey God and listen to Him we are considered His beloved. And when we disobey Him we are considered harlots.

And a relationship in marriage is like a relationship with God in that we can't just snap our fingers and achieve a beautiful relationship with God or with our spouse. It takes time and effort.

The halakhah intentionally divides the marriage ceremony into two distinct ceremonies, which in the time of the Mishnah were often a year apart. First there was an *erusin*, a betrothal that bound the man and the woman to each other but did not permit them to live as husband and wife, and only after that was the *nisuin*, the marriage canopy, which permitted them to live together as husband and wife. Even today we retain both of these parts of the ceremony and we don't go straight to the *nisuin*. There needs to be an *erusin*, followed by a formal break (usually the reading of the

Ketubah), and only then the *nisuin*. This underscores the idea that spousal love requires time to develop and grow.

So our relationship with God is like a spousal relationship in this crucial aspect: it takes time to develop and grow, and the more effort and time we put into it, the greater the relationship will be.

But there is another way in which our relationship with our spouse is like our relationship with God. This way is a little less cheerful.

First, let's return to parashat Eikev. When Moshe goes up the mountain for the third time, he is told to bring with him tablets of stone for Hashem to engrave upon them the second set of Ten Commandments, and he is also commanded to make an ark of wood, an *aron etz*.

This wooden ark requires an explanation. We know that ultimately the tablets would be housed in an ark, but that ark would be made of gold and wood, and not just wood. Furthermore, that ark would be made by Betzalel, the chief artisan of the Mishkan, and not by Moshe. For this reason, Rashi (10:1) adopts the interpretation that the wooden ark that Moshe made was *in addition* to a second ark that Betzalel would make, which would ultimately hold the second set of *luchot* in the Holy of Holies in the Mishkan.

If the second ark is the one that will eventually hold the *luchot*, what is going to happen with this first ark? Rashi explains that this ark would be the ark that went into battle with the Jewish people when they fought their wars. And what would be contained in this ark? The answer is that it would hold the broken set of tablets, as the Midrash says, *"Shivrei ha-luchot hayu sham"* (see Ramban, 10:1).

What is the reason that the wooden ark – or this second ark – containing the broken tablets was the ark that was chosen to go into battle with the Jewish people?

The reason for this is that when we go into battle we are often confident and even overconfident. We think we are strong – stronger than our enemies; we think we are righteous, much more virtuous than our hated enemies. So we are being reminded as we march out to war that we are not as strong as we think we are, and we are not as righteous as we think we are. We look at the broken tablets in the ark and we remember how we once sinned with the golden calf and how our entire people were almost wiped out on that one day on the seventeenth of Tamuz, and we remember our sins. And when we do that we remember not to be overconfident. We remember to serve God properly and to invest more time and effort in our battle and our mission.

The lesson of the broken tablets coming out to battle with us is that we live a fragile existence and we should not be overconfident.

Of course, this is not true just for going out to an actual battle, but it is true for all the battles we face in our lives. We must always have a picture of the broken tablets in mind. And it is not true only of "battles"; it is also true of missions that we have; things we work for our whole lives can never be taken for granted. They are all fragile.

Here, too, we see the metaphor of a marriage. Marriage is an amazing relationship; it is so passionate and enriching and beautiful, but it is fragile.

It is fragile for two reasons. First, no matter how many years a couple is together a marriage can always be severed and end in divorce. Second, a marriage is naturally fragile, as the normal order of the world is that a marriage relationship will end. When a spouse dies, the marriage is severed. Unlike other faiths, we don't believe you remain married after death.

A marriage is different than a sibling relationship or a parent-child relationship. Those relationships will always endure beyond fights or deaths. A parent who doesn't talk with his child is still his parent. But a spousal relationship can be terminated. It is naturally fragile.

Indeed, the Midrash even compares Moshe's breaking of the tablets to the ripping up of a *ketubah* in order to terminate a marriage (Shemot Rabbah 43:1). This is precisely why we always need to remember the broken set of tablets: to remind us to always work on our relationships, on improving them and strengthening them. Our relationship with God is like our relationship with our spouse and on a lesser level with all our significant interpersonal relationships. Our relationships are fragile and they need to be strengthened at all times. We must constantly work to improve them or else we run the risk of them disintegrating in a moment.

The month of Elul, coming as it does right before Rosh Hashanah, is the time of the year to start recognizing that we must improve our eternally fragile relationship with God. It can take an entire year to build up that relationship, but we can destroy it in a second. So we must be vigilant and guard the relationship closely. Rosh Chodesh Elul is the first step in marking our path toward Yom Kippur. Historically, Rosh Chodesh Elul was the first day of Moshe's final forty days up the mountain. It was the final push toward atonement for our people by means of a pure connection with to God.

Parashat Eikev often intersects with the month of Elul. Elul is the time of the year to improve all our relationships – our relationships with each other, our relationship with our spouse, and most importantly (for it is at the core of all our relationships) our relationship with God.

I AM FOR MY BELOVED

Re'eih

"*Ani le-dodi ve-dodi li* – I am for my beloved and my beloved is for me" (Shir ha-Shirim 6:3). The rabbis connect the first letters of this verse to spell the month Elul, the month of intense repentance leading up to Rosh Hashanah. But it is so much more than just an acrostic. The verse relates to a feeling that we have as the month of Elul comes upon us.

I remember very vividly the first time I went away from home to study in yeshivah. It was the first night of Elul. I had gone to sleep and suddenly I was awoken in the middle of the night by what seemed to be endless shofar blasts. I had no idea what was going on. I quickly got dressed and ran to the *beit midrash* to discover that Sephardic Jews were waking in the middle of the night to recite *selichot* prayers and blast the Shofar.

As an Ashkenazic Jew I was not familiar with this custom. The midnight devotion of the Sephardic Jews demonstrates the excitement and anticipation that comes upon us in this season. As soon as Elul begins we start to blast the shofar at the end of every davening. We also add psalm 27 to our morning and evening prayers. And in this psalm we declare, "We want but one thing from you, Hashem: to dwell in the house of the Lord for the length of days, to see the pleasantness of God, and to visit His sanctuary" (Tehillim 27:4).

We can barely wait for Rosh Hashanah and the shofar blowing, so we start earlier. It is an overwhelming excitement.

This is why the rabbis use the phrase "I am for my beloved" to describe Elul. We are like two lovers who have been distant from each other. They have an appointment to meet in a month. For the entire month before they meet, they prepare and eagerly await the moment of reunion. So too, as Elul begins we start preparing for our moment to meet with Hashem on Rosh Hashanah. Our entire focus, our learning, our liturgy, everything, leads us to Rosh Hashanah and Yom Kippur. It is for this reason that it is a custom that the *chazzan* who will lead the congregation in prayers on Rosh Hashanah also davens on the Shabbat that we usher in Rosh Chodesh Elul with a prayer known as *birkat ha-chodesh,* the blessing for the new month. All our energy now turns to the *yamim noraim,* the Days of Awe.

In that spirit, there are three lessons from parashat Re'eih that directly relate to the month of Elul.

First we turn to the opening verse of the parashah:

רְאֵה אָנֹכִי נֹתֵן לִפְנֵיכֶם הַיּוֹם בְּרָכָה וּקְלָלָה:

See, I place before you today blessings and curses.
(Devarim 11:26)

Hashem tells Moshe that when the Jewish people enter the land they should go to the valley near Elon Moreh. Half of the tribes should ascend Mount Gerizim and half should ascend Mount Eval. The tribes on Mount Gerizim will hear the blessings that will fall upon them if they follow God's way, and those on Mount Eval will hear the curses that will be if they reject the commandments.

The message is a fundamental message for us to remember in the month of Elul. We have a choice in life, and it is a simple choice: do we want to follow God's ways or not?

Sometimes we make choices and the consequences are not readily apparent. But in this case they are. Pedagogically, the Jewish people are placed on two separate mountains to show that there is a stark difference between the two choices we make. Each tribe could see the results and the distance between the two choices.

The rabbis say, "If you abandon me for one day, then in the end I will have abandoned you for two days" (tractate Berakhot 14:4; and cited in Rashi, Devarim 11:13). This is not a punishment from God but a measure of how we grow distant from Him. If two people each walk for one day in opposite directions then they are no longer one day apart, but two days apart. This is what being on the mountaintops shows the tribes. You can easily grow more and more distant from Hashem.

For many of us, this is what happens to us during the course of a year. We get caught up in other things that distract us from God. As the year progresses we grow farther and farther away. But then Elul comes and invites us to close that gap and draw closer to God. Elul reminds us to go back to basics. We have two choices in life and we need to make the right choice.

So the first lesson to remember as Elul begins is that we need to *choose* to close the gap with Hashem.

The second lesson is that we must especially *focus* in the month of Elul.

Abrabanel in his commentary to parashat Re'eih points out that the parashah draws a contrast to the way idolaters worship and the way we must worship. Idolaters worship wherever they want and however they want. But we cannot do that.

The Torah says that when it comes to worship, the Jewish people should not just do whatever finds favor in their eyes (12:8), and they should "be careful not to make a sacrifice in whatever place you see" (12:13). The Torah is commanding us that we must focus our worship in accord with the commandments of God. If we are not focused on what God wants from us, in the end we are just worshiping ourselves.

Elul is the time to focus ourselves and to remind ourselves to follow God's direction. The blueprint for this focus is the Torah, and even if we have grown distracted Elul is the moment to channel our attention properly.

Having focus is something that our society especially struggles with. There are so many great ways to waste our time and distract us. Our attention span gets shorter and shorter. It used to be that based upon the time between television commercials, our attention span was fifteen minutes long. Now that YouTube mostly allows videos of only ten minutes in length, our attention span, it seems, is even shorter.

I remember watching athletes prepare for their contests at the Olympics. Before they compete, they completely change their focus. Their expressions change. Their faces grow tense. They close their eyes, change their breathing, and tune out the world. They recognize that the next thirty seconds or three minutes is what they have been working for their whole life. With every ounce of energy in their body, they want to succeed.

This is what the month of Elul is supposed to help us do. It reminds us to focus. It is so easy during the year to get distracted and grow apart from Hashem. We are supposed to repent every day, but how can we do that with all the noise going on in the world?

So Hashem gave us the month of Elul. It is the time to refocus and tune everything out. It is the time to remember that the next thirty days are what we have been working toward in our life.

This leads to a third lesson about how to succeed in the month of Elul.

The Torah warns us in parashat Re'eih not to eat the blood of an animal: "*Rak chazak le-vilti akhol ha-dam* – Only be strong and do not eat the blood" (12:23). Why does the Torah have to tell us: "Be strong"? Of all the temptations to sin that I have encountered in life, the desire to eat blood ranks way down at the bottom. Rashi (12:23) explains that the Torah is teaching us that if the warning against eating blood, which is such an easy commandment to observe, requires enormous vigilance, how much more so do the other mitzvot of the Torah require vigilance.

Elul is the month of vigilance. We naturally let our vigilance down during the year. It is hard to be vigilant for 365 days. But for one month we can be *chazak*. We can be strong and we can grow and succeed.

But the way to succeed is through vigilance about the mitzvot. It is often the case that we attend to our mitzvot in a distracted fashion. In Elul, we should pay closer attention to the commandments; we should perform them with greater intensity and greater scrupulousness. We should set higher bars for ourselves in our devotion to God.

In Elul, we must choose, we must focus, and we must be vigilant.

As a community we add mitzvot in the month of Elul. We add the shofar and we add a psalm. On an individual level, if we want to succeed we need to do this as well. If there are commandments we have been lax in, now is the time to rise. Whether it be prayer, study, charity, or interpersonal behavior, Elul demands more.

Sometimes people think of the shofar as a siren. It is a warning for us to wake up before we miss the whole season of repentance. But I prefer to think of it as a musical instrument – God's musical instrument. Hashem is serenading and inviting us to come closer and closer to Him. He is calling us to His chamber. He is telling us that He loves us and is inviting us to love Him back. Will we allow ourselves to listen to His call?

THE FIVE-MINUTE SERMON
Shoftim

Parashat Shoftim at its core is about the Torah's approach to a human justice system. It teaches us about the need to establish courts, the need for us to listen to our judges, our priests (*kohanim*), our king, and our witnesses. It also establishes the concept of a city of refuge where we must go in order to escape retribution from a blood avenger.

If one kills by accident, without intent, then one runs to an *ir miklat*, a city of refuge, where he is protected from the family of the deceased, who would otherwise have an obligation to bring him to justice.

The city of refuge is administered by Levi'im, and this ensures that the city is not just a physical protection but also a spiritual refuge. The Torah says that the purpose of the city is to provide a safe haven to prevent innocent blood from being spilled (Devarim 19:10), and this is also true as it relates to a spiritual refuge. The *ir miklat* served to keep the person on the right spiritual path before he did an even worse sin. It is for this reason that the Talmud, tractate Makkot (10a), teaches that the rabbi of the person who was forced to run to the *ir miklat* was required to run there with him as well.

Today we no longer have an *ir miklat*. So we must look for our spiritual refuge in other places. I personally look at the month of Elul and the High Holidays as a spiritual refuge to protect us from doing worse sins and to remind us to remain focused lest we forget our true purpose in this world.

It is so easy to get lost in the status quo and to forget about our ultimate purpose in this world and how little time we have to accomplish it.

I will never forget how I was once officiating at a service in a cemetery. After we placed the coffin in the ground and finished the service, we began to walk out of the cemetery. I was still moved by the moment and engrossed in my own thoughts. A butterfly caught my eye, and I started watching it. I followed it as it fluttered this way and that way, seemingly without purpose. As I continued watching it, it flew right near a tombstone. I looked down at the tombstone and something struck me as odd. I wasn't sure what it was, but something was off. Then it hit me like a thunderbolt. I looked at the words on the tombstone and I nearly fainted. In big letters staring me straight in the face was the word *Herzfeld*. I was at Herzfeld's plot. I was standing at Herzfeld's grave. Herzfeld is not an exceedingly rare name, but it is not that common either. It was quite shocking to see my name on the tombstone.

My first thought was, "That could be me. That could be my tombstone." But then I quickly corrected my wishful thinking. "That *will* be me. That will certainly be me."

The Mishnah (Pirkei Avot 2:10) teaches: "*Shuv yom echad lifnei mitatekha* – Repent one day before you die." Of course one should repent one day before one dies. Who wouldn't? But as the students asked their rebbe, Rabbi Eliezer: "Does a person really know when exactly he will die?" Rabbi Eliezer answered his students, "Certainly one should repent every day, lest he die tomorrow" (recorded in *Avot de-Rebbe Natan* 15:4).

What do we mean by the word *repent*? It means to constantly examine ourselves and prepare ourselves for God. To ask ourselves every day, "Is this the way we want to go to meet our Maker? Do we have anything left to do or take care of? Do we have any habits to change?"

The sage R. Yochanan ben Zakkai described this phenomenon with a parable in the Talmud (Shabbat 153a). There was a king who invited his servants to a meal with him but he did not tell them when the meal would be. The smart servants prepared themselves every day for the meal. They wore nice clothing and sat at the king's entrance and declared, "Is there anything beyond the king's capabilities?" The foolish ones ignored the invitation and returned to their everyday labors. Suddenly, the king called them all to the meal. The smart ones entered in a clean state and dressed properly, while the foolish ones entered all dirty.

Do we want to meet our Maker while we are dirty or clean?

Shoftim always coincides with the month of Elul. This is the most appropriate time to try to change our direction. Change is never easy. We allow ourselves to get into a routine, into bad habits. It is difficult to overcome our current state. But if we will ever change for the better, then this is the easiest time to do it.

The reason this time of year is considered appropriate for change is because historically this is the moment when God forgave us. After *bnei Yisrael* had sinned with the golden calf and Moshe broke the Ten Commandments, Moshe then went up Mount Sinai for a second time to ask for forgiveness for his people. The day Moshe went up the mountain was the first day of the month of Elul. Forty days later, on Yom Kippur, *bnei Yisrael* were forgiven.

From this we learn that the month of Elul is the time for each of us to start the climb up our own mountains. Now is the time for all of us to ascend so that we too can be forgiven.

The High Holidays have always been my favorite time of the year. But my love for them has increased dramatically ever since I became a rabbi. Once I became a rabbi I started preparing much more for the holidays. I reviewed the liturgy in advance. I read more books about High Holiday themes. I tried to internalize more. In doing so, when the High Holidays finally came, I found them to be even more spiritually uplifting.

If we prepare for the High Holidays, then we will be blessed by the power of the days. But if we ignore them, then of course they will have no impact upon us. I recommend that everyone prepare thoroughly: read a book about repentance or Rosh Hashanah, review the liturgy, or attend a class in your synagogue or community. We can achieve change and holiness on the High Holidays only through preparation.

The very word Elul teaches us how best to make these preparations. The preparations should not be a labor of pain, but a labor of love. Our rabbis explain that the month of Elul is an abbreviation of "*Ani le-dodi ve-dodi li* – I am for my beloved and my beloved is for me" (Shir ha-Shirim 6:3). God is our beloved and we are His. Have you ever heard of lovers in which there was only a one-way relationship? Where only one person beseeched and loved, while the other one was indifferent? It can't work. So, too, our relationship with God. God does love us and He will always love us. But during this month we must remind ourselves to love Him.

Perhaps this is the reason why we blast the shofar every morning in the month of Elul. The shofar is many things. It is a siren, a wake-up call. And it is a prayer. But it can also be the music of a beloved. It is called *kol shofar*, the sound of a shofar. The word *kol* also appears in the context of lovers, as in, "*kol dodi dofek* – the sound of my beloved is knocking" (Shir ha-Shirim 5:2).

Every day in the month of Elul we are calling out to God like a lover calls to their beloved. God, we love You. God, we want to serve You. God, we want to feel Your presence. And when we call, we do it with urgency. We do it with the urgency of a lover, who feels their beloved is slipping away, who feels that they are running out of time. We can reunite with God. But we can also lose the moment. The choice is ours. We have the ability to make a choice. But we must all make the right choice.

This is the month of Elul. It is a reminder to choose correctly; to change before it is too late; to choose to ascend the mountain; to choose God.

In 1986, a rabbi in Tampa delivered a sermon about the explosion of the Space Shuttle *Challenger*.[1] The rabbi pointed out that even after the *Challenger* blew up, the astronauts did not die right away. It was proven that their actual death only came when their capsule hit the water. He said, "For perhaps as much as five minutes, the astronauts were alive and conscious and yet knew that death was certain."

He then went on to ask his congregation to consider the question: "What would you do if you had five minutes to live?" He challenged his congregation to live their lives as though they had five minutes left. Not in a cynical way – saying "What's the point?" – but in a spiritual way, a way that will help us channel our direction. He spoke about serving God in those five minutes and expressing our love for our loved ones.

This rabbi's name was Rabbi Kenneth Berger. He used to be a rabbi right here in Greenbelt, Maryland, before moving to Tampa. Less than three years later, the rabbi was with his wife and two of his children on United Airlines flight 232 to Philadelphia. After the engines failed, the flight was forced to make an emergency landing. In the landing 185 out of 285 passengers were killed, including Rabbi Berger and his wife, Aviva. During those moments as the plane was descending rapidly to an uncertain fate, Rabbi Berger probably thought about his own sermon.

Three years earlier, he had had the foresight to remind himself that life is not forever and that he only had five minutes left. He was lucky enough to understand the lesson of "Repent one day before you die."

Elul is the time for all of us to do *teshuvah*, to begin the process of returning to Hashem. Maybe we have a month until the "Day of Judgment," but maybe we have only one day; and maybe we have only one hour.

---

1. This sermon was shown to me by Phil Lehman.

Whenever the moment comes, if we are not prepared for it, then it will feel sudden.

We might not realize it yet, but we all only have five minutes left. The clock is ticking....

THE TORAH'S ATTITUDE
TOWARD BEHAVIOR IN WAR
Ki Teitzei

Parashat Ki Teitzei begins with a law that reflects the barbaric aspects of war. We are told of a case of a soldier who goes out to war, and in the process of winning this war he captures a beautiful woman and takes her home to be his wife. The Torah commands the soldier to shave this woman's head, let her fingernails grow long, and let her remain in the house crying for an entire month. Only then can the soldier marry this woman (21:10–14).

This law is very much a product of ancient society where people were routinely taken as slaves during war. The Torah is speaking to such a society. Rather than outlaw the practice, which probably would never have been accepted, the Torah chooses instead to limit it through legislation. The Torah wishes to control the manner in which the Jewish soldiers treated their prisoners.

What is the reason for these strange laws associated with the prisoner? Why does this woman captive grow her nails, shave her head, and sit there crying for an entire month?

Here are three distinct approaches to this question. Rashi (21:11) writes that the Torah is recognizing the evil inclinations of men. The Torah understands that ancient soldiers in the heat of battle cannot be told not to take captives. It is a prohibition that would be ignored. Instead the Torah tries to mitigate the desires of the soldier and cause the captive woman to be repulsive to him. She shaves her head and grows her nails long, so that she will appear disgusting to her captor. It's true the Torah allows the soldier to capture her. But before the soldier can marry her as a wife, the

Torah wants to certify that this soldier is marrying her despite the fact that she appears ugly and repulsive to him.

Rashi is stating that the Torah recognizes the weak inclinations of man, and therefore adds laws to this common ancient practice to combat these weaknesses.

On the other hand, Ramban (21:11) offers an entirely different approach. In fact, Ramban's approach is quite shocking. The reason why this woman captive grows her nails long, shaves her head, and cries for a month, he explains, is because she is in terrible mourning. She is in mourning because she is being forcibly converted to Judaism, forcibly taken from her homeland and thrust upon another people.

Ramban's position troubles me on a moral level because he is stating that the Torah allows the soldier to forcibly convert this woman to Judaism. That concept of forcing our religion upon someone else bothers me a great deal. Yet, within Ramban's approach there is also great mercy, for Ramban is also saying that the Torah commands the soldier to allow this woman slave the time to grieve, the time to mourn her family. Moreover, not only is she allowed the time to grieve, but the soldier must watch her for a month. He must watch her crying and realize what he did to her life. How he destroyed her entire life because he desired to take her home with him. And only after watching all that, can he decide to marry her.

Ramban's position has elements of both mercy and harshness. Harshness in that the woman might be forcibly converted and forced to marry without consent, but mercy in the fact that Torah forces the soldier to directly confront what he is doing to this woman.

Rambam (Hilkhot Melakhim 8:1–7) raises a third approach. Although the Torah does allow an initial sexual encounter while the soldier is in the battlefield, Rambam argues that the period of thirty days granted to this woman is to allow her the time to decide if she wants to convert. For, according to Rambam, she is under no circumstances allowed to be forcibly converted, rather her captor can only attempt to convince her of the truth of the Jewish religion. But if at the end of the thirty days, the woman decides that she does not wish to accept Judaism, then not only can she not be forcibly converted, but she must not even be sold or treated as a slave. In fact, she must be set free.

Although the entire law is difficult to understand, from a liberal, modern perspective Rambam's approach is certainly the most appealing. The Torah recognizes that a soldier wishes to conquer a foreign woman, and rather than letting him have free reign, the Torah allows him a thirty-day cooling-off period. The soldier has thirty days to convince her, or else she returns to her homeland.

So we have seen three positions: Rashi, who argues that the Torah is trying to wrestle with the basest instincts of soldiers; Ramban, who contends that the woman can be forcibly converted, but the Torah wants the soldier to witness what he is doing to her; and Rambam, who suggests that the Torah is acting in a completely merciful way out of respect for the independence of this captured woman.

While all of these positions have a lot of power, it is the position of Rambam that speaks most strongly to me today. And it's also the position that fits in best within the context of the entire parashah. While the parashah begins with this passage of the captured woman, it ends with the battle with Amalek, where the Jewish people are commanded to eternally wipe out the memory of Amalek.

What was the terrible sin of Amalek? So they attacked the Jews.... Perhaps they even had a right to attack the Jews. After all, Amalek was a tribe living in the desert, where resources are scarce and valuable. Suddenly, the Jews appeared from out of nowhere and began utilizing the same limited resources as the Amalekites. So maybe Amalek was justified in attacking them.

The eternal crime of Amalek was that they attacked *"ha-necheshalim acharekha* – the weak ones who were lagging behind you" (25:18). The great sin of Amalek was they attacked the weak and defenseless; they attacked people who posed no threat at all to them physically.

This sin of Amalek contrasts starkly with the Torah's approach to the captive woman. The captive woman is treated in such a way as to force her captors to see her as a person, to realize what they are doing to her.

The history of commentary on the biblical teaching of the captive woman – whether it is Rashi's, Ramban's, or Rambam's approach – shows the great sensitivity that the Torah teaches we must have to those rendered defenseless by the horrors of war.

The Torah is teaching us that even within war, there is a moral way to conduct ourselves. War is obviously not an ideal situation, and we are always going to be in morally challenging situations. Still, the Torah is commanding us, within reason, to be sensitive to the defenseless and the weak, to be careful about not oppressing them, and to always be conscious of the moral aspect to the war we are waging.

Although the law of the captive woman does not represent an ideal world, neither does war. It is a violent, horrible, but sometime necessary part of life. As Jews, we should be proud of our long tradition of conducting ourselves in a moral manner when faced with the horrors of war. And we as Jews should be equally proud of the way the Israeli army is conducting itself today. Here is an example of what I mean.

Matanya Robinson was the son of dear friends of mine. Matanya died at the age of twenty-one in April, 2002, while his unit of the Israeli Defense Forces was going door to door in Jenin searching for terrorists. One of the reasons Matanya died was because the Israeli army made a policy decision to risk the lives of their own soldiers in searching for terrorists rather than to merely bomb from the air the building it thought the terrorists were hiding in. The reason for this policy was so as not to unnecessarily risk the lives of Palestinian civilians.

The Israeli policy of singling out individual terrorists for attack – even when it places their own soldiers at greater risk – strikes me as a difficult policy, but a necessary one. It is the most moral approach to a terrible situation. We regard every life as precious; we mourn before Pesach for the Egyptians whose lives were lost while Jews were saved. But terrorists who have already committed horrible murders must be held accountable for the horrors that they are routinely inflicting. The Israeli policy recognizes the need to catch the terrorists and balances it with the need to protect civilian life.

Israel's response to this from a moral perspective far outshines the normal response of the rest of the world.

As Jews living in America, we should be proud that our brothers and sisters in the Israeli army are continuing the tradition taught by the Torah with respect to the captive woman: of waging our wars with great decency and great morality.

THE JOY OF SELICHOT

Ki Tavo

If we would have been living in Russia or Poland two hundred years ago, we could have expected the following scenario to happen on the Saturday night before Rosh Hashanah. After Shabbat we would have gone to sleep and then a few minutes before midnight we would have heard three knocks on our door. The town crier would have shouted in our window: "*Uru na*, wake up, *hitorreru na*, awaken, *kumu na*, arise, *la'avodat ha-Borei*, to serve the Creator." And everyone would then quickly arise for Selichot prayers – men, women, and children.[1]

We are not living in Russia in the year 1800. But I always tell everyone in my shul: I give you fair warning – today, instead of a town crier, I have a cell phone and text messaging!

Selichot are penitential prayers that we begin in the middle of the night, on the first Saturday night that is at least four days prior to Rosh Hashanah. In this prayer service we ask God to hear our prayers and have mercy upon us. We beg Hashem over and over again for forgiveness.

Many of the Selichot prayers are difficult for us to understand because we are not used to some of the words and also because each day has at least one specific poem or *piyyut* added to the service. Since the *piyyut* is poetry, it requires heavy analysis for proper understanding. But the central part of Selichot is easy to understand. It is where we continually ask Hashem to use His

---

1. See Shai Agnon, ed., *Yamim Noraim* (Tel Aviv: Schocken, 1998), 38. Also published in English as *Days of Awe*.

thirteen attributes of mercy when judging us. The theme of Selichot is asking God to hear our prayers and forgive us.

The minimum of at least four days of penitential prayers corresponds to the number of days one must observe an animal designated for sacrifice before offering it on the altar. An animal must be watched for four days to make sure it does not have a *mum*, or a disqualifying blemish. So, too, we must watch ourselves for a minimum of four days before we come to Hashem in prayer.[2]

There are two reasons why we always start Selichot on a Saturday night. One reason is practical. We want to standardize our liturgy so people do not get confused and for this reason we always begin on a Saturday night.[3]

A second reason is recorded in the work *Leket Yosher*, a fifteenth-century Austrian work written by R. Yosef ben Moshe. According to the *Leket Yosher*, we start Selichot on a Saturday night because it is close to Shabbat. On Shabbat people have off from work and thus have more time to engage in Torah study. Thus on Saturday night the people rejoice from having studied Torah all day and also from the general delight of the Shabbat.[4] And the rabbis teach in the Talmud, tractate Shabbat (30b), that the Divine Presence will only rest upon us when we have *simchah*, rejoicing. "Thus it is most appropriate to pray with *simchah shel mitzvah*, the rejoicing of the mitzvah."

At first glance, this idea is counterintuitive. Usually when we ask for forgiveness from a person we express contrition, not overwhelming joy. But when we ask forgiveness from Hashem we are joyous because we know that He will grant it. The *Leket Yosher* teaches us that when it comes to the penitential prayers of Selichot, the key to their success is reciting them with joy. The teaching is that we need joy in order to bring Hashem's presence upon us. If

---

2. Ibid., 37.

3. Ibid.

4. Ibid., 38.

we are not happy then God does not want to rest upon us. Indeed, we declare in Selichot, "I shall bring them to My holy mountain, and I shall make them *rejoice* in my holy prayer" (Isaiah 56:7).

It is for this reason that in our congregation we always have a small gathering of simple singing known as a *kumzitz* before our Saturday night Selichot service. We want to get in the proper framework of joy and gladness, so that we can genuinely recite the *piyyut* that night, "*lishmoah el ha-rinah* – to hear the sounds of our joyous song."

The necessity of joy in serving God appears twice in parashat Ki Tavo, once as a prohibition and once as a charge.

The parashah lists terrible curses that will come upon us as a nation. The curses are so horrific that we wonder what we did wrong to receive this punishment. Says the Torah, we are punished with the curses "because we did not serve God *with rejoicing and a full heart*" (28:47). It is not because we did not serve God that we are punished, but because we did not serve God with rejoicing. If we don't have joy in our hearts when we serve Hashem then we are missing the essence of the prayers, which is to express gratitude to Hashem for all that He does for us.

Such joy based upon gratitude for Hashem is the essential aspect of the *bikurim* ceremony that begins the parashah. We are commanded to take our first fruits, go up to the Temple, and say to Hashem: Thank you for taking us out of Egypt and for bringing us to this land and making us into a great nation (26:1–11). And when we bring up the *bikurim* we are supposed to rejoice, as God commands us, "*Ve-samachta be-khol ha-tov* – You must be happy for all the good that God has given you" (26:11).

So we have to be joyous to truly feel God's presence. How do we attain such joy in our lives? It is not so easy. I know…it is true…you can come and dance and sing before the prayer service. But that is just to prepare us for the prayer service. That is a momentary joy. How do we attain a lasting joy? We can attain a truly lasting joy by making ourselves complete. The purpose of the extra Selichot prayers we recite is supposed to focus us on making ourselves complete.

The Israeli Nobel Prize laureate for literature, Shai Agnon, records a story about a man who came to visit the holy rabbi, Reb Mordechai of Nadvorne. Since it was just before Rosh Hashanah, the visitor asked permission to leave early. The Rebbe said to him: "What is your hurry?"

The visitor replied, "I need to study the prayer book before the holiday."

The Rebbe responded: "The Machzor is exactly the same as last year. You are better off studying yourself instead!"[5]

Ultimately, our rabbis teach us that we make ourselves complete by helping others. In his *Hilkhot Teshuvah* (4:5), Rambam singles out *ba'alei lashon hara*, people who are serial gossipers, as an example of egregious sinners who are denied a place in the World to Come. We cannot expect to be complete in our service of God unless we are sensitive to others. And, more than that, the more we work on helping others in this holy period, the closer we will come to God and the more joyous our prayers will be.

This idea is told beautifully in a short story by the Yiddish author I.L. Peretz, called "If Not Higher."[6] Even if you are familiar with this story, it is worth reviewing it again.

> Every year on Friday morning, at the time of Selichot, the Rebbe of Nemirov would vanish. No one knew where he was.
>
> The Chassidim believed he was surely in heaven taking care of his important business before the Days of Awe. The Rebbe was surely up there arguing on behalf of Jews and defending them from Satan.

---

5. Ibid., 47.

6. Peretz died in Warsaw in 1915. The full story can be found at http://www. is.wayne.edu/mnissani/esl/higher.htm.

But there was one Litvak in the town. He was a cynic, and he laughed at the chasidim. The Litvak said that even Moshe did not actually go up to heaven, so how could this Rebbe go up to heaven every Friday.

The Litvak took it upon himself to discover where the Rebbe was. That night, after Ma'ariv, the Litvak snuck into the rabbi's room and hid under the bed. He kept himself awake by reciting passages from the Talmud by heart, all the while waiting to see where the Rebbe would go.

Meanwhile the Rebbe lay awake all night. The Litvak heard him groaning and moaning and sobbing all night. When the Rebbe of Nemirov groaned he was groaning for all of Israel. So much suffering lay in each groan!

Finally, the Litvak heard the beds in the house creak; he heard people running around and leaving for shul. Everyone in the house left, except the Rebbe.

Then the Rebbe got out of bed. He went to the closet and took out peasant clothes: linen trousers, high boots, a coat, a big felt hat, and a long, wide leather belt studded with brass nails. The Rebbe stopped in the kitchen and picked up an axe.

The Litvak followed the Rebbe to a forest that stood on the outskirts of the town.

The Rebbe entered the forest. The Litvak watched as the Rebbe cut down a small tree and chopped it into a bundle of wood. Then the Rebbe made his way back to town.

He stopped at a back street besides a small, broken-down shack and knocked at the window.

"Who is there?" asked a frightened voice. The Litvak recognized it as the voice of a sick Jewish woman.

"I," answered the rabbi in the accent of a peasant.

"What do you want?"

"I have wood to sell, very cheap." And not waiting for the woman's reply, he went into the house.

A sick woman, wrapped in rags, lay on the bed. She complained bitterly, "Buy? How can I buy? Where will a poor widow get money?"

"I'll lend it to you," answered the Rebbe. "It's only six cents."

"And who will kindle the fire?" asked the widow. "Have I the strength to get up? My son is at work."

"I'll kindle the fire," answered the Rebbe.

As the Rebbe put the wood into the oven he recited, in a groan, the first portion of the Selichot.

As he kindled the fire and the wood burned brightly, he recited, more joyously, the second portion of Selichot. When the fire was set, he recited the third portion, and by this time the Rebbe was beaming with joy.

From then on, when another disciple would tell how the rabbi of Nemirov ascended to heaven at the time of the Penitential Prayers, the Litvak always added, "If not higher."

When the time for Selichot comes we too have a chance to go higher. We can do so by completing ourselves through helping others and being sensitive to their needs. And if we can do that, then we can hope to feel the joy of God's presence when we pray.

RETURNING TOGETHER

Nitzavim

One of the highlights of my rabbinate took place on September 14, 2004, when along with a group of nine other rabbis from across the denominations of Judaism I organized a one-day conference called Lishmah (which literally means "for the sake of Hashem"). In the end nearly 1,500 people gathered for Lishmah. It was an intense day of Torah study. The speakers and participants came from the entire spectrum of denominations.

At the time of the conference the idea of gathering across the denominations of Judaism for a day of Torah study was relatively rare in the American Jewish community; now it is common, but then it was something new. So much so that at the time Yeshiva University refused to participate and the *Jewish Press* wrote an editorial criticizing us because the conference will "accord legitimacy to non-Orthodox movements."

The energy in the room that day was overwhelming; the excitement was contagious; the feeling in the air was that we were all at the start of something much larger. Subsequent to that conference similar interdenominational Torah gatherings in America were launched, and I like to think that Lishmah played a small part in inspiring them. Fundamentally, I think that what Lishmah stood for was not just a nice, innocuous day of Torah study but rather something core to the future of our faith.

Parashat Nitzavim contains within it the source for the mitzvah of *teshuvah*, repentance. Says the Torah: "You shall return with all of your hearts" (30:2). The mitzvah of *teshuvah* is often thought of as a very personal mitzvah, one that one does through personal introspection and reflection. It is often assumed to be a mitzvah of personal growth. However, the context of this commandment does not refer to an imperative to return on an individual level. If you read the commandment closely, you will see that it is a commandment on a *national level*.

Pay close attention to the context in which the mitzvah is commanded.

וְהָיָה כִי יָבֹאוּ עָלֶיךָ כָּל הַדְּבָרִים הָאֵלֶּה הַבְּרָכָה וְהַקְּלָלָה אֲשֶׁר נָתַתִּי
לְפָנֶיךָ וַהֲשֵׁבֹתָ אֶל לְבָבֶךָ בְּכָל הַגּוֹיִם אֲשֶׁר הִדִּיחֲךָ ה' אֱלֹקֶיךָ שָׁמָּה:
וְשַׁבְתָּ עַד ה' אֱלֹקֶיךָ וְשָׁמַעְתָּ בְקֹלוֹ....

There will come a time when you shall experience all the words of the blessings and the curses that I have promised to you; you will remember them among all the nations where God has banished you. And you shall return to God and listen to His voice.... (Devarim 30:1–2)

The context of this commandment is very clearly the obligation to return to God. But it is an obligation, first and foremost, upon the nation as a whole. Of course, the individual needs to do *teshuvah* and return, also. But the central obligation exists not for the individual, but for the community as a whole. If we are serious about *teshuvah*, this is the lesson that we need to remember. *Teshuvah* is something that should be done together by the whole community. The source of the commandment requires a communal response.

It's no accident that the words of this commandment, from parashat Nitzavim, make up the central element of the *tefillah la-medinah*, prayer for the welfare of the State of Israel. Every week we say, "If members of your people are cast out to the corners of the earth, from the farthest corners, God will gather them in."

Why are these words, which come from the commandment to repent, placed in the *tefillah la-medinah*? There is recognition that when we are returning, the return has to cast a wide net. The return can't come from only a portion of the Jewish people; it has to include the whole of the Jewish people. A personal *teshuvah* or even a local, communal *teshuvah* is important. But if that becomes the goal, then it misses the entire essence of the mitzvah. The mitzvah is for everyone to return together.

Just like there can be no communal redemption without there first being a personal redemption, so too there cannot be a true personal redemption unless it is made in the context of a complete communal redemption.

In these days, when Jews are so divided, how can we even begin to think of returning together? How could reform Jews return with Orthodox Jews? What would the minyan look like? Who would cater the Kiddush after davening? There seems to be nothing that we can agree upon.

A member of the board of a non-Orthodox school told me that his school was once in desperate need of space. They approached an Orthodox day school, which they noticed had excess space, and asked if temporarily they could share space. They didn't want to share the schools, just the space. The Orthodox school responded: "Our kids wear tzitzit, yours don't. We don't want our kids near yours."

That's an example of an approach that focuses on what divides us. Sure there are divisions, even very significant ones. We can choose to focus on those divisions. But if we continue to do that, we are going down a road of becoming a separate people.

Instead, what we should be doing is focusing not on what divides us, but on what unites us. What unites us today is the study of Torah. We all share a common library – the Torah. We all value the importance of studying the library. We don't always agree on the way to interpret those texts, but we can at least study those texts together. As one of the organizers of the Lishmah conference, Eliyahu Stern, told me: "If prayer is the way that Jews speak to God, then the study of Torah is the way Jews speak to each other."

Torah is called "light." Perhaps Torah is called light because like light, Torah unifies. Torah, like light, is something that everyone is drawn to. But light doesn't only unify. When light reflects back on you it merges with the uniqueness of each individual. When light shines on you it is absorbed in each person differently. Light unifies, but it also shines on us in a way that gives us more and more unique qualities.

Lishmah was founded by a group of rabbis, and we met every other week for a year. Those meetings had a big impact on me and were themselves an inspiring experience. We not only helped plan a day of intense study, but it was also a growth process for all of us. The common light of Torah did not take away our uniqueness, just the opposite – by illuminating the richness of our own distinct lives, it has made our lives even richer.

Lishmah is about building a community of Jews that surrounds itself around the commonality of the study of Torah. It is about building a community that loves Torah and seeks to impart its energy, values, poetry, and beauty to as many people as possible. It's about building a community that thirsts for Torah so deeply that it seeks out Torah in traditional and in untraditional places. It's about building a community that seeks to engage people on an ongoing basis in the full depth and breadth of Torah study. It's about building a community that recognizes the relevance of serious Torah study to our daily lives. It's about building a community that says, come, study Torah with me, whether or not we agree.

At the time we thought Lishmah was a novel idea. But as I become an older rabbi I realize that we were wrong. The idea of Lishmah was not novel at all. It is found on every page of the Talmud, where rabbis are allowed to suggest radical ideas, which are then discussed and debated. And it is found in the fundamental concept of *teshuvah*, which makes clear that if we don't all return together, then there cannot be a complete return.

CROWD CONTROL
Vayeilekh

I had a rebbe in Israel, an extremely devoted Zionist, who once said something very provocative to us. He admitted that he was bothered when he would see large crowds waving Israeli flags, an image that was common on Yom ha-Atzmaut, Israeli Independence Day. The crowds made him nervous because historically it was often the case that large crowds were a precursor to violence or would turn into powerful, uncontrollable forces.

A mass of people gathered together is an extremely powerful force. For some reason, when people are in a crowd they are swayed into doing things that they would absolutely never do on their own.

Take a benign example. I no longer enjoy going to sporting events. I find it to be spiritually unhelpful, but on rare occasions I will go because my kids will beg me to take them, and I also remember fondly going to such events with my own father.

But the events themselves are spiritually concerning. Some anonymous person on a large screen tells you to cheer, so you cheer. He tells you to get up in the seventh inning and stretch, so you and fifty thousand other people get up and stretch. He tells you to do a chicken dance; you do a chicken dance in front of the entire world. He tells you to make noise, so you yell at the top of your lungs. How many of us would act that way if we weren't in a crowd? It's clear that the power, the force of the crowd, causes us to act differently. It's almost as though we are intoxicated by the crowd. Like after drinking alcohol, we lose partial control of our mental faculties and are overwhelmed into following the decisions of the crowd.

How concerned must we be about getting caught up in a crowd of people?

In this context, there is one mitzvah in the Torah that especially comes to mind. This is the mitzvah of *hakhel*. In parashat Vayeilekh, the Torah says that every seven years, on the festival of Sukkot:

הַקְהֵל אֶת הָעָם הָאֲנָשִׁים וְהַנָּשִׁים וְהַטַּף וְגֵרְךָ אֲשֶׁר בִּשְׁעָרֶיךָ לְמַעַן
יִשְׁמְעוּ וּלְמַעַן יִלְמְדוּ וְיָרְאוּ אֶת ה' אֱלֹקֵיכֶם וְשָׁמְרוּ לַעֲשׂוֹת אֶת כָּל
דִּבְרֵי הַתּוֹרָה הַזֹּאת:

> Gather together men, women, children, and the strangers that live amongst you, so that they will hear and so that they will learn to fear God and to observe all the words of this Torah. (Devarim 31:12)

The mitzvah of *hakhel* is for all the Jewish people to gather together every seven years in order to teach them to better observe the Torah. How does this work? Why if we gather together will we be any better at observing the Torah than we would if we just studied in small, intimate groups?

One approach to this question explains that the mitzvah of *hakhel* is intimately connected with the concept of crowd psychology.

Says Rambam in his great work, the *Moreh Nevuchim* (*Guide for the Perplexed* 3:46), the reason for this mitzvah is: "Such a gathering results in a renewal of the Torah, this being a result of the people being affected by it and the fraternity that comes about among them because of it."

Let's analyze what Rambam said. What is the purpose of this mitzvah? To renew the Torah. How is this purpose accomplished? It's a result of *the people being affected by the fraternity*. Notice what Rambam is arguing – the people will believe in the Torah because when they are gathered together in a large group of people they will be convinced of the correctness of their decision. To me, this sounds like a very dangerous idea: convince the masses through the emotional bonding of large, enthusiastic crowds. This is a dangerous idea because when it is manipulated by people with bad intentions – and this has happened far too frequently in our history – it can be used powerfully as a tool for evil.

In a similar manner, the *Sefer ha-Chinukh* (mitzvah 612) explains that *hakhel* is a little bit like a spiritual press conference. People will ask: What is this large crowd doing gathered here? And the answer will be that the people are gathered to hear the words of the Torah, and as a result people will start discussing the greatness of the Torah.

If we combine these answers, we see that the mitzvah of *hakhel* is cleverly intended to attract large numbers of people, and to cause these people to bond together so that they will accept the Torah.

This approach seems somewhat problematic to me. After all, it's as though we're not allowing people to make up their own minds freely. It's almost as though the Torah is using this manipulative force – this idea of crowds and mobs of people – to convince us that the message of the Torah is correct.

An alternative suggestion of Rabbi Moshe Alshekh, a seventeenth-century scholar, in his commentary *Torat Moshe*, moves away from these psychological theories. He writes that the mitzvah of *hakhel* is given to the Jewish people in order to counteract the sin of the golden calf.

What happened during the sin of the golden calf? Writes the Torah, the people realized that Moshe was slow to descend from the mountain, "and the people gathered around Aharon" (Shemot 32:1). The sin of the golden calf came about because the people gathered, *va-yikahel*. The gathering of people, this enormously strong force, caused the greatest sin in the history of the Jewish people.

Rabbi Moshe Alshekh explains, this sin of the Jewish people, which came about through the gathering of a crowd, needs to be rectified through the gathering of another type of crowd. Therefore the Torah commands us to gather every seven years for the mitzvah of *hakhel*.

The Torah knows the potential evil involved in a mass gathering; the crowd is the massive force that caused the sin of the golden calf. Still the Torah is telling us, just because this force has been used for wicked purposes, doesn't mean that we should be afraid to use it for positive purposes. Grab the force, harness it, use it productively. Gather together every seven years and promote the Torah using these same methods.

Just before we enter the land of Israel, the Torah reminds us: Yes, this dangerous force caused you to sin. But, don't be afraid. Realize that when you are building a land in Israel, you should use these same tactics for your own purposes.

This is the idea behind the mitzvah of *hakhel*. Even today, countries are using these same manipulating maneuvers to control the minds of large numbers of people. Still, the message of the Torah is: don't allow the evil forces of the world to own this powerful weapon. We should seize this same idea – that there is so much power and energy in a gathering of people – and use it to counteract the evil of the world.

WRITE FOR YOURSELVES
THIS SONG

Ha'azinu

In 2010, my sixth-grade daughter got an unusual homework assignment. She needed to find an article in the entertainment section of the newspaper, clip it out, and bring it in to school. When she told me she needed a newspaper, I told her to just go on the Internet and type in the web address. But that wasn't sufficient. The teacher required them to actually purchase a physical newspaper, clip out the article, and bring it in. The teacher wanted them to know how to hold a newspaper in their hands.

I was skeptical about this assignment. Why would a teacher require a student to learn how to use a dying technology? After all, who really thinks that an actual physical, daily newspaper will exist in fifty years in the manner in which it exists today?

Technologies always change. And very soon after the technology has changed we look back at the old technology in amazement at how rudimentary it was. For example, who would ever think of publishing a book on papyrus or parchment today? But when those technologies were introduced they were huge innovations. And soon after the newest technology is replaced, who remembers the old technology at all?

It is a custom to read the book of Kohelet on the holiday of Sukkot, which takes place right after we have read parashat Ha'azinu. These two texts offer powerful ideas about the value of writing things down.

Kohelet makes the point about the futility of outdated technology over and over again in his writings: "*Havel havalim, hakol*

298

havel – Emptiness of emptiness, the world is entirely ephemeral" (Kohelet 1:2). As Kohelet teaches us, "No one will remember the ancient things, nor will anyone remember the newest things that will one day be invented – no one will remember those either" (ibid. 1:11).

Kohelet reminds us of the transience of life. We put our energies into matters that are just a drop in the bucket, that are here today and tomorrow are no longer. Is it any surprise that Kohelet ends his work by giving the following instructions to his child: "Above all, my child, be careful: the making of many books is without limit" (Kohelet 12:12)? He warns his child: Do not waste your time writing pointless books that already fill the world without limit. It's a waste of time. Like a newspaper. Here one day, gone tomorrow.

Kohelet's final instructions to his child are especially jarring when we compare them with the final words of Moshe to *bnei Yisrael* in the Torah. At the end of the Torah, Hashem instructs Moshe, "Now write for yourselves this song" (Devarim 31:19). This is understood by some rabbis to refer to just parashat Ha'azinu, as the song of Ha'azinu immediately follows this command. But other rabbis say that this verse contains the commandment to write the entire Torah. Either way, it is definitely a commandment to write down a portion of the Torah – either just Ha'azinu or else the whole Torah.

But this commandment is expanded even more by later authorities.

There is a classic medieval work called *Sefer ha-Chinukh*. It is an anonymous thirteenth-century work written by a father for a child, where the father instructs his son in all the 613 commandments of the Torah.

The very last commandment (the 613th) listed in *Sefer ha-Chinukh* is the commandment to write a Torah scroll. In contrast to Kohelet, who ends his work by telling his child not to waste his time writing or reading books of fleeting significance, the *Sefer ha-Chinukh* ends his work by expanding the specific mitzvah of writing a Torah. He says: "*Beni*, my child, even though the biblical obligation is only to write a Torah, there is no doubt that [rabbinically because of this commandment] we are commanded to purchase other works that were composed in explanation of the Torah."

Kohelet tells us not to waste our time with pointless books, but Kohelet is only referring to books that are easily outdated. Here one generation, and completely forgotten soon after. In contrast, the Torah ends with Hashem exhorting us to spend our time on *the* book of eternal value. More specifically, we are commanded to write down the Torah, and according to some authorities, this is also a commandment to write and purchase books that are a commentary to the Torah.

The commandment to write a Torah scroll on parchment is thus understood as an eternal commandment for every generation. Regarding the mitzvah of writing a Torah scroll, we are taught in the Talmud (Sanhedrin 21b): "Even though one might have a Torah scroll already from his father, *mitzvah likhtov mi-shelo*, it is a mitzvah to write a Torah for oneself."

This is a unique law. If one inherits an *etrog* or a pair of tefillin, one can simply use that *etrog* or tefillin and fulfill the mitzvah. Not so for a Torah. One cannot fulfill the mitzvah of writing a Torah by merely having it in one's possession. In order to fulfill the mitzvah you need to be directly involved in the process of making the Torah.

Some commentators (like the ninth-century author of *Ba'al Halakhot Gedolot*) understand that this mitzvah is a communal commandment – that every *community* is required to write a new Torah. But most authorities understand that this is a personal commandment. Rambam teaches: "There is a positive commandment for every person to write a Torah for themselves. And if he does not know how to write a Torah, then he may hire others to write it for him" (*Hilkhot Tefillin, Mezuzah, ve-Sefer Torah* 7:1).

But still we wonder... You know, my *bookshelf* is extremely erudite. It is filled with books that I have not yet read. Shouldn't the Torah have commanded us as the last mitzvah to *read the Torah*? Instead, why does it focus on telling us to write or purchase a Torah? What is the reason that the Torah gave us this mitzvah and emphasized it so much by making it the very last mitzvah of the Torah?

There are many reasons suggested.

The *Sefer ha-Chinukh* (mitzvah 613) at first suggests a practical reason. "It is known that people carry out all matters according to the resources that are available to them. Thus the Torah wants every single Jew to have a Torah scroll at hand so that he can read it always and will not need to go to a friend's home in order to read the Torah."

The modern commentator Torah Temimah (in his commentary on Devarim, chapter 31), suggests, "The essential reason for the mitzvah is in order to make as many Torah scrolls in the world as possible, for in this manner we will be glorifying the Torah." And indeed, the Talmud tractate Baba Batra (14a) tells us that the sage Rabbi Ami wrote four hundred Torah scrolls.

Another answer given by *Sefer ha-Chinukh* (mitzvah 613) is especially relevant to a new community. He emphasizes that the reason why it is not sufficient to rely upon the Torah scrolls of previous generations is because each individual in Israel must read from a new Torah scroll: "For we are concerned that people's spirits may become weary if they are only reading from the old scrolls that have been left to them by their parents."

According to this reason, each person should write a new Torah scroll so that the Torah appears fresh to them; so that they are excited and eager and energized by the sight of their Torah; and so that every time they hold the Torah scroll in their hands that they literally wrote or commissioned, their souls will soar with a desire to listen and heed the words of the Torah.

This is true on both a practical and a symbolic level. On a symbolic level it means that we should all try to create our own

Torah; we should all endeavor to fashion our own insights and homilies from the words of the Torah.

But on a practical level it is an injunction to every community to write its own Torah, and it is a reminder for each of us as individuals to participate in the project. When I read this explanation of the *Sefer ha-Chinukh* I immediately thought of our own congregation. Even though the actual mitzvah is assumed by most commentators to be a personal mitzvah, there is clearly a communal mitzvah on a symbolic level as well. I thought of the excitement we all had in our shul after we commissioned a new Torah scroll. Every time the Torah that our generation wrote circles the sanctuary or is carried or read by one of our children, we all feel especially proud. We all listen to that Torah with extra attention and it is an even greater part of our lives.

Finally, there is one other reason for the mitzvah of writing a *sefer Torah*. Rambam teaches: "If one actually writes the Torah with his own hands, then it is as though he literally received it on Mount Sinai" (*Hilkhot Tefillin, Mezuzah, ve-Sefer Torah* 7:1). When we fulfill the mitzvah of writing a *sefer Torah*, it is as though we are all one generation standing with our ancestors and our future descendants. Just as our ancestors stood at Sinai, we too are standing with them. And yet, at the same time, we cannot only rely upon the fact that our ancestors received the Torah. We are reminded that this is the one mitzvah that we cannot inherit. We must perform this mitzvah on our own.

When we perform this mitzvah, we are recognizing that it is both new for every generation and, at the same time, eternal. We recognize that everything is transient, except for the eternality of the Torah!

This is why when we finish reading the Torah we immediately start over. Even though we have read it again and again, we will continue to read it again and again, each time feeling like it is the first time; and each time we will read it as though the Torah was written just for us.

Kohelet is teaching us that the other books of the world are transitory and easily outdated, but the Torah…it is and will always be eternal. And when we participate in the mitzvah of writing the Torah, we too will forever be linked to this eternal tradition, linking us simultaneously to past, present, and future.

OH, HOW I MISS
THE HOLIDAYS!

Ve-Zot ha-Berakhah

Often I have an experience in my week that goes something like this. My two-year-old asks me for a lollipop. He will ask me what feels like several hundred times until I will finally relent and say "fine." Then the second I give him the lollipop, he will look at me with a devilish smile and say, "I want two lollipops." One time I made the mistake of giving him two lollipops and he immediately said, "I want three."

No matter what you give the two-year-old he is never satisfied. He always wants more. I can't blame him because that's the nature of a two-year-old.

But how much different are we grown-ups? Whenever we get something, we want more and more and more. It is never enough.

We need to learn to be satisfied in life without the lollipops. We need to find satisfaction in the spiritual.

But even as it relates to the spiritual, we are always seeking more and more. We are never satisfied. This is one reason why in many communities there is what is known as a *netiah le-chumra*, a tendency towards stringency. People are always seeking more and more mitzvot and supererogatory behavior because they feel like they have not achieved their goal. We feel incomplete and so we seek more, even and especially in the realm of the spiritual.

There is a verse from the book of Kohelet (5:10) that states, "One who loves money will never be satisfied with money." But a teacher of mine, Rabbi Elchanan Adler, who is now a *rosh yeshivah* at Yeshiva University, once quoted a teaching of our rabbis that states: "One who loves mitzvot will never be satisfied with the mitzvot that he has performed." He will always seek to do more in service of God and to look for more ways to please Him. This desire will arise from a feeling of inadequacy and distance from Hashem. Even in the realm of the spiritual we will always feel incomplete.

This is what the holiday of Shemini Atzeret speaks about.

Traditionally. there are two fundamental questions that bother people when they think about Shemini Atzeret. Shemini Atzeret is a very strange holiday as it is bereft of any unique mitzvah or custom. It follows on the heels of our cycle of holidays, which have such a rich plethora of mitzvot. Rosh Hashanah has the majestic shofar and the sweetness of the honey; Yom Kippur has the purity of fasting and the cleansing of wearing white garments; Sukkot has the frailty of the temporary sukkah and the mystical nature of the four species, the *daled minim*; and even Chol ha-Moed has the powerful Hoshanah Rabbah with the *aravah* – the willows that we beat into the ground. And immediately following Shemini Atzeret we have Simchat Torah with its endless rejoicing over the Torah, which is one of the most joyous of all our holidays. And sandwiched in between all of these holidays is Shemini Atzeret, a holiday that seems to lack identity and a unique custom or ritual. Why is that?

A second fundamental question: Sukkot is the holiday of joy. We celebrate Sukkot when we lovingly and joyously "gather in our crops from the threshing floor and from the vat" (Devarim 16:13). About all the other holidays mentioned in the Torah, it mentions *simchah* (joy) only once (about Shavuot in Devarim 16:11), but about Sukkot it says it three times: first in Vayikra (23:40) and twice in Devarim, when it says, *"ve-samachta be-chagekha*, you shall rejoice on your holiday" (16:14); and *"ve-hayita akh same'ach*, and you should only be happy" (16:15).

Our rabbis understand this to mean that there is a special mitzvah to be extra happy on the holiday of Sukkot. In this spirit,

I remember as a boy that we rarely had liquor or alcohol around the house, but on Sukkot we would bring beer into the sukkah, because it is an extra mitzvah to be happy on Sukkot. On Sukkot there is a custom to throw sukkah parties that recall the amazing party in the Beit ha-Mikdash known as the *simchat beit ha-sho'evah*. And Shemini Atzeret is followed by Simchat Torah, which is a post-biblical holiday that is an entire day of pure rejoicing.

So it is a season of joy. But in between these two joyous holidays is Shemini Atzeret; a day of muted joy; a day with the cries of Yizkor; a day where we pray for rain using the solemn tunes of Yom Kippur. What is that about?

Both of these questions point to the *sui generis* nature of Shemini Atzeret. It is about the recognition of what Kohelet says: "One who loves money will never be satisfied with money" – true happiness is contained within ourselves. To be truly happy, a person must find happiness without all the toys that we bring into our lives to get us through the day. So too, the mitzvot; even though they are a gift from Hashem to help us achieve happiness, they are not the final step of spiritual bliss. The final step is to be able to get to the highest level of happiness before Hashem without clinging to additional mitzvot.

Shemini Atzeret is the model for how we can live the rest of the year once the holidays are over; it teaches us how we can bring the spirit of the holidays into our daily lives.

As we step away from the holiday season and return to our daily lives, we begin to feel bereft. Where are all our additional mitzvot? What are we going to do without the shofar for an entire year? Oh, how I already miss saying a blessing on the *daled minim* and how I dread saying good-bye to the sukkah! I want to take these mitzvot with me! I need them.

But the teaching of Shemini Atzeret is that we have gained so much from the mitzvot and the *chagim* that we now know how to achieve happiness even without turning every day into a *chag*. By using the spiritual growth that we have gained from the holidays, we can achieve this elevated spiritual level on a daily basis in our regular lives even without the additional rituals of the holidays. If we cling to the regular observance and teachings of the Torah then we won't need a daily, supercharged lift from the holidays.

This idea is also the very last teaching that Moshe Rabbeinu ever taught in the Torah.

Here in the Diaspora we celebrate Shemini Atzeret as one day and Simchat Torah as the second day. Of course, in Eretz Yisrael it is all combined into one day. So in Israel the Torah reading for Shemini Atzeret is the last portion of the Torah known as *Ve-Zot ha-Berachah*, which in the Diaspora is read on Simchat Torah.

Ve-Zot ha-Berachah translates as "this is the blessing" – this is the final blessing that Moshe gave to the children of Israel before he died. With his final breaths he calls everyone together and tells them that Hashem loves us so much that He has given us something we can carry with us at all times. Moshe says:

תּוֹרָה צִוָּה לָנוּ מֹשֶׁה מוֹרָשָׁה קְהִלַּת יַעֲקֹב:

Moshe commanded the Torah to us, an eternal heritage for the congregation of Yaakov. (Devarim 33:4)

He then proceeds to bless all the tribes, and then he concludes – and these are the very last words Moshe speaks in his life – with the following phrase:

וַיִּשְׁכֹּן יִשְׂרָאֵל בֶּטַח בָּדָד עֵין יַעֲקֹב אֶל אֶרֶץ דָּגָן וְתִירוֹשׁ אַף שָׁמָיו
יַעַרְפוּ טָל: אַשְׁרֶיךָ יִשְׂרָאֵל מִי כָמוֹךָ עַם נוֹשַׁע בַּה' מָגֵן עֶזְרֶךָ....

Israel shall thus dwell securely, alone in a land of grain and wine, just like Yaakov; your heavens shall drip with dew. Happy are you, Israel! Who is like you? [You are] a nation delivered by God, the Shield who helps you…. (Devarim 33:28–29)

The meaning of this is that we will be fortunate and happy when we are secure with the Torah. All we need to be happy is to cling to the Torah and then even just a little grain, rain, and wine will suffice.

So we have seen that Shemini Atzeret is a model for how we can live our lives throughout the whole year even without all the extra mitzvot of the holidays. All we need to do is to cling to the Torah and we will have enough.

This is the secret of why Moshe doesn't enter into Eretz Yisrael. Right after these words appear in the Torah, Moshe ascends the mountain and looks at the land of Canaan, and God tells him: You will not cross over the Jordan. You will not make it to Canaan (34:4).

But now we know why Moshe doesn't go into Eretz Yisrael. Earlier in the Torah we were told that Moshe doesn't go in because he is punished for hitting a rock in order to draw out water. But now the Torah simply says he is not crossing the Jordan River, and it no longer explicitly states that he is being punished.

You know why he doesn't he go into Israel now? He no longer needs to. As he dies, Moshe understands that the essence of Hashem and the Torah can get him to where he needs to go even if he is missing out on the mitzvah of crossing the Jordan into the land of Canaan. Don't misunderstand: the rest of us desperately need Eretz Yisrael and the 613 mitzvot, but by this time in his life Moshe had achieved the highest level of spirituality even without the land. He didn't need the land in order to ascend to Hashem.

He had internalized the mitzvot to such a degree that he was high enough to return to Hashem.

On Shemini Atzeret we have a custom to say the prayer for rain known as *tefillat geshem*. In this prayer we cry out to Hashem: "Remember Moshe who was drawn forth in a basket from the water…. When Your treasured people thirsted for water, he hit the rock and out came water. *Be-tzidko*, in the merit of his righteousness, grant us water." In this prayer we don't mention that Moshe will be punished for hitting the rock on another occasion. Just the opposite, we are praising him. He was righteous even as he died.

Now we see that when Moshe hit the rock he was teaching us a fundamental lesson that would carry on after his death. Moshe taught us how to get water from a rock. Water is life and a rock, in its simplicity, is the Torah. By dying before he entered into Eretz Yisrael, Moshe taught us how to get life from the Torah.

Let us think of the holidays as a ledge that we can hold on to. The whole year we are in a raging sea of tsunamis and earthquakes. Our lives beat us up and down and toss us all around. But then comes the *yamim noraim* and we grasp a hold of these ledges to help us survive.

But then the ledge leaves, so what are we to do? That's the lesson of Shemini Atzeret: we can survive even without the ledge, even without the extra mitzvot, because the whole year we have the Torah. The Torah is our ledge and will be our protector and we cling to the Torah knowing that we will be happy and secure no matter what the year might bring.